STEP-BY-STEP
desserts

Caroline Bretherton
Kristan Raines

Penguin Random House

DK LONDON

Project Editor Martha Burley
Senior Art Editor Sara Robin
Project Art Editor Vicky Read
Editorial Assistant Alice Kewellhampton
Design Assistant Laura Buscemi
Managing Editor Dawn Henderson
Managing Art Editor Christine Keilty
Senior Jacket Creative Nicola Powling
Pre-Production Producer Dragana Puvacic
Senior Producer Stephanie McConnell
Creative Technical Support Sonia Charbonnier
Deputy Art Director Maxine Pedliham
Publisher Peggy Vance

DK INDIA

Senior Art Editor Ira Sharma
Editors Neha Samuel, Seetha Natesh
Art Editors Zaurin Thoidingjam, Tashi Topgyal Laya
Deputy Managing Editor Bushra Ahmed
Managing Art Editor Navidita Thapa
Pre-production Manager Sunil Sharma
DTP Designer Rajdeep Singh

Published in Great Britain in 2015 by
Dorling Kindersley Limited
80 Strand, London, WC2R 0RL

2 4 6 8 10 9 7 5 3
001 – 278606 – Sept/2015

Copyright © 2015
Dorling Kindersley Limited
A Penguin Random House Company

A CIP catalogue record for this book is available
from the British Library

ISBN 978-0-2411-8909-2

Colour reproduction by Altaimage Ltd

Printed and bound in China

Discover more at **www.dk.com**

Contents

Sweet success

Desserts are more indulgent, daring, and fabulous than ever. Treat yourself to dinner at a good restaurant, and you can choose a dessert that is just as exciting as your main course. Today's dessert recipes draw influences from all cuisines, play with new ingredients, and introduce fresh flavour pairings. They are the finishing touch to a meal, and show-stoppers in their own right.

Recipes to impress

To celebrate the buzz around desserts, *Step-by-Step Desserts* is a unique collection of over 400 recipes. With a comprehensive collection of luscious recipes and simple guidance to help you on your way, here are endless ideas and inspiration for that sweet treat at the end of a meal.

Within the three chapters – Hot, Cold, and Frozen – you can find every classic dessert recipe that a home cook needs, shown step by step. Each classic is followed by creative variations, so if you are looking for inspiration for a mid-week dessert or wish to prepare an impressive finale to a celebration dinner, you can find the ideal recipe. Alongside the recipes are fun feature panels that share ideas for decoration

techniques – so you can drip, drizzle, melt, marble, pipe, crimp, skewer, shape, or dust your way to truly sensational desserts.

Making desserts is creative and fun, but it does require attention to detail and precision. Before you begin to cook, read the recipe carefully and check that you have all the ingredients, time, and equipment you need. If your dessert needs to bake in the oven, set the shelf at the correct height before you heat it up, and keep in mind that the top of the oven can be a lot hotter than the bottom. Unless stated otherwise in the recipe, you should bake your dessert on the centre shelf so that it cooks evenly. Here is some more expert guidance that can help you.

Pastry know-how

Home-made pastry can become tough, crumbly, or difficult to handle. Don't panic – before you resort to shop-bought pastry, there are some simple steps that can give you fabulous results.

▪ **Chill pastry**, well wrapped in cling film, for at least 30 minutes before rolling. This allows the gluten in the flour to relax and stops the pastry toughening on baking.

▪ **Avoid over-flouring** the work surface. Use as little flour as you can – extra flour absorbs into the pastry and makes it dry once baked.

▪ **Avoid over-working** the pastry. For all stages of pastry making, use as light a hand as possible. Avoid re-rolling where possible, as the pastry may toughen and be liable to shrinkage.

▪ **Roll your pastry** into a tin using a rolling pin. Transferring pastry to a tin is tricky, so to avoid breakage, simply roll it up around your rolling pin, then unroll it gradually into the tin.

Rolled pastry is delicate, so handle it with care.

For best results, whisk the egg whites until they are stiff and glossy.

Mastering meringue

Delicate meringue is a very simple combination of egg whites and sugar, but it can be difficult to perfect. From preparing your bowl to separating eggs, here are some expert tips to help you.

- **Separate the eggs** one by one in a smaller bowl before combining them. Any trace of egg yolk will spoil a meringue – so this method means that even if a yolk breaks, only a single egg is lost.
- **Remove small pieces of eggshell** from the egg whites using another broken egg shell. The albumen inside the shell attracts the smaller piece, making it easy to scoop out.
- **Whisk egg whites** in a scrupulously clean bowl. If in doubt, run the cut-side of a lemon around the inside of the bowl to remove any residual grease, then dry with a piece of kitchen paper.

All about cakes and tortes

Baking itself is a science, but there is an art to a light and airy sponge or a rich and dense torte – choosing your ingredients carefully is key.

- **Make sure your eggs** are at room temperature. They whisk more easily, so this means you can incorporate more air into your cake – giving you a light and aerated sponge.
- **Start with butter** that is softened at room temperature, unless otherwise stated in the recipe. If you are short of time, dividing it into small cubes helps it to soften more quickly.
- **Use unsalted butter.** If the recipe calls for additional salt, use good-quality sea salt, which has a softer flavour than table salt.
- **Measure your tins.** The size is vital because the depth of the batter can affect a cake's cooking time.

Make sure that all your ingredients are at room temperature.

HOT

Cobblers, crumbles, and crisps ▪ Pâtisserie
Bakes and batters ▪ Cakes and tortes
Puddings ▪ Cooked fruit

INGREDIENTS

675g (1½lb) blueberries
2 tbsp cornflour
3–4 tbsp caster sugar
pinch of salt
grated zest of 1 lemon
2 tsp lemon juice

For the topping

185g (6½oz) plain flour
1¾ tsp baking powder
pinch of salt
4 tbsp caster sugar
85g (3oz) unsalted butter,
   chilled and diced
180ml (6fl oz) double
   cream, plus extra
   for brushing
¼ tsp ground cinnamon
whipped cream, to serve
   (optional)

SPECIAL EQUIPMENT

1.7 litre (3 pint) deep
ovenproof dish

55 mins plus cooling   **SERVES 6**

COBBLER blueberry

A cobbler is a simple alternative to a pie or crumble – perfect for when you are short of time in the kitchen. You can choose any seasonal fruit filling, top it with this sweetened scone mix, and bake to create a warm and homely dessert.

1

Preheat the oven to 190°C (375°F/Gas 5). Combine the blueberries, cornflour, sugar, salt, and lemon zest and juice in a bowl.

2

For the topping, sift the flour, baking powder, salt, and 3 tablespoons of the sugar into a large bowl. Rub in the butter until the mixture resembles coarse breadcrumbs. Add the cream and bring the mixture together to form a dough.

3

Transfer the blueberry mixture to the ovenproof dish, spreading it out evenly. Divide the dough into six equal portions and place it on top of the blueberries. Combine the cinnamon and remaining sugar in a small bowl.

Make sure you leave enough space for the dough to spread.

4

Brush the dough with a little double cream, then sprinkle over the cinnamon mixture. Bake for 25–30 minutes, until golden and bubbling. Insert a skewer into the topping – it should come out clean. Remove and leave to cool for 5 minutes. Serve warm with whipped cream, if desired. You can store the cobbler in the fridge for up to 2 days.

🕐 **1 hr**
plus cooling 🍴 **SERVES 6**

COBBLER cranberry and pear

The combination of tart cranberries and sweet pears gives this recipe a tempting contrast of colour, flavour, and texture.

INGREDIENTS
100g (3½oz) light brown sugar
½ tsp ground cardamom
¼ tsp ground cinnamon
2 tbsp cornflour
salt
115g (4oz) cranberries
900g (2lb) pears, peeled, cored, and thinly sliced
juice of ½ orange
whipped cream, to serve

For the topping
185g (6½oz) plain flour
1¾ tsp baking powder
4 tbsp caster sugar
85g (3oz) unsalted butter, chilled and diced
180ml (6fl oz) double cream, plus extra for brushing
¼ tsp ground cinnamon

SPECIAL EQUIPMENT
1.7 litre (3 pint) ovenproof dish

1 Preheat the oven to 190C°(375°F/Gas 5). Combine the brown sugar, cardamom, cinnamon, cornflour, and a pinch of salt in a large bowl. Add the cranberries, pears, and orange juice. Mix well, spread the mixture in the ovenproof dish, and set aside.

2 For the topping, sift the flour, baking powder, 3 tablespoons of caster sugar, and a pinch of salt into a large bowl. Rub in the butter until the mixture resembles breadcrumbs. Add the cream and bring the mixture together to form a soft, sticky dough.

3 Place 6 heaped tablespoons of the dough over the fruit, leaving space for it to spread. Brush with a little cream. Mix the cinnamon and remaining sugar in a bowl and sprinkle over the dough.

4 Bake for 35–40 minutes, until the cobbler is golden and bubbling, and an inserted skewer comes out clean. Cover with foil if the topping browns too quickly. Cool for 5 minutes, then serve warm with whipped cream. You can store the cobbler in the fridge for up to 2 days.

🕐 **55 mins**
plus cooling 🍴 **SERVES 6**

COBBLER peach

Fragrant summer peaches require nothing more than this soft and yielding topping to soak up their juices.

INGREDIENTS
50g (1¾oz) caster sugar
8 ripe peaches, peeled, stoned, and quartered
1 tsp cornflour
juice of ½ lemon

For the topping
185g (6½oz) plain flour
1¾ tsp baking powder
75g (2½oz) caster sugar
pinch of salt
½–¾ tsp ground cinnamon, to taste

75g (2½oz) unsalted butter, chilled and diced
1 egg
100ml (3½fl oz) buttermilk
1 tbsp soft light brown sugar
custard or cream, to serve (optional)

SPECIAL EQUIPMENT
1.7 litre (3 pint) ovenproof dish

1 Preheat the oven to 190ºC (375ºF/Gas 5). Heat the sugar and 4 tablespoons of water in a large, lidded, heavy-based saucepan. Add the peaches once the sugar has dissolved. Cover and cook for 2–3 minutes over a medium heat, stirring occasionally, until the peaches are well coated in the mixture. Reduce the heat to low.

2 Mix the cornflour and lemon juice in a bowl to a paste. Add to the pan, and cook the mixture, uncovered, until thickened to a syrup-like consistency. Transfer to the ovenproof dish and spread out the peach filling into an even layer.

3 For the topping, sift the flour, baking powder, caster sugar, salt, and cinnamon into a bowl. Rub in the butter until the mixture resembles breadcrumbs. Whisk the egg and buttermilk in a separate bowl and combine with the dry ingredients to form a dough. Use to cover the fruit (see Cranberry and pear cobbler, step 3).

4 Sprinkle over the brown sugar. Bake for 25–30 minutes, until done (see Cranberry and pear cobbler, step 4). Cool for 5 minutes, then serve with custard or cream, if desired. You can store the cobbler in the fridge for up to 2 days.

⏱ **1 hr 20 mins**
plus cooling   🍴 **SERVES 6**

COBBLER apple and blackberry

Enhance the flavour of your cobbler with a mix of tart and sweet apples. This blend ensures that some apple pieces stay firm enough to have a nice bite to them.

INGREDIENTS

900g (2lb) mixed tart and sweet apples, peeled, cored, and thinly sliced

100g (3½oz) dark brown sugar

2 tbsp cornflour

1 tsp ground cinnamon

¼ tsp ground cloves

juice of ½ lemon

350g (12oz) blackberries

whipped cream, to serve

For the topping

185g (6½oz) plain flour

1¾ tsp baking powder

pinch of salt

4 tbsp caster sugar

85g (3oz) unsalted butter, chilled and diced

180ml (6fl oz) double cream, plus extra for brushing

¼ tsp ground cinnamon

SPECIAL EQUIPMENT

1.7 litre (3 pint) ovenproof dish

1 Preheat the oven to 190C°(375°F/Gas 5). Combine the apples, brown sugar, cornflour, cinnamon, cloves, and lemon juice in a large bowl. Transfer the mixture to the ovenproof dish and bake for 20 minutes, until the apples are slightly tender. Remove and fold in the blackberries.

2 For the topping, sift the flour, baking powder, salt, and 3 tablespoons of caster sugar into a bowl. Rub in the butter until the mixture resembles breadcrumbs. Add the cream and bring the mixture together to form a dough. Use to cover the fruit (see Cranberry and pear cobbler, step 3).

3 Combine the cinnamon with the remaining sugar in a bowl. Brush the dough with cream and sprinkle over the cinnamon and sugar mixture.

4 Bake for 35–40 minutes, or until done (see Cranberry and pear cobbler, step 4). Cool the cobbler for 5 minutes, then serve it warm with whipped cream. You can store the cobbler in the fridge for up to 2 days.

🕐 **1 hr 10 mins**
plus resting

🍴 **MAKES 6–8**

CRUMBLE apple and cinnamon

This is a beloved British dessert, and deservedly so. A good crumble topping should be loosely patted down over the filling, and made with irregular-sized lumps of butter that melt and create a fudge-like texture during the bake.

INGREDIENTS

250g (9oz) plain flour
150g (5½oz) caster sugar
1 tsp cinnamon
150g (5½oz) unsalted butter, softened and diced

For the filling

8–10 dessert apples, peeled, cored, and diced into 2cm (¾in) pieces
2 heaped tbsp soft light brown sugar

1 heaped tbsp plain flour
½ tsp ground cinnamon
25g (scant 1oz) butter, softened and diced
double cream, to serve (optional)

SPECIAL EQUIPMENT
23cm (9in) ovenproof dish, about 7.5cm (3in) deep

1 Preheat the oven to 180°C (350°F/ Gas 4). Combine the flour, sugar, and cinnamon in a large bowl. Rub in the butter until the mixture resembles coarse breadcrumbs, making sure you leave a few small lumps of butter.

2 For the filling, place the apple pieces in the ovenproof dish. Scatter over the sugar, flour, and cinnamon. Toss well to combine. Gently pack the filling into the dish.

3 Dot the filling with butter. Then spoon the flour topping over and spread it out gently. Lightly shake the dish to help settle the topping into an even layer.

4 Bake for 45 minutes, until the top is golden brown and the filling is soft when pierced with a sharp knife. Remove and leave to rest for 5 minutes. Serve warm with cream, if desired. You can store the crumble, covered in the fridge, for up to 3 days.

SMULPAJ rhubarb

A Swedish favourite, smulpaj features a layer of fruit topped with an oaty crumble.

INGREDIENTS
50g (1¾oz) plain flour

75g (2½oz) soft light brown sugar

75g (2½oz) unsalted butter, softened

75g (2½oz) oats

½ tsp ground cinnamon

For the filling
300g (10oz) rhubarb, trimmed and chopped into 2cm (¾in) chunks

4 tbsp caster sugar

1 tsp cornflour

For the custard
375ml (13fl oz) whole milk

75ml (2½fl oz) double cream

3 large egg yolks, at room temperature

1½ tbsp caster sugar

1 tbsp cornflour

½ tsp vanilla extract

SPECIAL EQUIPMENT
20cm (8in) round ovenproof dish

1 Preheat the oven to 190ºC (375ºF/Gas 5). Combine the flour and brown sugar in a bowl. Rub in the butter until the mixture resembles coarse breadcrumbs. Add the oats and cinnamon, mix well, and set aside.

2 For the filling, combine the rhubarb, caster sugar, and cornflour in the ovenproof dish. Gently pack the filling down, spread the flour topping over the top, and shake the dish lightly so it settles. Place it on a baking sheet.

3 Bake for 30 minutes, until the top is golden and the filling is soft when pierced with a knife. Remove and leave to rest for 5–10 minutes. Meanwhile, for the custard, heat the milk and cream in a heavy-based saucepan for 5–6 minutes, until steaming.

4 In a heatproof bowl, whisk the egg yolks, caster sugar, cornflour, and vanilla extract until well combined. Gradually add the milk mixture, whisking until the sugar has melted. Pour the custard back into the pan.

5 Cook the custard over a gentle heat for a further 5–8 minutes, stirring constantly, until it is thick enough to coat the back of a spoon. Remove from the heat and serve warm with the smulpaj. You can store the smulpaj, covered, in the fridge for 1–2 days.

CRISPS summer berry

These pots are ideal when you need to plan ahead. Prepare the components in advance for a no-fuss finish to your meal.

INGREDIENTS
100g (3½oz) rolled oats

1 tsp cinnamon

3 tbsp soft light brown sugar

60g (2oz) unsalted butter, melted

200ml (7fl oz) single cream

2 egg yolks

½ tsp vanilla extract

4 tbsp caster sugar

500g (1lb 2oz) mixed berries, chopped into small pieces

125ml (4¼fl oz) double cream

SPECIAL EQUIPMENT
4 x 350ml (12fl oz) wide-mouthed jam jars

PLAN AHEAD
You can prepare and store the oat mixture in an airtight container up to 2 days ahead. You can prepare and store the custard in an airtight container in the fridge up to 2 days ahead.

1 Preheat the oven to 180°C (350°F/Gas 4). Combine the oats, cinnamon, brown sugar, and butter in a bowl. Spread the mixture on a heavy baking sheet. Bake on the top shelf of the oven for 12–15 minutes, until golden. Leave to cool.

2 Heat the single cream in a heavy-based saucepan over a low heat, until steaming. Whisk the egg yolks, vanilla extract, and 3 tablespoons caster sugar in a heatproof bowl. Pour in the hot cream and whisk until the sugar melts.

3 Pour the mixture back into the pan. Cook over a low heat for 8–10 minutes, stirring continuously, until it is thick enough to coat the back of a spoon. Transfer the custard to a bowl and leave to cool. Cover the surface with cling film, and chill until needed.

4 Combine the berries and remaining caster sugar in a bowl and leave to macerate for 20 minutes. In a separate bowl, whisk the double cream to form stiff peaks. Then whisk in the chilled custard until well combined.

5 Place one-eighth of the berries in each jam jar in an even layer. Top with one-eighth each of the custard and the oat mixture. Repeat to add one more layer each of the fruit, custard, and oat mixture. Chill for at least 30 minutes, before serving on the same day.

🕐 **1 hr 20 mins** plus cooling and resting   🍴 **SERVES 6-8**

CRUMBLE autumn fruit

Walnuts give fantastic crunch and texture to this crumble filling, and cranberries provide a tangy brightness of flavour.

INGREDIENTS

225g (8oz) plain flour

150g (5½oz) soft light brown sugar

½ tsp ground cinnamon

175g (6oz) unsalted butter, softened and diced

100g (3½oz) rolled oats

vanilla custard, to serve

For the filling

60g (2oz) walnuts

½ tsp cinnamon

2 heaped tbsp soft light brown sugar

4-5 apples, peeled, cored, and cut into cubes

2-3 pears, peeled, cored, and cut into cubes

100g (3½oz) cranberries

1 heaped tbsp plain flour

SPECIAL EQUIPMENT

23cm (9in) ovenproof dish, about 7.5cm (3in) deep

1 Preheat the oven to 180°C (350°F/Gas 4). Combine the flour, brown sugar, and cinnamon in a large bowl. Rub in 150g (5½oz) of the butter until the mixture resembles coarse breadcrumbs. Add the oats, mix well, and set aside.

2 For the filling, spread the walnuts on a baking sheet and bake for 5 minutes. Gently rub them with a kitchen towel to remove the skin. Leave to cool before chopping them into small pieces. Transfer to the ovenproof dish along with the cinnamon, sugar, and fruit.

3 Mix the filling and pack it down gently. Dot with the remaining butter. Then spread the flour topping over the top (see Rhubarb smulpaj, step 2).

4 Bake for 45-50 minutes, until the top is golden and the filling is soft when pierced with a knife. Remove the crumble from the heat and leave to rest. Serve it warm with vanilla custard. You can store the crumble, covered, in the fridge for 1-2 days.

Simple alternatives

A simple Apple and cinnamon crumble (see pp14-15) is a time-honoured classic, but you can swap in a variety of fruits and spices to create fabulous alternatives.

Pear and nutmeg Omit the cinnamon from the recipe (see Apple and cinnamon crumble, pp14-15). Use 8 peeled, cored, and diced, just-ripe pears instead of the apples. Add ½ tsp grated nutmeg to the filling and 1 tsp to the topping and continue.

Plum Replace the apples (see Apple and cinnamon crumble, pp14-15) with 16-18 halved and pitted firm plums and continue with the recipe.

Damson These are a little-known fruit, smaller and tarter than plums. Use 18-20 halved and pitted damsons instead of the chopped apples (see Apple and cinnamon crumble, pp14-15).

Peach Omit the cinnamon from the recipe (see Apple and cinnamon crumble, pp14-15). Use 10 halved, stoned, and quartered peaches instead of the apples. Serve the crumble at room temperature with vanilla ice cream.

Gooseberry and elderflower For this summer-time recipe, toss 800g (1¾lb) hulled, ripe gooseberries in a little elderflower cordial and 60g (2oz) caster sugar, and omit the cinnamon (see Apple and cinnamon crumble, pp14-15).

Banana and mango Omit the cinnamon from the recipe (see Apple and cinnamon crumble, pp14-15). Use 2-3 large bananas, cut into 2cm (¾in) thick slices with 2 mangos, diced into 2cm (¾in) pieces instead of the apples. For best results, use fruit that is just ripe.

Rhubarb and strawberry Use 400g (14oz) rhubarb, cut into 2.5cm (1in) pieces, and 400g (14oz) hulled strawberries, and omit the cinnamon (see Apple and cinnamon crumble, pp14-15).

Cherry and almond Omit the cinnamon from the recipe (see Apple and cinnamon crumble, pp14-15). Use 700g (1lb 8oz) pitted cherries and 100g (3½oz) roughly chopped raw almonds instead of the apples.

1 hr 25 mins
plus resting

SERVES 6–8

Also great
COLD

STRUDEL apple and almond

Strudel dough is tricky to get right, but this recipe guarantees success. The breadcrumbs in the filling help to soak up juices from the apple that could make the pastry soggy – leaving you with perfectly crisp and flaky pastry.

INGREDIENTS

185g (6½oz) plain flour, plus extra for dusting

¼ tsp salt

1 tsp caster sugar, plus extra for dusting

100g (3½oz) unsalted butter, diced, plus extra for greasing

1 large egg, beaten

½ tsp cider vinegar

1 tbsp icing sugar, for dusting

For the filling

900g (2lb) tart apples, such as Granny Smith, peeled, cored, and thinly sliced

grated zest of ½ lemon

30g (1oz) breadcrumbs

100g (3½oz) caster sugar

3 tbsp dark brown sugar

1 tsp ground cinnamon

¼ tsp grated nutmeg

45g (1½oz) sliced almonds

¼ tsp vanilla extract

1

Combine the flour, salt, and caster sugar in a large bowl. Rub in 30g (1oz) of the butter until the mixture resembles rough breadcrumbs. Whisk the egg, vinegar, and 60ml (2fl oz) water in a separate bowl. Add the liquid mixture to the dry ingredients and mix well to form a loose dough.

2

Add 1–2 teaspoons flour if the dough seems too wet. Throw the dough against a lightly floured work surface repeatedly for about 10–15 minutes until it is shiny, smooth, and elastic. Place it in a lightly greased bowl, cover, and leave to rest for 30 minutes.

3

Preheat the oven to 190°C (375°F/Gas 5). Line a baking sheet with baking parchment and set aside. For the filling, combine all the ingredients in a large bowl and set aside. Cover a work surface with a large, clean, kitchen towel and flour it lightly. Place the pastry on top.

Start at the centre and work outwards to stretch out the pastry.

4

Roll out the pastry to a large rectangle of even thickness. Then gently stretch it out, until it is very thin and translucent. The stretched pastry should be about 40 x 61cm (16 x 24in) in size.

5

Melt the remaining butter in a saucepan over a low heat and brush generously over the pastry. Place the filling at one end of the pastry, leaving a wide edge. Lift the edges of the kitchen towel and slowly roll up the strudel, working gently but firmly, making sure the filling does not fall out.

6

Place the strudel on the baking sheet. Curve it into a crescent and brush with butter. Sprinkle over the caster sugar and trim the edges. Bake for 35–40 minutes, until golden. Sprinkle with icing sugar and serve warm. Best served on the same day.

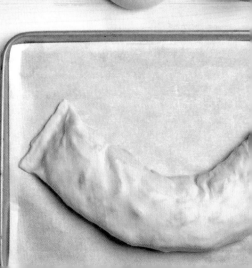

⏱ **1 hr 20 mins** plus resting and cooling   🍴 **SERVES 6-8**   🌡 Also great **COLD**

STRUDEL ricotta and raisin

In the style of Eastern European sweetened-cheese strudels, this recipe uses ricotta for a sweet, creamy, and delicious filling.

INGREDIENTS
185g (6½oz) plain flour, plus extra for dusting
¼ tsp salt
1 tsp caster sugar
100g (3½oz) unsalted butter, softened, plus extra for greasing
1 large egg, beaten
½ tsp cider vinegar
1-2 tbsp icing sugar, to serve

For the filling
60g (2oz) raisins
3 tbsp rum or Port
350g (12oz) ricotta cheese
50g (1¾oz) caster sugar, plus extra for dusting
1 tsp vanilla extract
⅛ tsp salt
grated zest of 1 lemon
1 large egg
1½ tbsp breadcrumbs

1 Preheat the oven to 190°C (375°F/Gas 5). Combine the flour, salt, and caster sugar in a bowl. Rub in 30g (1oz) butter until the mixture resembles breadcrumbs. In a separate bowl, whisk the egg, vinegar, and 60ml (2fl oz) water. Add it to the dry mixture and bring together to form a smooth dough.

2 Add 1-2 teaspoons of flour if the dough seems too wet. Then throw it against a floured surface repeatedly for 10-15 minutes, until shiny, smooth, and elastic. Place it in a lightly greased bowl, cover, and leave to rest for 30 minutes.

3 For the filling, combine the raisins and rum in a bowl and leave to soak. In a separate bowl, combine the ricotta, caster sugar, vanilla extract, salt, lemon zest, and egg. Cover a work surface with a large kitchen towel and flour it lightly. Place the pastry on top and roll it out to a large rectangle.

4 Gently stretch the pastry, working outwards from the centre to form a 40 x 61cm (16 x 24in) translucent rectangle. Use a slotted spoon to combine the raisins with the ricotta mixture. Melt the remaining butter and use to brush over the pastry.

5 Scatter 1 tablespoon of the breadcrumbs at one end of the pastry, leaving a wide edge. Top with the filling, and then the remaining breadcrumbs. Lift the edges of the cloth to roll the strudel, gently but firmly, making sure the filling does not fall out. Place it on a baking sheet lined with baking parchment.

6 Shape the strudel into a crescent and brush with the remaining butter. Sprinkle with caster sugar and trim the excess pastry. Bake for 30-35 minutes, until golden. Cool for 5-10 minutes. Dust with icing sugar and serve warm. You can store the strudel in an airtight container in the fridge for up to 1 day.

⏱ **1 hr 20 mins** plus resting   🍴 **SERVES 6-8**   🌡 Also great **COLD**

STRUDEL plum

For a twist on classic fruit strudel, finely dice plums and mix them with walnut and fragrant cardamom.

INGREDIENTS
185g (6½oz) plain flour
¼ tsp salt
1 tsp caster sugar
100g (3½oz) unsalted butter, softened
1 large egg, beaten
½ tsp cider vinegar
1-2 tbsp icing sugar, to serve

60g (2oz) breadcrumbs
100g (3½oz) soft light brown sugar
3 tbsp caster sugar
1 tsp ground cinnamon
¼ tsp cardamom
60g (2oz) chopped walnuts
¼ tsp vanilla extract

For the filling
675g (1½lb) plums, stoned and thinly sliced

1 Preheat the oven to 190°C (375°F/Gas 5). Prepare the pastry, transfer it to a greased bowl, and leave to rest for 30 minutes (see Ricotta and raisin strudel, steps 1-2).

2 For the filling, combine all the ingredients in a large bowl and set aside. Cover a work surface with a large kitchen towel and flour it lightly. Place the pastry on top and roll it out to a large rectangle.

3 Gently stretch out the pastry to form a 40 x 61cm (16 x 24in) translucent rectangle (see Ricotta and raisin strudel, step 4). Melt the remaining butter and brush generously over the pastry.

4 Place the filling at one end of the pastry, leaving a wide edge. Roll the strudel and transfer to a lined baking sheet (see Ricotta and raisin strudel, step 5). Sprinkle with caster sugar and trim the excess pastry at the ends.

5 Bake for 30-35 minutes, until golden. Remove the strudel from the heat and leave to rest for 5-10 minutes. Dust with icing sugar and serve warm. You can store it in an airtight container in the fridge for up to 1 day.

🕐 **2 hrs 5 mins–2 hrs 25 mins**
plus cooling   🍴 **MAKES 36**   Also great
COLD

BAKLAVA

This crisp Middle-Eastern pastry is sure to impress. It is layered with chopped nuts and spices, then drenched in an orange flower and honey syrup.

INGREDIENTS

250g (9oz) walnut pieces, coarsely chopped

2 tsp ground cinnamon

large pinch of ground cloves

50g (1¾oz) caster sugar

250g (9oz) unsalted and skinned pistachios, coarsely chopped

500g pack of filo pastry

250g (9oz) unsalted butter

For the syrup

200g (7oz) caster sugar

250ml (9fl oz) runny honey

juice of 1 lemon

3 tbsp orange flower water

SPECIAL EQUIPMENT

30 x 40cm (12 x 16in) deep baking tray

1 Preheat the oven to 180°C (350°F/Gas 4). For the filling, place the walnuts, cinnamon, cloves, and sugar in a large bowl. Then add the pistachios, reserving 3–4 tablespoons, and stir to mix. Set aside.

2 On a damp kitchen towel, unroll the pastry sheets and cover with a second dampened towel. Melt the butter in a saucepan over a gentle heat. Brush the baking tray with a little butter and line it with a sheet of pastry. Fold over the ends to fit the tray.

3 Brush the pastry with butter and gently press it into the corners and sides of the tray. Repeat to form layers with one-third of the pastry, brushing each layer with butter. Scatter over half the filling.

4 Repeat with another third of the pastry sheets. Sprinkle over the remaining filling and layer with the remaining pastry sheets. Trim off any excess and pour over any remaining butter.

5 Gently score 4cm (1½in) wide and 1cm (½in) deep diamond shapes into the pastry. Bake on the bottom shelf of the oven for 1¼–1½ hours, until golden on top and an inserted skewer comes out clean.

6 For the syrup, heat the sugar and 250ml (9fl oz) water in a saucepan, stirring occasionally, until dissolved. Add the honey, stir to mix, and bring to the boil. Cook for 25 minutes, without stirring, until drops of the cooled mixture can be shaped into soft balls.

7 Remove and cool the syrup to lukewarm, stir in the lemon juice and orange flower water, and pour over the pastry. Use a sharp knife to cut along the marked lines on the pastry, almost to the bottom, and leave to cool.

8 Cut through the marked lines, and carefully place the pastries on a large serving plate. Sprinkle with the reserved pistachios, and serve warm. You can store the baklava in an airtight container for up to 5 days.

1 hr
plus chilling

MAKES 8

GALETTES apple and almond

This classic French dessert features layers of light, flaky pastry decorated with a sweet topping and baked in the oven. Quicker to prepare than a tart or pie, galettes are equally stunning – the open form beautifully showcases the apple filling.

INGREDIENTS
plain flour, for dusting
600g (1lb 5oz) ready-made all-butter puff pastry

For the filling
215g (7½oz) marzipan
8 small, tart dessert apples, peeled, cored, and thinly sliced
juice of ½ lemon

50g (1¾oz) caster sugar
icing sugar, for dusting
double cream, to serve (optional)

PLAN AHEAD
You can prepare and store the pastry and marzipan rounds, covered in the fridge, up to 2 hours ahead of baking.

1 On a floured surface, roll out half the pastry to a 35cm (14in) square, about 3mm (⅛in) thick. Use a 15cm (6in) plate to cut out four rounds. Place them on a baking sheet lightly sprinkled with water.

2 Make four more rounds with the remaining dough and place them on another baking sheet. Prick them with a fork, avoiding the edges, and chill all the pastry for 15 minutes. Cut the marzipan into eight equal portions and roll them into balls.

Leave a border of at least 1cm (½in) around the edge.

3 Set one of the marzipan balls between two sheets of baking parchment and roll it out to a 12cm (5in) round. Place it on top of a pastry round and repeat with the remaining marzipan. Chill for 15 minutes.

4 Preheat the oven to 220°C (425°F/Gas 7). Toss the apple slices with the lemon juice in a bowl. Arrange them in an overlapping spiral over the marzipan, leaving a thin border around the edge.

5 Bake for 15–20 minutes, until the pastry edges have risen around the marzipan and are lightly golden. Sprinkle the apples evenly with caster sugar, and return the galettes to the oven.

6 Bake for a further 5–10 minutes, until the apples have caramelized around the edges and are tender when tested with a knife. Transfer the galettes to warmed serving plates and dust with icing sugar. Serve immediately, with double cream if desired.

🕐 **50 mins**   🍴 **MAKES 4**

GALETTES pineapple and rum

Griddling the pineapple first helps to caramelize it, and produces this attractive charred design. A sweet, heady rum-laced sauce adds a tropical twist.

INGREDIENTS

½ ripe pineapple, skin removed and cored

3 tbsp unsalted butter, melted, for brushing

plain flour, for dusting

25cm (10in) square sheet of ready-made, all-butter puff pastry

2 tbsp soft light brown sugar

For the sauce

60g (2oz) unsalted butter

60ml (2fl oz) golden rum

60g (2oz) soft dark brown sugar

125ml (4¼oz) double cream

vanilla ice cream, to serve

PLAN AHEAD

You can wrap the pastry squares in cling film and chill for up to 2 days ahead.

1 Heat a griddle pan to very hot. Cut the pineapple in half. Slice each piece into eight thin slices, each 7.5cm (3in) in length. Pat the slices dry with kitchen paper and brush them lightly with the butter on both sides. Griddle the slices for 2 minutes, on each side, until golden.

2 Preheat the oven to 200°C (400°F/Gas 6). On a floured surface, cut the pastry into four equal-sized squares. Prick each square with a fork, leaving a 2cm (¾in) border around the edge. Sprinkle with the brown sugar and transfer them to a baking sheet sprinkled with a little water.

3 Layer each pastry with four overlapping pineapple slices, leaving the border. Brush the galettes with butter and place them on the top shelf of the oven. Bake for 17–20 minutes, until the pastry is golden and puffed up and the pineapple is soft.

4 For the sauce, gently heat the butter, rum, and sugar in a saucepan, stirring occasionally, until the sugar has melted. Bring to the boil, then reduce the heat to a simmer. Add the cream and cook for 10 minutes, until the sauce is thick and syrup-like. Drizzle the sauce over the galettes and serve warm with vanilla ice cream.

🕐 **55 mins** plus cooling   🍴 **SERVES 6–8**

GALETTES des rois

This layered galette from France was traditionally prepared to celebrate the feast of Epiphany.

INGREDIENTS

plain flour, for dusting

500g (1lb 2oz) ready-made, all-butter puff pastry

1 egg, beaten, to glaze

For the frangipane

100g (3½oz) unsalted butter, softened

100g (3½oz) caster sugar

1 egg

100g (3½oz) ground almonds

1 tsp almond extract

1 tbsp brandy

PLAN AHEAD

You can prepare and store the frangipane in an airtight container in the fridge, up to 3 days ahead.

1 Preheat the oven to 200°C (400°F/Gas 6). For the frangipane, place the butter and sugar in a large bowl and whisk until light and fluffy. Add the egg and whisk well until combined. Then add the ground almonds, almond extract, and brandy and whisk the mixture to form a thick paste.

2 On a lightly floured surface, roll out the pastry to a 50 x 25cm (20 x 10in) rectangle, at least 3–5mm (⅛–¼in) thick. Fold it in half and use a 25cm (10in) plate to cut out two rounds.

3 Place one of the rounds on a non-stick baking sheet. Spread the frangipane on the pastry, leaving a 1cm (½in) border along the edges. Brush the border with a little of the beaten egg.

4 Place the remaining pastry round on top and pinch together the edges to seal. Use a sharp knife to score spiralling slivers on the top of the pastry, making sure they do not meet in the centre.

5 Brush the top with beaten egg. Bake on the top shelf of the oven for 30 minutes, until golden brown and puffed up. Leave the galette to cool on the baking sheet for about 5 minutes. Serve warm. You can store the galette in an airtight container in the fridge for up to 3 days.

🕐 **1 hr**
plus chilling and cooling

🍴 **SERVES 6–8**

GALETTE plum and thyme

Fold over the pastry edges to make this free-form tart – this process helps to contain the juices of the sweet, sticky plums. You could also replace the plum with another orchard fruit.

INGREDIENTS

225g (8oz) plain flour, plus extra for dusting

25g (scant 1oz) caster sugar

125g (4½oz) unsalted butter, chilled and diced

pinch of salt

1 tbsp milk

3 sprigs of thyme

single cream, to serve

For the filling

1 tbsp ground almonds

3 tbsp caster sugar

3 large ripe plums, stoned and thinly sliced

1 Sift the flour and sugar into a large bowl and mix well. Rub in the butter until the mixture resembles fine breadcrumbs. Add the salt and 3 tablespoons of ice-cold water to the bowl.

2 Use your fingertips to bring the mixture together to form a dough, adding more cold water if needed. Transfer the dough to a lightly floured surface and knead it gently and briefly until smooth. Wrap it in cling film and chill for at least 1 hour.

3 Preheat the oven to 200°C (400°F/Gas 6). On a lightly floured surface, roll out the pastry to a 30cm (12in) round. Transfer it to a large baking sheet sprinkled with a little water.

4 For the filling, combine the almonds and 1 tablespoon of the sugar in a bowl. Sprinkle it over the pastry, leaving a 5cm (2in) border.

5 Arrange the plum slices over the filling in a spiral pattern. Fold the pastry edges over them, pressing down lightly to enclose the filling. Brush the pastry edges with the milk, sprinkle the plums with the remaining sugar, and place the thyme in the centre.

6 Bake in the oven for 35–40 minutes, until the plums are soft and the pastry is golden. Remove from the heat and leave to cool for 10 minutes. Then remove the thyme and serve warm with single cream.

 1 hr 40 mins plus chilling **SERVES 8** Also great **COLD**

DOUBLE-CRUST PIE
cherry

This pie is an American classic. Ripe cherries give off a lot of luscious juice once cooked, so add cornflour to transform the liquid into a thick, sticky sauce that keeps the filling together when you slice it.

INGREDIENTS
300g (10oz) plain flour, plus extra for dusting

1 tsp salt

2 tbsp caster sugar

225g (8oz) unsalted butter, chilled and diced

2 tsp apple cider vinegar

For the filling
50g (1¾oz) caster sugar, plus extra for sprinkling

30g (1oz) cornflour

1 tbsp lemon juice

zest of ½ lemon

pinch of salt

½ tsp vanilla extract

900g (2lb) sweet cherries, pitted

1 tbsp unsalted butter, chilled and diced

1 large egg, lightly beaten, to glaze

SPECIAL EQUIPMENT
23cm (9in) round pie dish, about 5cm (2in deep)

PLAN AHEAD
You can prepare and store the dough, covered in the fridge, up 2 days ahead.

Gently stir the liquid and flour mixtures until clumps form.

1 For the pastry, place the flour, salt, and sugar in a large bowl and mix well. Rub in the butter and mix well until the mixture resembles coarse breadcrumbs. Combine the vinegar with 180ml (6fl oz) chilled water in a separate bowl.

2 Gradually add 4 tablespoons of the liquid mixture to the dry ingredients, using two forks to fluff and stir, until well combined. The mixture should resemble shaggy crumbs. If the dough seems dry, add a little more of the liquid mixture and combine.

Knead the dough only until it is just smooth.

KNOW-HOW Handle the dough very gently and be careful not to knead it too much. Overworking the dough can cause the pastry to become tough.

Make sure that one portion of the dough is roughly double the size of the other.

3 On a lightly floured work surface, turn out the mixture and bring it together to form a loose dough. Knead the dough gently for 4–5 minutes, until soft.

4 Divide the dough into one-third and two-thirds of the total quantity so you have two portions. Wrap them both in cling film and chill for at least 30 minutes, or preferably overnight.

 On a floured surface, roll out the larger portion of the pastry to a 30–33cm (12–13in) circle, about 3mm (⅛in) thick. Use it to line the pie dish, leaving a 2cm (¾in) overhang. Chill the pie base until needed.

 Preheat the oven to 200°C (400°F/Gas 6). For the filling, place the sugar, cornflour, lemon juice, zest, salt, and vanilla extract in a large bowl and stir well to combine. Add the cherries, toss well to coat, and leave to macerate for 10–15 minutes.

Crimp the edges of the pastry to your liking (see p35).

KNOW-HOW It is important to cut slits in the pie before baking, as it allows steam to escape and prevents the filling from leaking.

7 Transfer the filling to the pie base and dot with the butter. Roll out the smaller portion of the pastry to a circle slightly larger than the pie dish. Place it on top of the filling and seal the edges. Chill in the freezer for 15–20 minutes.

 Brush with the beaten egg and sprinkle over the sugar. Cut four slits on top of the pie. Bake for 35–45 minutes, then reduce the temperature to 180°C (350°F/Gas 4). Bake for a further 15–20 minutes, until golden. Remove and serve warm. You can store the pie in the fridge for 1–2 days.

🕐 **1 hr 20 mins** plus chilling   🍴 **SERVES 6–8**   🌡 Also great **COLD**

DOUBLE-CRUST PIE
pear and walnut

Ground nuts are a delicious addition to sweet pastry. Here, the mellow flavours of pear contrast with the nutty pastry.

INGREDIENTS
60g (2oz) walnut pieces

135g (5oz) caster sugar, plus extra for sprinkling

250g (9oz) plain flour, sifted, plus extra for dusting

1 egg

150g (5½oz) unsalted butter, softened, plus extra for greasing

½ tsp salt

1 tsp ground cinnamon

For the filling

875g (1lb 15oz) pears, trimmed, cored, and quartered

½ tsp freshly ground black pepper

juice of 1 lemon

SPECIAL EQUIPMENT
23cm (9in) loose-bottomed tart tin

PLAN AHEAD
You can prepare and store the pastry, covered in the fridge, up to 2 days ahead.

1 In a food processor, pulse the walnuts and half the sugar to a fine powder. Combine with the flour in a bowl. Make a well in the centre. Add the egg, butter, salt, cinnamon, and the remaining sugar. Combine well.

2 Gradually work the flour into the egg mixture until it resembles coarse breadcrumbs. Bring the mixture together to form a dough and knead gently on a floured surface for 1–2 minutes, until smooth. Shape into a ball, wrap in cling film, and chill for 30 minutes until firm.

3 Preheat the oven to 190°C (375°F/Gas 5). Grease the tin. On a floured surface, roll out two-thirds of the pastry to a 28cm (11in) circle. Use it to line the tin, pressing it up the sides. Trim and chill for 1 hour. Add the trimmings to the reserved pastry, re-wrap, and chill.

4 For the filling, remove any hard fibres from the pears and place them in a bowl. Toss to coat with the pepper and lemon juice. Shake off any excess juice and arrange them in a spiral pattern in the pastry case.

5 Roll out the reserved pastry to a 25cm (10in) circle and drape over the pears. Trim the edges, brush with water, and seal. Sprinkle with sugar and chill for 15 minutes. Place on a baking sheet and bake for 35–40 minutes, until brown on top. Remove and serve hot.

🕐 **1 hr 5 mins** plus chilling and cooling   🍴 **MAKES 6**   🌡 Also great **COLD**

HAND PIES peach

These individual pies, filled with gently spiced peaches, are perfect for picnics.

INGREDIENTS
150g (5½oz) plain flour, plus extra for dusting

½ tsp salt

1 tbsp caster sugar, plus extra for sprinkling

115g (4oz) unsalted butter, chilled and diced

1 tsp apple cider vinegar

For the filling

350g (12oz) peaches, peeled and cut into 2.5cm (1in) pieces

½ tsp vanilla bean paste

50g (1¾oz) dark brown sugar

1 tsp cinnamon

¼ tsp salt

1 tbsp plain flour

1 large egg, lightly beaten

PLAN AHEAD
You can prepare and store the pastry, covered in the fridge, up to 2 days ahead.

1 Combine the flour, salt, and caster sugar in a bowl. Rub in the butter until the mixture resembles coarse breadcrumbs. Combine the vinegar with 120ml (4fl oz) chilled water in a separate bowl. Gradually add 4 tablespoons of the liquid mixture to the dry ingredients, using two forks to fluff, until it resembles shaggy crumbs.

2 Add a little more liquid, if needed. On a floured surface, bring the mixture together to form a dough and gently knead it 3–6 times. Shape into a ball and wrap in cling film. Chill for 30 minutes, preferably overnight.

3 For the filling, combine the peaches and vanilla bean paste in a bowl. Mix the brown sugar, cinnamon, salt, and flour in a separate bowl and toss with the peaches.

4 On a floured surface, roll out the pastry to a 24 x 37cm (9½ x 15in) rectangle, about 2.5cm (1in) thick. Cut out six 12cm (5in) squares. Transfer to a baking sheet and lightly dampen the edges of the pastry squares.

5 Use a slotted spoon to place equal quantities of the filling on one side of each square. Fold the pastry over to enclose the filling and seal the edges. Crimp the edges and chill the pies for about 20 minutes. Preheat the oven to 190°C (375°F/Gas 5).

6 Brush the pies with the beaten egg. Cut two small slits on top of each pie. Sprinkle the pies with caster sugar and bake them for 30–35 minutes, until golden brown. Remove from the heat and leave to cool slightly. Serve warm.

DOUBLE-CRUST PIE
Alternative fillings

A home-made Cherry double-crust pie (see pp26–29) is a comforting treat, but there are so many alternative fillings to try using the same pastry recipe as a base.

◄ Blueberry and peach
Instead of the cherries, combine 600g (1lb 5oz) peeled, stoned, and thickly sliced ripe peaches with 300g (10oz) blueberries. Add them to the other filling ingredients (see pp26–29, step 6).

▲ Apricot and pistachio
Use 1.1 kg (2½lb) halved, stoned, and quartered just-ripe apricots in place of the cherries. Combine them with 30g (1oz) roughly chopped shelled raw pistachios and add to the other filling ingredients (see pp26–29, step 6).

◄ Apple and cinnamon
Use 1.35kg (3lb) peeled and diced tart apples instead of the cherries. Add 50g (1¾oz) dark brown sugar, ½ tsp cinnamon, ¼ tsp cloves, and ¼ tsp grated nutmeg to the rest of the filling ingredients (see pp26–29, step 6).

◄ Blackberry and apple
Replace the cherries with 450g (1lb) each of blackberries and peeled, cored, and diced apples. Add them to the rest of the filling ingredients (see pp26–29, step 6).

Rhubarb and strawberry ►
For the perfect summer filling, chop 450g (1lb) rhubarb into 2cm (¾in) chunks and combine with the same quantity of hulled strawberries. Add them to the rest of the filling ingredients (see pp26–29, step 6).

▲ Yellow plum
In place of cherries, add the same amount of halved and stoned yellow plums to the rest of the filling ingredients (see pp26–29, step 6). Plums can give off a lot of liquid if they are very ripe, so use only just-ripe smaller plums.

INGREDIENTS

200g (7oz) plain flour, plus extra for dusting

100g (3½oz) unsalted butter, chilled and diced

1 egg, beaten

For the topping

75g (2½oz) plain flour

30g (1oz) soft light brown sugar

½ tsp cinnamon

75g (2½oz) unsalted butter

45g (1½oz) rolled oats

45g (1½oz) chopped pecans

salted caramel ice cream, to serve (optional)

For the filling

250g (9oz) blueberries

250g (9oz) apples, peeled, cored, and diced into about 1cm (½in) cubes

2 tbsp cornflour

3 tbsp caster sugar

SPECIAL EQUIPMENT

23cm (9in) deep-sided, loose-bottomed tart tin

baking beans

PLAN AHEAD

You can store the blind-baked pastry case in an airtight container in the fridge up to 2 days ahead.

🕐 **1 hr 35 mins**
plus chilling and cooling

🍴 **SERVES 8**

🌡 Also great
COLD

SINGLE-CRUST PIE
blueberry and apple

A simple streusel topping is quick to make, and creates a beautifully textured topping for this soft blueberry filling. You will need to blind bake the pastry case before filling to give the pie a crisp and golden base.

1

Place the flour in a bowl and rub in the butter until the mixture resembles fine breadcrumbs. Add the egg, and bring together to form a smooth dough. Wrap in cling film and chill for 30 minutes. Preheat the oven to 180°C (350°F/Gas 4).

2

On a floured surface, roll out the pastry to a circle, 5mm (¼in) thick, and use it to line the tin. Trim the overhang, prick the pastry, and line the base with greaseproof paper. Fill with baking beans and bake for 20 minutes. Remove the beans and paper, and bake for a further 5 minutes. Remove and leave to cool.

3

Leave a few small lumps of butter in the flour mixture.

Increase the oven temperature to 190°C (375°F/Gas 5). For the topping, combine the flour, sugar, cinnamon, and butter into a coarse mixture. Stir in the oats and pecans.

4

For the filling, place all the ingredients in a bowl. Toss well to coat the fruit in the cornflour and sugar.

KNOW-HOW The apple cubes should be small enough to cook through while baking but not lose their texture.

5

Spread the filling in the pastry case evenly and pack it down slightly. Then heap the topping in the centre and spread it out loosely and evenly.

Bake for 40–45 minutes. Cover loosely with foil if it browns too quickly. Cool for 30 minutes. Remove from the tin and serve warm with salted caramel ice cream, if desired. You can store the pie in the fridge for up to 2 days.

6

⏱ **1 hr** plus chilling   🍴 **SERVES 6**   🌡 Also great **COLD**

SINGLE-CRUST PIE mincemeat

Many people find Christmas pudding dense and heavy. Try this flaky pie instead – it features all the familiar festive flavours.

INGREDIENTS

60g (2oz) dried cranberries,
150g (5½oz) each sultanas and raisins
30g (1oz) candied peel
150g (5½oz) apples, peeled, cored, and grated
2 tbsp brandy
30g (1oz) walnuts, chopped
grated zest and juice of 1 orange
½ tsp ground cinnamon
¼ tsp grated nutmeg
⅛ tsp ground cloves
15g (½oz) flaked almonds
icing sugar, for dusting
150g (5½oz) plain flour, plus extra for dusting
25g (scant 1oz) caster sugar
85g (3oz) unsalted butter, chilled and diced
1 egg, beaten

For the frangipane

100g (3½oz) unsalted butter, softened
100g (3½oz) caster sugar
2 large eggs
100g (3½oz) ground almonds
30g (1oz) plain flour

SPECIAL EQUIPMENT

23cm (9in) loose-bottomed tart tin
baking beans

1 For the filling, chop the cranberries, sultanas, raisins, and candied peel finely. Mix them with the apples, brandy, walnuts, orange zest and juice, and spices in a large bowl. Cover with cling film and chill overnight.

2 For the pastry, combine the flour and caster sugar in a bowl. Rub in the butter until the mixture resembles breadcrumbs. Add the egg and bring the mixture together to form a smooth dough. Wrap it in cling film and chill for 30 minutes. Preheat the oven to 180°C (350°F/Gas 4).

3 On a floured surface, roll out the pastry to a circle, 5mm (¼in) thick, and use to line the tin. Prick the pastry, line with greaseproof paper, and fill with baking beans. Bake for 20 minutes. Remove the beans and paper, and bake for 5 more minutes, until lightly coloured. Remove and set aside.

4 For the frangipane, whisk the butter and caster sugar in a bowl until light and fluffy. Add the eggs, one at a time, and whisk well after each addition until combined. Fold in the almonds and flour and combine well.

5 Spread the filling evenly in the pie case. Top with an even layer of the frangipane and sprinkle the flaked almonds over the top. Bake for 40 minutes, until light brown all over. Cool in the tin for 10 minutes, before turning it out. Dust with icing sugar and serve warm. You can store the pie in an airtight container for up to 3 days.

⏱ **35 mins** plus chilling and cooling   🍴 **MAKES 4**   🌡 Also great **COLD**

PIES plum and blackberry

These freeform pies are open in the centre, and so make the most of an attractive autumnal fruit filling.

INGREDIENTS

200g (7oz) plain flour, plus extra for dusting
50g (1¾oz) caster sugar
100g (3½oz) unsalted butter, chilled and diced
2 large plums, stoned and roughly chopped into 2cm (¾in) cubes

200g (7oz) blackberries
1 tbsp ground almonds
1 tbsp soft light brown sugar, plus extra for dusting
½ tsp lemon zest
1 egg, beaten to glaze
custard, to serve

1 Sift the flour and caster sugar into a bowl. Rub in the butter until the mixture resembles coarse breadcrumbs. Add 3–4 tablespoons of chilled water and bring the mixture together to form a smooth dough. Wrap in cling film and chill for 30 minutes.

2 Preheat the oven to 200°C (400°F/Gas 6). Combine the plums, blackberries, almonds, brown sugar, and lemon zest in a large bowl. Divide the pastry into four equal portions and shape them into balls. On a lightly floured surface, roll out each ball to a 20cm (8in) round.

3 Place one-quarter of the filling in the centre of each round. Pull up the pastry edges and crimp them together, leaving an opening in the centre to show the filling. Brush the pies with the beaten egg and sprinkle with brown sugar.

4 Place the pies on a large non-stick baking sheet and bake for 20 minutes, until they are crisp underneath and golden brown on top. Remove from the heat and leave to cool for 10 minutes. Serve warm with custard. Best served on the same day.

Crusts and crimping

Add style to a pastry crust. Line a traditional pie dish with pastry and trim the excess. Just before you blind bake, embellish the crust.

Crimped Pinch the pastry with the thumb and forefinger of one hand, from the outside in, to create a lip. At the same time, use your other forefinger to push the pastry between the thumb and forefinger from the inside out. Repeat the process around the dish.

Plaited Use a sharp knife to cut three 1 x 23cm (½ x 9in) pastry strips. Plait them on a flat surface, and use egg wash to stick one plait down on top of your crust. Repeat this process with two more plaits of the same size, until the plait reaches around the whole circumference.

Leaf Cut out about 40 leaves using a small leaf-shaped cookie cutter, and use the tip of a small, sharp knife to score a vein design on each one. Use egg wash to attach them to the pastry crust, overlapping as you go. Brush the top with egg wash.

Twisted ribbon Cut two 2.5 x 38cm (1 x 15in) pastry strips. Twist one loosely between your hands and use egg wash to fix it around the crust, pressing it down lightly to secure it. Twist and adhere the second strip to complete the circumference of the pie.

⏱ **40 mins** plus cooling   🍴 **MAKES 6**   🌡 Also great **COLD**

PIES peach and raspberry

Thanks to shop-bought filo pastry, these delicacies are so easy to make. They are the perfect finale to a summer's meal.

INGREDIENTS

3 sheets ready-made filo pastry

flour, for dusting

30g (1oz) unsalted butter, melted, plus extra if needed

30g (1oz) ground almonds

1 tbsp pistachios, finely chopped

Greek yogurt, to serve

For the filling

2 ripe peaches, peeled, stoned, and thinly sliced

125g (4½oz) raspberries

1 heaped tbsp soft light brown sugar

SPECIAL EQUIPMENT

6-hole muffin tin, about 6cm (2½in) deep

1. Preheat the oven to 190°C (375°F/Gas 5). On a well-floured work surface roll out one sheet of the pastry and brush with a little butter. Cover with a second layer of pastry, brush with butter, and cover with the final pastry sheet. Cut it into 6 equal pieces.

2. Grease the muffin tin and line with the pastry pieces. Gently push the pastry into the sides, until it ruffles up in places. Brush the edges of the pastry with butter and cover the tin with a damp kitchen towel. For the filling, combine all the ingredients in a large bowl.

3. Divide the almonds evenly between the pastry cases and top with equal quantities of the filling, allowing it to pile up in the centre. Bake for 15–20 minutes, until the pies are crisp and golden, and the filling is soft.

4. Remove from the heat and leave the pies to cool in the tin for 5 minutes. Then turn them out and place on a wire rack to cool a little more, before topping them with pistachios and serving them warm with Greek yogurt. Best served on the same day.

1 hr 10 mins
plus chilling

SERVES 4–6

Also great
COLD

TARTE TATIN apple

According to legend, this tart is named after two French sisters who created the recipe by accident in the 19th century. To create an even layer of caramelized fruit on top of the pastry, fill all the gaps between the apple slices with smaller apple pieces.

INGREDIENTS

175g (6oz) plain flour, sifted, plus extra for dusting

25g (scant 1oz) caster sugar, sifted

100g (3½oz) unsalted butter, chilled and diced

vanilla ice cream, to serve

For the topping

150g (5½oz) caster sugar

30g (1oz) unsalted butter

4–5 dessert apples, such as Gala or Cox, peeled, cored, and cut into eighths

SPECIAL EQUIPMENT

23cm (9in) ovenproof frying pan

Place the flour and sugar in a large bowl. Rub in the butter until the mixture resembles coarse breadcrumbs. Add 3 tablespoons of ice-cold water, and bring together to form a smooth dough. Wrap in cling film and chill for 30 minutes.

1

For the topping, spread the sugar in the frying pan and heat gently until melting at the edges. Cook, stirring occasionally, until golden. Do not over-stir or the sugar will harden. Remove from the heat.

2

Stir in the butter until combined. Spread the caramel evenly in the pan, and leave to cool and harden. Preheat the oven to 200°C (400°F/Gas 6).

3

Place the apple slices evenly over the cooled caramel in a tight layer. Plug any gaps with small pieces of apple.

4

On a floured surface, roll out the pastry. Use a 24cm (9½in) plate to cut out a circle and drape over the apples. Tuck in the edges, creating a small lip around the fruit.

5

Bake on the top shelf of the oven for 30–35 minutes, until golden. Cool for 5 minutes, before carefully turning the tart out onto a large plate. Pour the excess caramel over the apples. Serve immediately with vanilla ice cream.

6

⏱ **30 mins**
plus cooling and chilling

🍴 **SERVES 4–6**

🌡 Also great
COLD

TARTE TATIN
fig with goat's cheese mascarpone

Sweet ripe figs create a wonderfully sticky topping for this tart. Serve it with mild tangy goat's cheese and creamy mascarpone for a delicious Middle-Eastern take on the French classic. It looks show-stopping and is so easy to make.

INGREDIENTS
60g (2oz) unsalted butter

60g (2oz) caster sugar

8 ripe figs, trimmed and halved lengthways

flour, for dusting

25cm (10in) square ready-made all-butter puff pastry

For the mascarpone
150g (5½oz) mascarpone, at room temperature

100g (3½oz) soft goat's cheese, at room temperature

6 tbsp single cream

6 tsp icing sugar

SPECIAL EQUIPMENT
23cm (9in) cast-iron frying pan

PLAN AHEAD
You can prepare and store the mascarpone, covered in the fridge, up to 3 days ahead.

1 Preheat the oven to 220°C (425°F/Gas 7). Place the butter and sugar in the frying pan over a medium heat. Cook, stirring constantly, until the sugar dissolves and the mixture is well combined. Remove and leave to cool.

2 Place the figs, cut-side down, over the caramel. On a floured surface, roll out the pastry and use a 24cm (9½in) plate to cut out a circle. Drape the pastry over the figs, tucking in the edges to create a small lip around the fruit.

3 Bake the tart on the top shelf of the oven for 20 minutes, until golden brown. Leave to cool for 5 minutes, before transferring it to a serving plate. Pour over any excess caramel.

4 Meanwhile, for the mascarpone, place all the ingredients in a large bowl. Beat the mixture until smooth and well combined. Chill until needed. Serve the tart warm, on the same day, along with the mascarpone.

⏱ **35 mins** plus cooling 🍴 **SERVES 4-6** 🌡 Also great **COLD**

TARTE TATIN
banana, maple, and rum

This tart is unashamedly sweet, with deep, rich notes of maple syrup alongside the soft sweetness of banana. You could serve with good-quality vanilla ice cream.

INGREDIENTS

2 tbsp maple syrup

30g (1oz) soft dark brown sugar

30g (1oz) unsalted butter

2 tbsp rum

4 slightly underripe bananas, cut into 2cm (¾in) slices

flour, for dusting

25cm (10in) square ready-made, all-butter puff pastry

SPECIAL EQUIPMENT

23cm (9in) cast-iron frying pan

1 Preheat the oven to 220°C (425°F/Gas 7). Place the maple syrup, sugar, butter, and rum in the frying pan over a medium heat. Cook, stirring constantly, until the sugar dissolves and the mixture is well combined.

2 Bring to the boil, then reduce the heat to a simmer. Cook for 2–3 minutes, until the caramel has reduced. Remove and leave to cool. Place the banana slices over the cooled caramel in tight concentric circles.

3 On a floured surface, roll out the pastry and use a 24cm (9½in) plate to cut out a circle. Drape the pastry over the bananas, tucking in the edges to create a small lip around the fruit.

4 Bake the tart on the top shelf of the oven for about 20 minutes, until golden brown. Leave to cool for 5 minutes, before transferring it to a large serving plate. Pour over any excess caramel and serve immediately.

Simple alternatives

Many fruits lend themselves to caramelizing. All you require is a good sweet pastry recipe, as shown for the classic Apple tarte tatin (see pp36–37) and an ovenproof frying pan.

Apple and blackberry Fill the gaps between the apple slices with blackberries (see p37, step 4). You will need one less apple, and 100g (3½oz) blackberries.

Pear Use slightly underripe pears in a tarte tatin. Peel, core, and quarter the same quantity of pears as apples (see pp36–37).

Pineapple The flavour of caramel works well with sweet and rich pineapple. Trim, core, and chop 1 medium-sized pineapple into 2cm (¾in) cubes and use in place of the apple (see pp36–37).

Apricot Halve and stone 8 large apricots. Use them instead of the apples in the recipe (see pp36–37). As with all soft fruit, make sure the apricots are not overripe or they may disintegrate before the pastry is fully cooked.

Plum Halve and stone 8 plums, and place them skin-side down over the caramel base instead of the apples (see pp36–37). Choose dark and firm plums.

Peach Halve, stone, and thickly slice 4–6 perfectly ripe peaches. Use in place of the apples for a summery alternative (see pp36–37).

🕐 **1 hr 30 mins**
plus chilling and cooling

🍴 **SERVES 8**

TART Normandy pear

Rich, crisp butter pastry makes this elegant French tart irresistible. The pairing of pears and frangipane is a classic of the Normandy region, but you could use apples instead for another traditional choice.

INGREDIENTS

75g (2½oz) unsalted butter, softened and diced, plus extra for greasing

175g (6oz) plain flour, sifted, plus extra for dusting

3 egg yolks

60g (2oz) caster sugar

pinch of salt

½ tsp vanilla extract

3–4 ripe pears, peeled, cored, and cut into wedges

juice of 1 lemon

double cream, to serve

For the frangipane

125g (4½oz) unsalted butter, softened

100g (3½oz) caster sugar

1 egg, plus 1 egg yolk, lightly beaten

1 tbsp Kirsch

125g (4½oz) ground almonds

2 tbsp plain flour, sifted

For the glaze

150g (5½oz) apricot jam

2–3 tbsp Kirsch or water

SPECIAL EQUIPMENT

23cm (9in) loose-bottomed, fluted tart tin

PLAN AHEAD

You can prepare and store the tart case in an airtight container in the fridge for up to 3 days ahead, or freeze it up to 12 weeks ahead.

1

Preheat the oven to 200°C (400°F/Gas 6) and grease the tart tin. Place the flour in a large bowl and make a well in the centre. Place the butter, egg yolks, sugar, salt, and vanilla extract in the well and mix to combine.

2

Use your fingertips to work the ingredients together to form a sticky dough, adding water if needed. Lightly knead the dough on a floured surface for 1-2 minutes, wrap in cling film, and chill for 30 minutes.

Knead the dough gently and work it only until the texture is just smooth.

3

On a floured surface, roll out the pastry to a 28cm (11in) circle. Use it to line the tin and trim any overhang. Prick the base with a fork and chill the tart case for 15 minutes, or until firm.

4

For the frangipane, beat the butter and sugar in a large bowl for 2-3 minutes, until fluffy. Add the egg and yolk, a little at a time, beating well after each addition. Stir in the Kirsch, ground almonds, and flour.

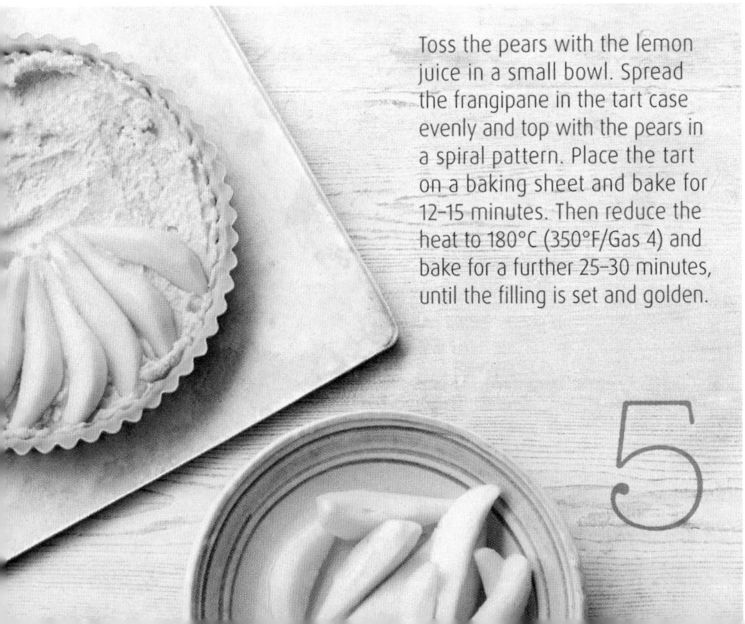

5

Toss the pears with the lemon juice in a small bowl. Spread the frangipane in the tart case evenly and top with the pears in a spiral pattern. Place the tart on a baking sheet and bake for 12-15 minutes. Then reduce the heat to 180°C (350°F/Gas 4) and bake for a further 25-30 minutes, until the filling is set and golden.

6

Leave to cool slightly, then remove the tart from the tin. For the glaze, push the jam through a sieve into a heatproof bowl. Add the Kirsch, melt over a saucepan of hot water, and brush over the tart. Serve warm with double cream. You can store the tart in an airtight container for up to 2 days.

🕐 **1 hr 15 mins**
plus chilling and cooling   🍴 **SERVES 8**

TART French apple

This stunning tart combines a layer of puréed cooked apple, topped with an overlapping spiral of finely cut fresh apple. Glazing makes a home-made tart look as appetizing as one in a French pâtisserie – use apricot jam for this recipe.

INGREDIENTS

plain flour, for dusting

375g (13oz) ready-made sweet pastry

2 tbsp apricot jam, sieved

For the filling

50g (1¾oz) unsalted butter

750g (1lb 10oz) cooking apples, cored and roughly chopped

125g (4½oz) caster sugar

finely grated zest and juice of ½ lemon

2 tbsp Calvados or brandy

2 dessert apples, cored and thinly sliced

SPECIAL EQUIPMENT

23cm (9in) loose-bottomed tart tin

baking beans

PLAN AHEAD

You can store the blind-baked tart case in an airtight container in the fridge up to 3 days ahead, or freeze it up to 12 weeks ahead.

1 On a lightly floured surface, roll out the pastry to a 28cm (11in) large and 3mm (⅛in) thick circle. Use the circle to line the tin, leaving an overhang of 2cm (¾in). Prick the base and chill for 30 minutes. Preheat the oven to 200°C (400°F/Gas 6).

2 Line the pastry base with greaseproof paper and fill with baking beans. Place the tin on a baking sheet and blind bake for 20 minutes. Then remove the beans and paper and bake for a further 5 minutes, until it is a light golden colour. Remove from the oven and trim the overhanging pastry. Set aside.

3 For the filling, melt the butter in a lidded saucepan over a low heat and add the cooking apples. Then cover and cook for 15 minutes, stirring, until soft. Push the cooked apple through a sieve to make a smooth purée.

4 Return the purée to the pan. Reserve 1 tablespoon of the sugar and stir the rest into the pan. Add the lemon zest and Calvados, and reduce the heat to a simmer. Cook the purée, stirring frequently, until thickened.

5 Spread the purée evenly in the tart case and top with the dessert apples, in a spiral pattern. Brush with the lemon juice and sprinkle over the reserved sugar. Bake for 30–35 minutes, until the apples are a pale gold in colour.

6 Leave to cool slightly in the tin, before transferring it to a plate. Warm the jam and brush over the top. Serve warm. You can store the tart in an airtight container in the fridge for up to 2 days.

TART custard

A great British classic, this tart is made with gently set home-made custard that is delicately flavoured with nutmeg.

INGREDIENTS

175g (6oz) plain flour, plus extra for dusting

100g (3½oz) unsalted butter, chilled and diced

50g (1¾oz) caster sugar

2 egg yolks

½ tsp vanilla extract

For the filling

2 eggs

30g (1oz) caster sugar

½ tsp vanilla extract

¼ tsp grated nutmeg

225ml (7¾fl oz) milk

150ml (5fl oz) double cream

SPECIAL EQUIPMENT

23cm (9in) loose-bottomed tart tin

baking beans

PLAN AHEAD

You can store the blind-baked tart case in an airtight container in the fridge up to 3 days ahead, or freeze it up to 12 weeks.

1 Place the flour in a large bowl and rub in the butter until the mixture resembles breadcrumbs. Stir in the sugar. In a separate bowl, beat together the egg yolks and vanilla extract until combined. Add the egg mixture to the dry ingredients and bring together to form a soft dough. Wrap in cling film and chill for 1 hour.

2 Preheat the oven to 180°C (350°F/Gas 4). Roll out the pastry and use it to line the tart tin (see French apple tart, step 1). Prick the base, chill, and then blind bake the tart case until light golden in colour (see French apple tart, step 2). Trim the overhanging pastry. Reduce the oven temperature to 170°C (340°F/Gas 3½).

3 For the filling, whisk the eggs, sugar, vanilla extract, and nutmeg in a bowl, until combined. Place the milk and cream in a saucepan, bring to the boil, and pour the hot mixture over the egg mixture, whisking to combine.

4 Place the tart case on a baking sheet, on an oven rack. Carefully pour in the filling and spread it out evenly. Bake for 20–25 minutes, until just set but with a slight wobble. Leave in the tin for 15 minutes, before transferring to a plate. Serve warm. You can store the tart in an airtight container in the fridge for up to 1 day.

TART treacle

The fillings for most classic treacle tarts include little more than breadcrumbs and syrup. This version is given a French twist with the addition of cream and eggs, for a just-set texture.

INGREDIENTS

150g (5½oz) plain flour, plus extra for dusting

100g (3½oz) unsalted butter, chilled and diced

½ tsp vanilla extract

1 egg yolk

50g (1¾oz) caster sugar

For the filling

200ml (7fl oz) golden syrup

200ml (7fl oz) double cream

2 eggs

finely grated zest of 1 orange

100g (3½oz) brioche or croissant crumbs

thick cream, to serve

SPECIAL EQUIPMENT

23cm (9in) loose-bottomed tart tin

baking beans

PLAN AHEAD

You can store the blind-baked tart case in an airtight container in the fridge up to 3 days ahead, or freeze it up to 12 weeks.

1 Place the flour in a large bowl and rub in the butter until the mixture resembles breadcrumbs. Beat the vanilla extract and egg yolk in a separate bowl. Add the egg mixture and sugar to the flour mixture and bring them together to form a soft dough, adding water if it seems dry. Wrap in cling film and chill for 30 minutes.

2 Preheat the oven to 180°C (350°F/Gas 4). Roll out the pastry and use it to line the tart tin (see French apple tart, step 1). Prick the base, chill it, and then blind bake the tart case until light golden in colour (see French apple tart, step 2). Trim the overhanging pastry. Reduce the heat to 170°C (340°F/Gas 3½).

3 For the filling, whisk the golden syrup, cream, eggs, and orange zest in a large bowl until combined. Gently fold in the brioche crumbs and combine well. Place the tart case on a baking sheet, on an oven rack. Carefully pour the filling into the tart case, ensuring that it spreads out evenly.

4 Carefully slide the rack into the oven and bake for 30 minutes, until the filling is just set. Leave to cool in the tin for 15 minutes, before transferring to a plate. Serve warm with thick cream. You can store the tart in an airtight container for up to 2 days.

🕐 **1 hr 35 mins**
plus cooling

🍴 **SERVES 8**

🌡 Also great
COLD

PIE pumpkin

Dark, rich, and sweet, this classic American pie has all the fragrance and flavours of autumn, wrapped in a crisp pastry shell. It is the perfect dessert to bring to the Thanksgiving table.

INGREDIENTS
115g (4oz) butter, chilled
  and diced, plus
  extra for greasing
150g (5½oz) plain flour,
  plus extra for dusting
1 tbsp caster sugar
½ tsp salt
1 tsp apple cider vinegar
whipped cream, to serve

For the filling
400g can pumpkin purée
120ml (4fl oz) whole milk
175g (6oz) dark brown
  sugar
1⅛ tsp ground cinnamon

½ tsp grated nutmeg
⅛ tsp ground allspice
½ tsp salt
2 large eggs

SPECIAL EQUIPMENT
23cm (9in) pie dish, about
  5cm (2in) deep
baking beans

PLAN AHEAD
You can store the blind-baked pastry case in an airtight container up to 3 days ahead.

The mixture
should resemble
shaggy crumbs.

1 Grease the pie dish. Combine the flour, caster sugar, and salt in a bowl. Rub in the butter with your fingertips until the mixture resembles coarse breadcrumbs. In a separate bowl, combine the cider vinegar with 120ml (4fl oz) chilled water.

2 Gradually add 8 tablespoons of the liquid mixture to the dry ingredients, using two forks to fluff and stir them together until clumps form. Add a little more of the liquid mixture if it seems too dry.

Knead the dough only
until it is just smooth.

KNOW-HOW Chilling the dough allows the gluten to relax, making the dough easier to roll out. It also helps prevent the pastry from shrinking.

 On a lightly floured surface, gently knead the mixture 3–6 times, until it comes together to form a dough. Wrap the dough in cling film and chill it for 30 minutes, or preferably overnight.

4 On a floured surface, roll out the pastry to a 30cm (12in) circle, 2mm (⅛in) thick. Use to line the pie dish, leaving an overhang of 1cm (½in). Crimp the edges of the pastry (see p35) and chill for 30 minutes. Preheat the oven to 190°C (375°F/Gas 5).

 Prick the bottom of the pie case. Then line it with greaseproof paper and fill with baking beans. Place on a baking sheet and bake for about 25 minutes, until lightly brown at the edges.

6 Remove the beans and paper. Bake for a further 6–10 minutes, until the pastry is golden. Remove from the oven, trim the pastry case, and leave to cool. Reduce the oven temperature to 180°C (350°F/Gas 4).

7 For the filling, whisk the pumpkin purée, milk, and brown sugar in a bowl, until smooth. Beat in the spices, salt, and eggs until smooth and well combined.

 Pour the filling into the pastry case, and place on a baking sheet. Cover the edges with foil, and bake for 35–40 minutes. Remove the foil and bake for a further 10 minutes, until set. Leave to cool slightly and serve warm with whipped cream. You can store the pie in an airtight container for up to 2 days.

🕐 **1 hr 40 mins**
plus chilling and cooling   🍴 **SERVES 8**   🌡 Also great **COLD**

PIE brûléed spiced pumpkin

This recipe packs a punch thanks to the cardamom and cloves. A brûlée topping is a caramelizing technique that gives a professional finish – try it with any just-set tart.

INGREDIENTS

115g (4oz) unsalted butter, chilled and diced, plus extra for greasing

150g (5½oz) plain flour, plus extra for dusting

2½ tbsp caster sugar

½ tsp salt

1 tsp apple cider vinegar

whipped cream, to serve

For the filling

400g can pumpkin purée

400g can condensed milk

1¼ tsp ground cinnamon

½ tsp grated nutmeg

¼ tsp ground cardamom

⅛ tsp ground cloves

½ tsp pure vanilla extract

¼ tsp salt

2 large eggs

SPECIAL EQUIPMENT

23cm (9in) pie dish, about 5cm (2in) deep

baking beans

small kitchen blowtorch

PLAN AHEAD

You can store the blind-baked pastry case in an airtight container up to 3 days ahead.

1 Grease the pie dish and set aside. Combine the flour, 1 tablespoon of sugar, and salt in a bowl. Rub in the butter until the mixture resembles coarse breadcrumbs. Mix the vinegar with 60ml (2fl oz) chilled water in a bowl.

2 Gradually add 8 tablespoons of the liquid mixture to the dry ingredients. Use two forks to fluff and stir the mixture until it forms clumps. On a floured surface, gently knead it 3–6 times to form a dough. Wrap in cling film and chill for 30 minutes, preferably overnight.

3 On a floured surface, roll out the pastry to a 30–33cm (12–13in) circle, 3mm (⅛in) thick. Use it to line the pie dish, leaving a 1cm (½in) overhang. Crimp the edges and chill for 30 minutes. Preheat the oven to 190°C (375°F/Gas 5).

4 Prick the bottom of the pastry, line with greaseproof paper, and fill with baking beans. Bake for 25 minutes. Then remove the beans and paper, and bake for a further 6–10 minutes, until lightly golden. Remove from the heat, trim the pastry, and leave to cool.

5 Reduce the temperature to 180°C (350°F/Gas 4). For the filling, whisk the pumpkin purée and milk in a bowl until combined. Then beat in the remaining ingredients until smooth.

6 Pour the filling into the pastry case and cover the edges with foil. Bake for 35 minutes, until set. Then remove the foil and bake for a further 10 minutes. Remove from the heat and leave to cool completely.

7 Sprinkle the remaining sugar over the pie and gently spread it out with the back of a spoon. Use the blowtorch to melt the sugar, sweeping it over gently to form a caramel. Serve at room temperature with whipped cream. You can store the pie in an airtight container for up to 2 days.

⏱ **1 hr 30 mins** plus chilling and cooling   🍴 **SERVES 8**   🌡 Also great **COLD**

PIE sweet potato

Another southern American holiday favourite, sweet potato pie has a light and velvet-like texture.

INGREDIENTS

1½ tbsp unsalted butter, melted, plus extra for greasing

270g (9½oz) sweet pastry (see Brûléed spiced pumpkin pie, steps 1-2)

550g (1¼lb) sweet potatoes, boiled and mashed

¼ tsp salt

200ml (7fl oz) condensed milk

120ml (4fl oz) evaporated milk

2 tbsp dark brown sugar

1¼ tsp ground cinnamon

½ tsp grated nutmeg

½ tsp vanilla extract

2 large eggs

whipped cream, to serve

SPECIAL EQUIPMENT

23cm (9in) pie dish, about 5cm (2in) deep

baking beans

PLAN AHEAD

You can store the blind-baked pastry case in an airtight container up to 3 days ahead.

1 Preheat the oven to 180°C (350°F/Gas 4). Grease the pie dish. Roll out the pastry, use it to line the dish, and blind bake it (see Brûléed spiced pumpkin pie, steps 3-4). Beat the potatoes, butter, salt, and both lots of milk in a large bowl, until smooth and well combined.

2 Add the brown sugar, cinnamon, nutmeg, vanilla extract, and eggs to the bowl. Beat until smooth, and pour the filling into the pastry case evenly. Cover the edges with foil.

3 Transfer the pie to the oven and bake for about 35 minutes, until the filling is set. Then remove the foil and bake for a further 10 minutes. Remove from the heat.

4 Leave to cool slightly in the dish. Then turn it out and place on a wire rack to cool completely. Serve at room temperature with whipped cream. You can store the sweet potato pie in an airtight container for up to 2 days.

⏱ **1 hr 30 mins** plus chilling and cooling   🍴 **SERVES 8**   🌡 Also great **COLD**

PIE pumpkin and pecan

This recipe requires a metal tart tin instead of a pie dish. The tin helps heat to conduct evenly, resulting in a super-crisp pastry.

INGREDIENTS

150g (5½oz) plain flour, plus extra for dusting

100g (3½oz) unsalted butter, chilled and diced

50g (1¾oz) caster sugar

1 egg yolk

½ tsp vanilla extract

For the filling

3 eggs

100g (3½oz) soft light brown sugar

1 tsp mixed spice

200ml (7fl oz) double cream

1 tsp ground cinnamon

2 tbsp maple syrup

400g can pumpkin purée

75g (2½oz) pecans, roughly chopped

SPECIAL EQUIPMENT

23cm (9in) loose-bottomed tart tin

baking beans

PLAN AHEAD

You can store the blind-baked pastry case in an airtight container up to 3 days ahead.

1 Place the flour in a bowl and rub in the butter until the mixture resembles breadcrumbs. Stir in the sugar. In a separate bowl, whisk the egg yolk and vanilla extract and add to the flour mixture. Bring them together to form a dough, adding a little water if it seems dry. Wrap in cling film and chill for 30 minutes.

2 Preheat the oven to 180°C (350°F/Gas 4). On a lightly floured surface, roll out the pastry to a 3mm (⅛in) thick circle. Use it to line the tin, leaving a 2cm (¾in) overhang. Prick the bottom of the pastry, line it with greaseproof paper, and fill with baking beans.

3 Place the pastry case on a baking sheet and bake for 20 minutes. Then remove the beans and paper, and bake for a further 5 minutes if the centre seems uncooked. Remove from the heat, trim the pastry, and leave to cool.

4 For the filling, whisk the eggs, brown sugar, mixed spice, cream, cinnamon, and maple syrup in a bowl, until combined. Then whisk in the pumpkin until well blended. Sprinkle the pecans in the pastry case. Place the tart case on a baking sheet, on an oven rack.

5 Carefully pour the filling into the pastry case, spread it out evenly, and bake for 45–50 minutes until set. Leave the pie to cool in the tin for 15 minutes before turning it out. Serve warm. You can store the pie, in an airtight container in the fridge, for up to 2 days.

🕐 **40 mins**
plus resting

🍴 **MAKES 12**

🌡 Also great
COLD

DOUGHNUTS jam

These airy and moreish delights are so much better than any shop-bought variety you have ever tried. They are also surprisingly easy to make – the trick is to achieve the right temperature for the oil, and to maintain it throughout cooking.

INGREDIENTS

150ml (5fl oz) whole milk

75g (2½oz) unsalted butter

½ tsp vanilla extract

2 tsp dried yeast

75g (2½oz) caster sugar, plus extra for coating

425g (15oz) plain flour, preferably "00" grade, plus extra for dusting

½ tsp salt

2 eggs, beaten

1 litre (1¾ pints) sunflower oil, plus extra for greasing

250g (9oz) good-quality raspberry, strawberry, or cherry jam, pulsed until smooth

SPECIAL EQUIPMENT

oil thermometer

piping bag with thin nozzle

PLAN AHEAD

You can store the unfilled doughnuts in an airtight container up to 1 day ahead.

1

Heat the milk, butter, and vanilla extract in a saucepan over a medium heat, until combined. Cool to lukewarm and whisk in the yeast and 1 tablespoon of sugar. Cover and leave for 10 minutes. Sift the flour, salt, and the remaining sugar into a large bowl. Whisk the eggs into the cooled milk mixture, until combined.

2

Make a well in the centre of the dry ingredients. Pour in the milk mixture and bring together to form a dough. On a floured surface, knead the dough for 10 minutes, until soft. Transfer to a greased bowl, cover with cling film, and leave in a warm place for 2 hours, to rise.

3

On a floured surface, knock back the dough until smooth. Divide it into 12 portions and shape into balls. Place them on non-stick baking sheets, spaced apart, and cover with cling film and a kitchen towel. Rest the dough balls in a warm place for 1–2 hours, until they double in size.

4

Heat the oil in a large, deep saucepan to 170–180°C (340–350°F). Carefully slide the doughnuts, rounded-side down, into the oil. Fry them for 1 minute on each side, until golden brown all over. Remove with a slotted spoon. Fry in batches to avoid overcrowding the pan.

5

Drain the doughnuts on plates lined with kitchen paper. Roll them in some sugar while they are still hot.

6

Place the jam in a piping bag. Pierce each doughnut on the side and gently squirt in a tablespoon of the jam, until it almost spills out. Dust with a little more sugar and serve warm. You can store them in an airtight container for up to 1 day.

🕐 **25 mins**   🍴 **MAKES 25–30**

FRITTERS apple and cinnamon

It is easy and quick to transform apples and some store-cupboard ingredients into these light and delicious fritters.

INGREDIENTS
120ml (4fl oz) whole milk
1 egg
30g (1oz) unsalted butter, melted and cooled
½ tsp vanilla extract
150g (5½oz) plain flour
1 tsp baking powder
½ tsp ground cinnamon
50g (1¾oz) caster sugar
2 dessert apples, peeled, cored, and finely diced
1 litre (1¾ pints) sunflower or other flavourless oil
icing sugar, for dusting

SPECIAL EQUIPMENT
oil thermometer

1 Whisk the milk, egg, butter, and vanilla extract in a large bowl, until well combined. Sift the flour, baking powder, cinnamon, and caster sugar into a separate bowl and mix well. Bring the wet and dry ingredients together to form a thick batter. Fold in the apples.

2 Heat the oil in a large, heavy-based saucepan to 180°C (350°F). Drop a small amount of the batter into the oil to test if it is hot enough – the batter should sizzle and turn golden brown in colour.

3 Carefully drop a few heaped teaspoons of the batter into the hot oil and cook them for 1–2 minutes on each side, until golden brown all over. Do not use large amounts of the batter or overcrowd the pan.

4 Remove the fritters with a slotted spoon. Leave them to drain on a plate lined with kitchen paper, or keep them warm in a preheated oven. Continue cooking until you have used all of the batter. Dust the warm fritters with a little icing sugar and serve immediately.

🕐 **25 mins**   🍴 **MAKES 25–30**

FRITTERS lemon and ricotta

These airy little puffs, straight from the pan, are so moreish – serve them at a dinner party and you will find it hard to fry them quickly enough for your guests.

INGREDIENTS
200g (7oz) ricotta cheese
2 eggs, beaten
½ tsp vanilla extract
2 tbsp unsalted butter, melted and cooled
100g (3½oz) plain flour
2 tsp baking powder
4 tbsp caster sugar
1 tsp lemon zest
1 tbsp lemon juice
1 litre (1¾ pints) sunflower or other flavourless oil
icing sugar, for dusting

SPECIAL EQUIPMENT
oil thermometer

1 Whisk the ricotta, eggs, vanilla extract, and butter in a small bowl, until well combined. Sift the flour, baking powder, and caster sugar into a separate bowl. Add the lemon zest, then bring the dry and wet mixture together to form a thick batter. Add the lemon juice and mix well to combine.

2 Heat the oil in a large, heavy-based saucepan to 180°C (350°F). Test to check if the oil is hot (see Apple and cinnamon fritters, step 2). Cook heaped teaspoons of the batter in the oil until golden brown all over (see Apple and cinnamon fritters, step 3).

3 Remove the fritters with a slotted spoon and drain them on a plate lined with kitchen paper, or keep them warm in a preheated oven. Continue cooking until you have used all of the batter. Dust the warm fritters with a little icing sugar and serve immediately.

⏱ **40 mins**
plus chilling and rising　　🍴 **MAKES 40**

BEIGNETS
pumpkin spice

This is a US-style recipe, popular in New Orleans. Beignets were first brought to Louisiana by French settlers in the 1700s.

INGREDIENTS

7g (1 heaped tsp) active
　dried yeast
100g (3½oz) caster sugar,
　plus a pinch extra
250ml (9fl oz) double
　cream
60g (2oz) butter
2 eggs
750g (1lb 10oz) plain flour,
　plus extra for dusting
1 litre (1¾ pints) peanut
　or sunflower oil

For the spice mix

1 tbsp ground cinnamon
½ tbsp ground ginger
½ tbsp grated nutmeg
½ tbsp ground cloves
75g (2½oz) icing sugar

SPECIAL EQUIPMENT

oil thermometer

1 Place 125ml (4¼fl oz) warm water in a bowl. Add the yeast and a pinch of caster sugar, and stir to dissolve. Leave to stand for 5–7 minutes, until it begins to bubble. For the spice mix, combine all the ingredients in a small bowl and set aside.

2 Heat the cream and butter in a large saucepan over a low heat until the butter melts. Transfer to a large bowl and add the yeast mixture, sugar, eggs, and half the flour. Stir well to combine. Then gradually add the remaining flour and stir well to form a smooth dough.

3 Knead the dough for 5–7 minutes until it is smooth, adding more flour if it is sticky and difficult to handle. Place the dough in a bowl, cover with cling film, and chill for 4–6 hours, until it doubles in size.

4 On a floured surface, roll out the dough to a large circle, about 1cm (½in) thick. Cut it into 40 squares, each about 4cm (1½in) in diameter. Heat the oil in a large, heavy-based saucepan to 190°C (375°F).

5 Cook the squares in batches for 1–2 minutes, on each side, until golden brown and puffed. Remove with a slotted spoon and place on a wire rack to cool slightly. Sprinkle the spice mix over the warm beignets and serve immediately.

⏱ **25 mins**
plus cooling　　🍴 **MAKES 20**

CHURROS with chocolate and chilli sauce

Sprinkled with cinnamon–sugar and served with a rich and spicy chocolate dipping sauce, these Spanish treats make the perfect accompaniment to after-dinner coffee.

INGREDIENTS

25g (scant 1oz) unsalted
　butter
200g (7oz) plain flour
1 tsp baking powder
50g (1¾oz) caster sugar
1 litre (1¾ pints) peanut
　or sunflower oil
1 tsp ground cinnamon

For the sauce

50g (1¾oz) good-quality
　dark chocolate, broken
　into pieces
150ml (5fl oz) double
　cream
1 tbsp caster sugar
1 tbsp unsalted butter
pinch of salt
¼ tsp chilli powder,
　to taste

SPECIAL EQUIPMENT

piping bag fitted with a
　2cm (¾in) star nozzle
oil thermometer

1 Place the butter and 200ml (7fl oz) boiling water in a jug and stir well. Sift the flour, baking powder, and half the sugar into a bowl. Make a well in the centre and gradually add the liquid mixture, beating continuously to form a thick batter. Leave to cool for 5 minutes.

2 Heat the oil in a large, heavy-based saucepan to 190°C (375°F). Spoon the batter into the piping bag and pipe 7cm (2¾in) lengths into the pan, in batches, using a pair of scissors to snip off the ends. Cook them for 1–2 minutes on each side, until golden brown all over.

3 Remove them with a slotted spoon and drain on a plate lined with kitchen paper. Combine the cinnamon and remaining sugar in a plate and use to lightly coat the churros while still hot. Leave to cool for 5–10 minutes.

4 For the sauce, melt the chocolate, cream, sugar, and butter in a heatproof bowl over a pan of simmering water, making sure it does not touch the water. Stir for 3–4 minutes, until the sauce thickens.

5 Remove from the heat, add the salt, and mix well. Add the chilli powder gradually, until it reaches the desired level of heat, then serve the sauce warm alongside the churros.

🕐 **1 hr 10 mins**
plus cooling

🍴 **MAKES 9**

🌡 Also great
COLD

BROWNIES triple chocolate chip

The best kind of brownie is crisp on the surface and gently yielding on the inside. If you prefer them really soft and gooey, bake them for 5 minutes less than suggested here. If you like them firm, add 5 minutes more to the cooking time.

INGREDIENTS

115g (4oz) unsalted butter, plus extra for greasing

175g (6oz) good-quality dark chocolate, finely chopped

60g (2oz) very dark chocolate, at least 85 per cent cocoa solids, finely chopped

2 tsp vanilla extract

200g (7oz) caster sugar

50g (1¾oz) dark brown sugar

2 large eggs

125g (4½oz) plain flour

3 tbsp natural cocoa powder

¾ tsp salt

¼ tsp baking powder

60g (2oz) good-quality milk chocolate chips

60g (2oz) white chocolate chips

vanilla ice cream, to serve (optional)

SPECIAL EQUIPMENT

20cm (8in) square cake tin

1 Preheat the oven to 180°C (350°F/Gas 4). Lightly grease and line the tin with baking parchment, leaving some overhang. Melt the butter and both lots of chocolate in a heatproof bowl over a saucepan of simmering water, making sure it does not touch the water. Stir until smooth, then leave to cool.

2 Gradually add the vanilla extract and both lots of sugar to the mixture and whisk well to combine. Then add the eggs, one at a time, whisking well after each addition until smooth. Place the flour, cocoa powder, salt, and baking powder in a separate bowl and mix well.

Use a spatula to fold the dry ingredients into the chocolate mixture and combine until smooth. Then mix in both lots of chocolate chips until evenly incorporated. Pour the brownie mixture into the prepared tin, and spread it out evenly.

4 Bake for 40–45 minutes, until an inserted toothpick comes out clean. Leave to cool slightly before removing the brownie from the tin. Then cut it into nine equal-sized pieces, cleaning the knife with a damp kitchen towel between cuts. Serve warm with vanilla ice cream, if desired. You can store them in an airtight container for up to 5 days.

🕐 **1 hr 10 mins** plus cooling | 🍴 **MAKES 9** | 🌡 Also great **COLD**

BROWNIES cheesecake

This rich and moist variety is rippled with sweetened cream cheese to provide a pleasing contrast in flavour and texture.

1 Preheat the oven to 180°C (350°F/Gas 4). Grease and line a 20cm (8in) square tin with baking parchment, leaving some overhang. Melt **85g (3oz) unsalted butter**, **75g (2½oz) finely chopped good-quality dark chocolate**, and **45g (1½oz) finely chopped good-quality very dark chocolate** in a heatproof bowl over a saucepan of simmering water, making sure it does not touch the water. Stir until smooth.

2 Leave the chocolate mixture to cool, then gradually whisk in **175g (6oz) caster sugar** and **2 tbsp dark brown sugar** to combine. Add **2 eggs**, one at a time, whisking well after each addition until smooth. Whisk in **1½ tsp vanilla extract**. Combine **85g (3oz) plain flour**, **½ tsp salt**, and **½ tsp baking powder** in a separate bowl and fold into the mixture.

3 Whisk **225g (8oz) full-fat cream cheese** in a separate bowl, until smooth. Add **1 tsp pure vanilla extract**, **⅛ tsp salt**, **1 large egg yolk**, and **50g (1¾oz) icing sugar**. Whisk to combine. Pour the chocolate mixture into the tin. Spoon over the cheese mixture and swirl the tip of a knife through it.

4 Bake for 40–45 minutes, until a toothpick inserted into the centre comes out with very few crumbs. Leave to cool slightly in the tin, then remove the brownie. Cut it into nine even-sized pieces and serve warm. You can store them in an airtight container in the fridge for up to 4 days.

🕐 **1 hr 5 mins** plus cooling | 🍴 **MAKES 24** | 🌡 Also great **COLD**

BROWNIES chocolate and raspberry

There are few better flavour combinations than raspberries and dark chocolate. Served warm with whipped cream, these brownies are truly decadent.

1 Preheat the oven 180°C (350°F/Gas 4). Lightly grease and line a deep **30cm (12in) baking tray** with baking parchment, leaving some overhang. Melt **115g (4oz) unsalted butter** and **225g (8oz) finely chopped good-quality dark chocolate** in a heatproof bowl (see Cheesecake brownies, step 1).

2 Leave the chocolate mixture to cool, then add **200g (7oz) dark brown sugar**, **100g (3½oz) caster sugar**, and **2 tsp vanilla extract**, whisking well to combine. Add **4 large eggs**, one at a time, whisking well after each addition until smooth.

3 Combine **150g (5½oz) plain flour**, **1 tsp salt**, and **1 tsp baking powder** in small bowl and fold into the brownie mixture until incorporated. Fold in **225g (8oz) raspberries** and **140g (5oz) milk chocolate chips**. Mix well and pour into the tray in an even layer.

4 Bake for 30–35 minutes, until a toothpick inserted into the centre comes out clean. Leave to cool slightly in the tin, then remove the brownie. Cut it into 24 equal-sized squares and serve warm. You can store them in an airtight container in the fridge for up to 3 days.

Chocolate and raspberry

Cheesecake

Salted peanut

Pecan blondies

BROWNIES
salted peanut

A pinch of good-quality sea salt can enhance the flavour of chocolate desserts. In this recipe, salted peanuts give the brownies a deliciously piquant edge.

1 Preheat the oven to 180°C (350°F/Gas 4). Grease and line a **20cm (8in) square cake tin** with baking parchment, leaving some overhang. Melt **85g (3oz) unsalted butter**, **125g (4½oz) finely chopped milk chocolate**, and **60g (2oz) finely chopped good-quality very dark chocolate** in a heatproof bowl (see Cheesecake brownies, step 1).

2 Leave the chocolate mixture to cool, then gradually add **200g (7oz) caster sugar**, **75g (2½oz) dark brown sugar**, and **2 tsp vanilla extract**. Whisk well to incorporate. Add **2 eggs**, one at a time, whisking well after each addition until smooth.

3 Combine **100g (3½oz) plain flour**, **½ tsp salt**, and **¼ tsp baking powder** in a medium bowl and fold into the chocolate mixture. Then add **75g (2½oz) chopped salted peanuts**, mix well, and pour the mixture into the tin in an even layer.

4 Bake for 40–45 minutes, until a toothpick inserted into the centre comes out clean. Leave to cool slightly in the tin, then remove the brownie. Cut it into nine equal-sized squares and serve warm. You can store them in an airtight container for up to 5 days.

BLONDIES pecan

Made with white chocolate, these brownies are creamy and rich. The chopped pecans add instant crunch. You could also try hazelnuts or pistachios.

1 Preheat the oven to 180°C (350°F/Gas 4). Grease and line a deep **30cm (12in) baking tray** with baking parchment, leaving some overhang. Melt **140g (5oz) unsalted butter** in a small saucepan over a gentle heat.

2 Remove from the heat and add **300g (10oz) light brown sugar** and **1½ tsp vanilla extract**. Whisk until combined. Add **3 large eggs**, one at a time, and whisk well after each addition until the mixture is smooth.

3 Combine **200g (7oz) plain flour**, **1 tsp salt**, and **1¼ tsp baking powder** in a separate bowl and fold into the mixture until combined. Then fold in **125g (4½oz) chopped pecans** and **175g (6oz) good-quality white chocolate chips**, mixing until evenly combined. Pour the mixture into the tray in an even layer.

4 Bake for 30 minutes, until a toothpick inserted into the centre comes out clean. Leave to cool slightly in the tin, then remove the blondie. Cut it into 24 even-sized pieces and serve warm. You can store them in an airtight container for up to 4 days.

⏱ **45 mins**
plus resting and cooling

🍴 **SERVES 6**

CLAFOUTIS cherry

First popular in 19th-century France, clafoutis combines the simplest ingredients to stunning effect. For best results, use a cast-iron frying pan, which helps to conduct the heat and cook evenly. Serve warm, direct from oven to table.

INGREDIENTS

2 tbsp unsalted butter, melted and cooled, plus extra for greasing

75g (2½oz) plain flour

75g (2½oz) caster sugar

2 eggs

125ml (4¼fl oz) whole milk

125ml (4¼fl oz) double cream

1 tsp vanilla extract

300g can pitted cherries, drained

icing sugar, for dusting

SPECIAL EQUIPMENT

25cm (10in) cast-iron frying pan or ovenproof dish

1 Preheat the oven to 200°C (400°F/Gas 6). Grease the frying pan and set aside. Combine the flour and caster sugar in a large bowl. Add the eggs, one at a time, whisking well after each addition until combined. Then whisk in the butter until it is well incorporated.

2 Add the milk and cream alternately, a little at a time, and whisk well to form a smooth batter. Add the vanilla extract and mix well to combine. Leave to rest at room temperature for 30 minutes.

Whisk the mixture well after each addition.

3 *Ensure that the batter and cherries are evenly distributed.*

Spread out the cherries in the pan in an even layer and carefully pour the batter over them.

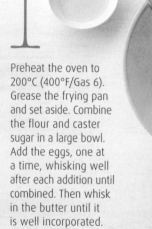

4 Bake on the top shelf of the oven for 30 minutes, until the top is golden brown and the centre is firm. Remove and cool for about 5 minutes. Dust with icing sugar, and serve warm, or at room temperature. Best served on the same day.

CLAFOUTIS blackberry and pear

This is an autumnal take on classic clafoutis. Use the ripest blackberries for added juice, but avoid choosing pears that are very ripe, as you will need the slices to keep their shape.

INGREDIENTS

75g (2½oz) plain four
75g (2½oz) caster sugar
2 eggs
3 tbsp unsalted butter, melted and cooled
125ml (4¼fl oz) whole milk
125ml (4¼fl oz) double cream
1 tsp vanilla extract
2 pears, peeled, cored , and cut lengthways into 8 slices each
150g (5½oz) blackberries

SPECIAL EQUIPMENT

25cm (10in) cast-iron frying pan

1 Preheat the oven to 200°C (400°F/Gas 6). Combine the flour and sugar in a large bowl. Add the eggs, one at a time, whisking well after each addition until combined. Whisk in 2 tablespoons of the butter.

2 Add the milk and cream, a little at a time, and whisk well to form a smooth batter. Then add the vanilla extract and mix well. Leave to rest at room temperature for 30 minutes.

3 Heat the remaining butter in the frying pan over a medium heat. Add the pears and blackberries, toss well to coat, and remove from the heat. Shake the pan lightly to spread out the mixture evenly. Pour the batter over the fruit mixture, making sure it is evenly distributed.

4 Bake on the top shelf of the oven for 30 minutes, until the top is golden brown and the centre is firm to the touch. Remove from the oven and leave to cool for 5 minutes. Serve warm or at room temperature. Best served on the same day.

🕐 **45 mins**
plus resting and cooling 🍴 **SERVES 6**

CLAFOUTIS apricot and almond

You only need store-cupboard ingredients to make this variety, so it is ideal for a last-minute dessert.

INGREDIENTS

2 tbsp butter, melted and cooled, plus extra for greasing
50g (1¾oz) ground almonds
25g (scant 1oz) plain flour
75g (2½oz) caster sugar
2 eggs
125ml (4¼fl oz) whole milk
125ml (4¼fl oz) double cream
1 tsp vanilla extract
425g can apricots, drained and halved
20g (¾oz) flaked almonds
icing sugar, for dusting

SPECIAL EQUIPMENT

25cm (10in) cast-iron frying pan

1 Preheat the oven to 200°C (400°F/Gas 6). Grease the frying pan and set aside. Combine the ground almonds, flour, and caster sugar in a large bowl. Add the eggs, one at a time, whisking well after each addition. Then whisk in the butter until incorporated.

2 Whisk in the milk and cream gradually (see Blackberry and pear clafoutis, step 2). Then add the vanilla extract and mix well. Leave to rest at room temperature for about 30 minutes.

3 Spread out the apricots evenly in the pan, cut-side down. Pour the batter over carefully, making sure the apricots are not displaced and the batter is evenly distributed. Scatter over the flaked almonds.

4 Bake for 30 minutes (see Blackberry and pear clafoutis, step 4). Remove from the oven and leave to cool for 5 minutes. Dust with icing sugar and serve warm or at room temperature. Best served on the same day.

🕐 **35 mins**
plus resting and cooling

🍴 **MAKES 12**

MINI CLAFOUTIS
raspberry

Mini clafoutis require less baking time than larger ones – perfect for delicate raspberries, as they can disintegrate during a long bake.

INGREDIENTS

2 tbsp butter, melted and cooled, plus extra for greasing

75g (2½oz) plain four

75g (2½oz) caster sugar

2 eggs, separated

120ml (4fl oz) whole milk

120ml (4fl oz) double cream, plus extra for serving

1 tsp vanilla extract

48 raspberries, about 175g (6oz) in total

icing sugar, for dusting

SPECIAL EQUIPMENT

12-hole deep muffin tin

1 Preheat the oven to 200°C (400°F/Gas 6). Grease the muffin tin and set aside. Place the flour and caster sugar in a bowl and mix well. Add the egg yolks and butter, whisking constantly until well combined.

2 Add the milk and cream, a little at a time, and whisk until smooth and well incorporated. Stir in the vanilla extract. Place the egg whites in a separate bowl and whisk to form soft peaks. Fold them into the batter and mix until just combined.

3 Place a tablespoon of batter in each hole of the muffin tin. Top with 4 raspberries each and pour over the remaining batter, making sure it is evenly distributed. Bake the mini clafoutis on the top shelf in the oven for about 20 minutes, until golden brown on top and firm to the touch.

4 Remove from the oven and leave them to rest for 10 minutes. Run a knife around the edge of each clafoutis to loosen and turn them out of the tin. Then place them on a wire rack to cool to room temperature. Dust with icing sugar and serve with double cream. Best served on the same day.

20 mins
plus resting　　**MAKES 8**

CRÊPES lemon and sugar

These rich and crisp crêpes are a great choice for a family gathering. It is so easy to serve them with a variety of toppings – as alternatives to lemon and sugar, you could bring honey, golden syrup, chocolate spread, and berries to the table.

INGREDIENTS
100g (3½oz) plain flour, sifted

2 tbsp caster sugar, plus extra for dusting

½ tsp fine salt

2 eggs

250ml (9fl oz) whole milk

2 tbsp unsalted butter, melted and cooled, plus extra for frying

1 lemon, cut into quarters, to serve

SPECIAL EQUIPMENT
25cm (10in) non-stick frying pan

PLAN AHEAD
You can prepare and store the batter, covered in the fridge, up to 1 day ahead. Bring to room temperature and whisk well before cooking.

1　Combine the flour, sugar, and salt in a large bowl. Add the eggs, one at a time, whisking well after each addition to form a smooth, thick paste.

2　Gradually pour in the milk and whisk well to incorporate. Add the butter and whisk well to combine. Pour the batter into a jug. Leave to rest for 30 minutes. Preheat the oven to 150°C (300°F/Gas 2).

3　Place the frying pan over a medium-high heat and melt a small knob of butter. When the butter begins to sizzle, use kitchen paper to wipe off any excess. Pour in enough batter to form a thin layer, tipping the pan quickly to spread it. Cook for 2 minutes, until the edges are browning and the underside is golden.

4　Flip and cook for a further 1–2 minutes. Remove from the heat, wrap the crêpe tightly in a clean kitchen towel, and place in the oven. Continue cooking with all of the batter. Dust the crêpes with sugar and serve warm with a squeeze of lemon.

🕐 **25 mins**   🍴 **SERVES 6–8**

CRÊPE CAKE Swedish-style

This stunning cake is a Swedish favourite. If time is short, you can use good-quality shop-bought crêpes and fill them with seasonal berries and whipped cream.

INGREDIENTS

200ml (7fl oz) double cream

240ml (8fl oz) crème fraîche

3 tbsp caster sugar

¼ tsp vanilla extract

250g (9oz) raspberries

6 crêpes (see p62, steps 1–4)

icing sugar, to serve

1 Place the cream in a large bowl and whisk to form stiff peaks. Add the crème fraîche, caster sugar, and vanilla extract, and whisk well to combine. Set aside four tablespoons of the mixture.

2 Reserve a handful of the raspberries and place the rest in a bowl. Crush them with the back of a fork. Gently fold the crushed raspberries into the cream mixture to create a ripple effect.

3 Place one crêpe on a platter, spread over one-fifth of the cream, and top with a second crêpe. Repeat with the remaining crêpes, spreading equal quantities of the raspberry cream mixture between each layer.

4 Spread the reserved cream mixture on top of the crêpe cake. Scatter over the reserved raspberries, dust with icing sugar, and serve immediately.

🕐 **25 mins** plus resting   🍴 **MAKES 8**

CRÊPES suzette

Give simple crêpes a flourish with a rich, buttery sauce made from fresh orange juice and orange liqueur.

INGREDIENTS

zest of 1 large orange, julienned

60g (2oz) unsalted butter

4 tbsp caster sugar

juice and grated zest of 2 oranges

2 tbsp Grand Marnier, or other orange liqueur

8 crêpes (see p62, steps 1–4)

1 Place the julienned orange zests in a saucepan half-full of boiling water. Allow to simmer for 2 minutes. Drain, and set aside to cool.

2 Heat the butter and sugar in a small, heavy-based saucepan over a low heat, stirring until the sugar has dissolved. Add the orange juice and zest, and bring to the boil, stirring frequently.

3 Reduce the heat to a simmer and cook the sauce for 5 minutes until thick and syrup-like. Then add the Grand Marnier and cook for a further 1–2 minutes, until it has reduced.

4 Remove the sauce from the heat and keep it warm. Fold the warm crêpes into quarters, and pour the sauce over the crêpes. Decorate each crêpe with the cooled orange strips, and serve immediately.

CRÊPES chocolate

Children and adults alike love these crêpes. Stack them with chocolate frosting for a delightful birthday cake.

INGREDIENTS

30g (1oz) unsalted butter, plus extra for frying

30g (1oz) good-quality dark chocolate

75g (2½oz) plain flour, sifted

25g (scant 1oz) cocoa powder

2 tbsp caster sugar

½ tsp fine salt

2 eggs

250ml (9fl oz) whole milk

PLAN AHEAD

You can prepare and store the batter, covered in the fridge, up to 1 day ahead. Bring it up to room temperature and whisk well before cooking.

1 Melt the butter and chocolate in a heatproof bowl over a saucepan of simmering water. Set aside to cool completely. Mix together the flour, cocoa powder, sugar, and salt in a large bowl. Add the eggs, one at a time, whisking to form a paste.

2 Gradually add the milk and whisk until incorporated. Add the cooled chocolate mixture to the bowl, a little at a time, whisking constantly to combine. Pour the batter into a jug and leave to rest for at least 30 minutes.

3 Preheat the oven to 150°C (300°F/Gas 2). Melt a little butter in a large non-stick frying pan over a medium heat. When the butter sizzles, use kitchen paper to wipe off excess. Pour in a thin layer of batter, tipping the pan to help it to spread.

4 Cook the crêpe for 2 minutes, until the underside looks golden. Flip and cook for a further 1–2 minutes. Remove and wrap in a clean kitchen towel. Keep it warm in the oven while you cook with the remaining batter. Serve warm.

BLINTZ with cherry sauce

These delicate stuffed crêpes hail from Eastern Europe. The soft, creamy filling and sharp, fruity sauce provide a beautiful contrast in flavour.

INGREDIENTS

200g (7oz) full-fat cottage cheese

100g (3½oz) full-fat cream cheese

2 tbsp icing sugar, plus extra for dusting

grated zest of ½ lemon

½ tsp vanilla extract

8 crêpes (see p62, steps 1–4)

knob of unsalted butter, for frying

For the sauce

450g can pitted dark cherries, quartered

60g (2oz) caster sugar

2 tbsp lemon juice

1 tsp vanilla extract

1 Pulse the cottage cheese in a food processor until smooth and transfer to a large bowl. Add the cream cheese, icing sugar, lemon zest, and vanilla extract. Whisk the mixture until smooth. Place a tablespoon of the filling in the centre of each crêpe. Fold the sides over the filling to make a parcel.

2 Preheat the oven to 150°C (300°F/Gas 2). Melt a knob of butter in a 25cm (10in) non-stick frying pan over a medium heat. Fry the blintz for 2 minutes on each side, until golden brown. Remove with a slotted spoon, place on a lined plate, and keep warm in the oven.

3 For the sauce, place all the ingredients in a small, lidded saucepan and bring to the boil. Then reduce the heat to a simmer, cover, and cook for 2–3 minutes.

4 Increase the heat to medium. Cook, uncovered, for 3–5 minutes, until the sauce is thick and syrup-like and the cherries are cooked but retain their shape. To serve, dust the blintz with icing sugar and pour over the cherry sauce.

🕐 **1 hr 5 mins**
plus cooling

🍴 **SERVES 8**

🌡 Also great
COLD

UPSIDE-DOWN CAKE
caramelized pear

The soft texture of lightly caramelized pears makes them a perfect match for delicate sponge. The cake tastes meltingly good fresh from the oven, but it is also great the next day, as the fruit continues to impart the sponge with flavour and juice.

INGREDIENTS
50g (1¾oz) unsalted butter, plus extra for greasing
125g (4½oz) soft light brown sugar
2 pears, peeled, cored, and chopped into 16 slices
single cream, to serve (optional)

For the sponge
115g (4oz) caster sugar

115g (4oz) unsalted butter, softened
2 eggs
1 tsp vanilla extract
200g (7oz) plain flour
1 tsp baking powder
100ml (3½fl oz) whole milk

SPECIAL EQUIPMENT
20cm (8in) round cake tin

1 Preheat the oven to 180°C (350°F/Gas 4). Grease the cake tin and set aside. Melt the butter in a small, heavy-based saucepan over a low heat. Increase the heat and add the sugar. Bring to the boil, stirring frequently, until the sugar has dissolved and the mixture has thickened.

2 Transfer the caramel to the cake tin and use a wooden spoon to spread it out into an even layer. Leave to cool slightly. Place the pear slices over the cooled caramel in a well-spaced spiral pattern. Set aside.

3 For the sponge, beat the sugar and butter in a bowl until fluffy. Add the eggs one at a time, beat well, and stir in the vanilla extract. Sift the flour and baking powder into a separate bowl. Add the dry mixture and milk to the egg mixture, alternately, and beat to combine.

Beat the sponge mixture until smooth.

4 Spoon the mixture into the tin and place on a baking sheet. Bake in the oven for 40–45 minutes. Cool for 5 minutes, before turning it out. Serve warm with cream, if desired. You can store the cake in an airtight container in the fridge for up to 3 days.

The finished cake will be golden and well risen.

⏱ 1 hr plus cooling 🍴 MAKES 4 🌡 Also great COLD

UPSIDE-DOWN CAKES pineapple

Give this classic dessert a contemporary makeover by serving it with a light cream sauce that is laced with fresh basil.

INGREDIENTS
125g (4½oz) unsalted butter, plus extra for greasing

100g (3½oz) soft light brown sugar

125g can pineapple chunks, in natural juice, chopped into small pieces

100g (3½oz) caster sugar

2 eggs

½ tsp vanilla extract

150g (5½oz) self-raising flour, sifted

100ml (3½fl oz) double cream

1 tsp finely chopped basil

1 tsp lime juice

SPECIAL EQUIPMENT
4 x 250ml (9fl oz) ramekins

1 Preheat the oven to 180ºC (350ºF/Gas 4). Grease the ramekins. Melt 50g (1¾oz) of the butter in a heavy-based saucepan over a medium heat. Add the brown sugar and cook for 2–3 minutes, stirring constantly, until dissolved. Divide evenly between the ramekins.

2 Drain the pineapple chunks, reserving the juice, and divide them between the ramekins. In a bowl, whisk the caster sugar and remaining butter until light and fluffy. Then whisk in the eggs and vanilla extract, until combined. Gently fold in the flour, until just combined.

3 Divide the mixture between the ramekins. Transfer to a baking sheet, and bake for 25–30 minutes, until well risen and golden. Remove and leave to cool slightly.

4 Meanwhile, bring the reserved pineapple juice to the boil in a small, heavy-based saucepan. Cook for 5 minutes, until the juice has reduced by half. Invert the ramekins onto serving plates. Leave for 2–3 minutes before removing, to allow the juices to drip down.

5 Add half the cream to the pan. Cook for 5–7 minutes, until reduced by half. Remove from the heat and whisk in the basil, lime juice, and remaining cream until thick. Serve the cream immediately, alongside the cakes.

⏱ 1 hr 25 mins plus cooling 🍴 SERVES 8 🌡 Also great COLD

UPSIDE-DOWN CAKE apple and blackberry

With a glorious orchard flavour, this cake is also delicious served with custard.

INGREDIENTS
150ml (5fl oz) maple syrup, plus extra to serve

150g (5½oz) unsalted butter, diced, plus extra for greasing

60g (2oz) soft dark brown sugar

2 eggs

200g (7oz) plain flour

2 tsp baking powder

½ tsp ground cinnamon

¼ tsp ground ginger

¼ tsp grated nutmeg

30g (1oz) soft light brown sugar

1 apple, peeled, cored, and quartered

100g (3½oz) frozen blackberries, halved, if large

whipped cream, to serve

SPECIAL EQUIPMENT
20cm (8in) deep cake tin

1 Preheat the oven to 160°C (325°F/Gas 3). Melt the maple syrup, butter, and dark brown sugar in a saucepan over a medium heat, stirring, until the sugar has dissolved. Transfer to a bowl and leave to cool.

2 Add the eggs to the cooled maple syrup, one at a time, beating well after each addition until combined. Sift the flour, baking powder, and spices into a bowl and make a well in the centre. Pour the wet mixture into the well and fold into the dry ingredients until just combined.

3 Grease the tin and sprinkle the light brown sugar over the bottom evenly. Slice the apple quarters lengthways, into 3 or 4 pieces. Place them in a well-spaced spiral over the brown sugar. Fill the spaces with the blackberries and pour the batter evenly over the top.

4 Bake for 50 minutes to 1 hour, until well risen and golden brown. Cover loosely with foil if it browns too quickly. Cool in the tin for 5 minutes, before turning it out. Serve warm or at room temperature with whipped cream. You can store the cake in an airtight container for up to 2 days.

🕐 **50 mins**
plus cooling

🍴 **MAKES 6**

🌡 Also great
COLD

UPSIDE-DOWN CAKES blueberry with crème anglaise

These mini dessert cakes, served with a light and pourable custard, are easy to make and look very impressive.

INGREDIENTS

115g (4oz) unsalted butter, softened, plus extra for greasing

30g (1oz) soft light brown sugar

100g (3½oz) frozen blueberries

115g (4oz) caster sugar

2 eggs

1 tsp vanilla extract

115g (4oz) self-raising flour

For the crème anglaise

1 vanilla pod, split in half, lengthways

200ml (7fl oz) whole milk

2 egg yolks

2 tbsp caster sugar

SPECIAL EQUIPMENT

6-hole deep muffin tin

1 Preheat the oven to 180°C (350°F/Gas 4). Grease the muffin tin. Sprinkle the brown sugar into each hole and top with equal quantities of the blueberries. Whisk the butter and caster sugar in a bowl until light and fluffy.

2 Add the eggs to the butter mixture, one at a time, whisking well after each addition until combined. Add the vanilla extract, sift in the flour, and fold in gently. Divide the batter evenly between the holes in the tin.

3 Bake for 20 minutes, until well risen and golden brown. Leave to cool slightly. For the crème anglaise, cook the vanilla pod and milk in a saucepan over a low heat for 5 minutes, until hot, but not boiling.

4 Remove the vanilla pod, scrape out the seeds, and add to the milk. In a heatproof bowl, whisk the egg yolks and caster sugar until combined. Pour in the hot milk and whisk until the sugar has dissolved. Pour the mixture back into the pan.

5 Cook the mixture over a low heat for 2–3 minutes, stirring constantly, until thick enough to coat the back of a spoon. Invert the muffin tin over a large serving plate and leave for 2–3 minutes before taking off the tin. Serve immediately with the crème anglaise.

Simple alternatives

It is very easy to adapt the Caramelized pear upside-down cake on pages 66–67 following the recipes below. You should caramelize just-ripe fruit, as it will keep its shape.

Apple and cinnamon Add a pinch of ground cinnamon to the caramel and 1 tsp of it to the cake mixture. Replace the pears (see p67, step 2) with 2 peeled, cored, and sliced apples.

Plum and almond In place of the pears (see p67, step 2), scatter slivers of raw almonds over the caramel and top with 6–8 stoned and quartered plums.

Peach Instead of the pears (see Pear upside-down cake, pp66–67), use 3 ripe, peeled, stoned, and quartered peaches, and 1 tsp finely chopped lemon verbena.

Cranberry and raspberry Use 150g (5½oz) raspberries and 50g (1¾oz) cranberries in place of the pears (see p67, step 2).

Banana Use 2 bananas, cut into 2cm (¾in) thick slices, in place of the pears for a gorgeously sticky dessert (see p67, step 2).

Chocolate and date For a rich variation, add 2 heaped tbsp cocoa powder to the cake mixture and use 100g (3½oz) roughly chopped dates instead of the pears (see p67, step 2).

Rhubarb, ginger, and orange Sprinkle the caramel with 1 tbsp finely diced crystallized ginger and top with 150g (5½oz) rhubarb, sliced into 2.5cm (1in) pieces. Add 1 tsp grated fresh ginger and the zest of 1 orange to the cake mixture (see p67, step 3).

Blackcurrant Instead of the pears (see p67, step 2), place 200g (7oz) blackcurrants, in a thick layer, over the caramel. For best results, serve the cake warm with whipped cream.

Apricot and lavender Use 4 halved, stoned, and quartered apricots in place of the pears (see p67, step 2). Add ¼ tsp finely chopped culinary lavender to the cake mixture.

35 mins plus cooling 🍴 **MAKES 4**

SOUFFLÉ vanilla

Many people assume that a soufflé is difficult to master, yet a few simple tips can help you to achieve a beautifully light and airy dessert. Make sure the ramekin is buttered and dusted, the mixture lightly folded, and that you serve it immediately.

INGREDIENTS

30g (1oz) unsalted butter, plus extra for greasing

50g (1¾oz) caster sugar, plus extra for dusting

2 tbsp plain flour

170ml (6fl oz) whole milk

¾ tsp vanilla extract

pinch of salt

3 large eggs, separated

pinch of cream of tartar

icing sugar, for dusting

SPECIAL EQUIPMENT

4 x 150ml (5fl oz) ramekins

PLAN AHEAD

You can prepare and store the batter, covered in the fridge, up to 1 day ahead.

1

Preheat the oven to 200°C (400°F/Gas 6). Grease the ramekins, dust lightly with caster sugar, and set aside. Melt the butter in a saucepan over a low heat. Add the flour and cook for 1 minute. Remove from the heat and whisk in the milk until smooth.

2

Bring the mixture to the boil over a low heat, stirring constantly. Then reduce the heat and simmer for 1–2 minutes. Remove from the heat and add the vanilla extract, salt, and 2 tablespoons of caster sugar. Stir until the sugar has dissolved.

3

Cool the milk mixture slightly. Then beat in the egg yolks, one at a time, until well combined and smooth. Set aside.

4

In a large bowl, whisk the egg whites and cream of tartar with a hand-held whisk to form medium peaks. Then whisk in the remaining caster sugar to form stiff peaks.

5

Gradually fold the egg white mixture into the milk mixture, until combined. Divide the batter evenly between the ramekins, filling them to the rim. Smooth over the batter and run a finger around the edge of each ramekin.

KNOW-HOW Running a finger around the edges of the batter creates an indentation, helping the soufflés rise upwards in a straight direction.

6

Place the ramekins on a baking sheet. Bake on the bottom shelf of the oven for 10–12 minutes, until well risen, golden, and an inserted toothpick comes out clean. Dust with icing sugar and serve immediately.

🕐 **35–40 mins** plus cooling   🍴 **MAKES 6**

SOUFFLÉ chocolate

Served straight from the oven, this deliciously rich soufflé is fantastic with a scoop of good-quality vanilla ice cream.

1. Preheat the oven to 200°C (400°F/Gas 6). Grease **six 150ml (5fl oz) ramekins** with **softened, unsalted butter** and dust with **caster sugar**. Dissolve **1 tsp instant espresso powder** into **3 tbsp double cream** in a heatproof bowl over a saucepan of simmering water, until smooth.

2. Add **115g (4oz) finely chopped good-quality dark chocolate** to the pan, stirring until melted. Remove and leave to cool. Whisk **3 large egg whites** with a **pinch of cream of tartar** in a bowl, until thick. Gradually add **50g (1¾oz) caster sugar**, whisking continuously until soft peaks form.

3. Beat **2 large egg yolks** into the cooled chocolate mixture, until smooth. Stir in **¼ tsp vanilla extract** and a **pinch of salt**. Fold in a little of the egg white mixture. Then gently fold in the remaining until combined.

4. Divide the mixture between the ramekins. Smooth them over, run a finger around the edges, and place them on a baking sheet. Bake on the bottom shelf of the oven for 12–15 minutes, until they are well risen and an inserted toothpick comes out clean. Dust with **icing sugar** and serve immediately.

PLAN AHEAD
You can prepare and store the batter, covered in the fridge, up to 1 day ahead.

Chocolate

Pistachio

🕐 **30 mins** plus cooling   🍴 **MAKES 6**

SOUFFLÉ pistachio

This is a fragrant dessert that combines pistachio, orange, and cardamom. Try serving it with crème fraîche, mixed with a little orange flower water.

1. Preheat the oven to 200°C (400°F/Gas 6) and prepare **six 150ml (5fl oz) ramekins** (see Chocolate soufflé, step 1). Pulse **85g (3oz) unsalted and skinned pistachios** with **2 tsp caster sugar** in a food processor, adding **1 tbsp water** if needed, to form a smooth, thick paste. Set aside.

2. Melt **3 tbsp unsalted butter** in a saucepan over a low heat. Add **2 tbsp plain flour** and cook for 1 minute. Then remove from the heat and whisk in **180ml (6fl oz) whole milk, at room temperature**, until smooth.

3. Bring the mixture to the boil over a low heat. Reduce the heat to a simmer, and cook for 1–2 minutes. Then remove from the heat and add **¼ tsp ground cardamom**, **1 tbsp orange juice**, **2 tbsp caster sugar**, and a **pinch of salt**. Stir until the sugar has dissolved, then leave to cool slightly.

4. Beat 3 tbsp of the pistachio paste and **2 large egg yolks** in a bowl and combine with the milk mixture until smooth. In a separate bowl, whisk **3 large egg whites** and a **pinch of cream of tartar** to form medium peaks. Whisk in **2 tbsp caster sugar** to form soft peaks and gradually fold it to the milk mixture until just combined.

5. Divide the mixture between the ramekins and place them on a baking sheet (see Chocolate soufflé, step 4). Bake on the bottom shelf of the oven for 10–14 minutes, until they are well risen and an inserted toothpick comes out clean. Dust with **icing sugar** and serve immediately.

PLAN AHEAD
You can prepare and store the batter, covered in the fridge, up to 1 day ahead.

🕐 **30–35 mins** plus cooling   🍴 **MAKES 6**

SOUFFLÉ raspberry

This white chocolate and raspberry soufflé is a summery take on the French classic. You could serve it with a cold raspberry coulis (see p215).

1 Preheat the oven to 200°C (400°F/Gas 6) and prepare **six 150ml (5fl oz) ramekins** (see Chocolate soufflé, step 1). Melt **85g (3oz) finely chopped white chocolate**, **2 tbsp double cream**, and a **pinch of salt** in a heatproof bowl over a saucepan of simmering water. Remove and leave to cool.

2 Pulse **200g (7oz) raspberries** in a food processor until smooth and strain into a bowl. In a separate bowl, whisk **4 large egg whites** and a **pinch of cream of tartar** until thick. Gradually whisk in **50g (1¾oz) caster sugar** to form soft peaks.

3 Whisk **3 large egg yolks** into the chocolate mixture, one at a time, until combined. Then whisk in **2 tbsp plain flour**, **¼ tsp vanilla extract**, and the raspberry purée, until smooth. Fold in a little of the egg white mixture. Then gently fold in the remaining mixture until combined.

4 Divide the mixture between the ramekins and place them on a baking sheet (see Chocolate soufflé, step 4). Bake for 10–12 minutes, until they are well risen, lightly golden, and an inserted toothpick comes out clean. Dust with **icing sugar** and serve immediately.

PLAN AHEAD
You can prepare and store the batter, covered in the fridge, up to 1 day ahead.

Lemon

🕐 **30–35 mins** plus cooling   🍴 **MAKES 6**

SOUFFLÉ lemon

A delicious palate-cleanser with a sharp–sweet flavour, this lemon soufflé works very well alongside a spoonful of cold double cream.

1 Preheat the oven to 200°C (400°F/Gas 6) and prepare **six 150ml (5fl oz) ramekins** (see Chocolate soufflé, step 1). Melt **2 tbsp unsalted butter** in saucepan over a low heat. Add **2 tbsp plain flour** and cook for 1 minute. Remove and whisk in **180ml (6fl oz) whole milk**, **at room temperature**, until smooth.

2 Bring the mixture to the boil over a low heat. Then reduce to a simmer and cook for 1–2 minutes, stirring constantly. Remove from the heat. Whisk in **¼ tsp vanilla extract**, **2 tbsp caster sugar**, and a **pinch of salt** until the sugar dissolves. Whisk in **zest and juice of 1 lemon** and leave to cool.

3 In a bowl, whisk **4 large egg whites** and a **pinch of cream of tartar** until thick. Gradually whisk in **25g (scant 1oz) caster sugar** to form medium peaks. Whisk **3 large egg yolks** into the cooled milk mixture, one at a time, until smooth. Fold in a little of the egg white mixture. Then gently fold in the remaining until combined.

4 Divide the mixture between the ramekins and place them on a baking sheet (see Chocolate soufflé, step 4). Bake for 10–12 minutes, until they are well risen, lightly golden, and an inserted toothpick comes out clean. Dust with **icing sugar** and serve immediately.

PLAN AHEAD
You can prepare and store the batter, covered in the fridge, up to 1 day ahead.

Raspberry

35 mins
plus resting and cooling

MAKES 4

FONDANT chocolate

Baking a fondant can seem daunting, as it is difficult to know just how molten the inside will be until you serve. However, think of it as a slightly undercooked chocolate cake – a careful eye on the clock guarantees a perfectly oozing centre.

INGREDIENTS
150g (5½oz) unsalted butter, plus extra for greasing

150g (5½oz) good-quality dark chocolate, at least 60 per cent cocoa solids

3 large eggs

75g (2½oz) caster sugar

1 heaped tbsp plain flour

cocoa powder, for dusting

double cream, to serve

SPECIAL EQUIPMENT
4 x 200ml (7fl oz) ramekins

PLAN AHEAD
You can prepare and store the batter, wrapped in cling film, in the fridge up to 3 days ahead, or freeze it up to 1 month ahead. Bring to room temperature before baking.

Preheat the oven to 200°C (400°F/Gas 6). Grease the ramekins and chill them in the fridge until needed. Melt the chocolate and butter in a heatproof bowl over a small saucepan of gently simmering water, making sure it does not touch the water. Leave to cool.

1

In a separate bowl, beat the eggs and sugar for 4–5 minutes, until the mixture has tripled in volume and is pale and fluffy. Fold in the cooled chocolate mixture and mix well. Then sift over the flour and fold it in gently.

2

Lightly dust the ramekins with cocoa powder, shaking off any excess. Divide the batter evenly between the ramekins, making sure that they are not filled to the top. Bake in the oven for 12 minutes, until set, but still soft to the touch in the middle.

3

Leave to rest for 1 minute. Run a sharp knife around the edges of the fondants and top with serving plates. Turn them over and gently remove the ramekins. Dust with cocoa powder and serve immediately with double cream.

4

🕐 **2 hrs 5 mins**
plus chilling and cooling   🍴 **MAKES 4**

FONDANT dulce de leche

Place small amounts of home-made dulce de leche inside your chocolate fondants – it transforms them into a show-stopping dessert.

1 Preheat the oven to 220°C (425°F/Gas 7). For the dulce de leche, pour **400g (14oz) sweetened condensed milk** into a **14cm (5¾in) pie dish**. Cover tightly with two sheets of foil and place the dish in a small roasting tin. Fill the tin with enough hot water to come halfway up the sides of the pie dish, making sure the water does not splash onto the foil.

2 Bake in the middle of the oven for 1–1½ hours, stirring every 15 minutes, until small holes appear on the surface of the foil and the milk is a golden, caramel colour. Check the water level regularly and add more if it has evaporated. Transfer the dulce de leche to a shallow dish. Cool completely, before chilling. Reduce the oven temperature to 200°C (400°F/Gas 6).

3 Grease **four 200ml (7fl oz) ramekins** with **unsalted butter** and place in the fridge to chill. Melt **150g (5½oz) finely chopped good-quality dark chocolate** and **150g (5½oz) unsalted butter** in a heatproof bowl over a small saucepan of simmering water. Make sure the base of the bowl does not touch the water. Stir well and leave to cool.

4 Whisk **3 large eggs** and **75g (2½oz) caster sugar** in a large bowl, until fluffy and tripled in volume. Whisk in the cooled chocolate mixture until combined. Sift **1 heaped tbsp plain flour** into the mixture and gently fold it in.

5 Lightly dust the ramekins with **cocoa powder**, shaking off any excess. Half-fill the ramekins with the fondant mixture and spread to form an even base. Shape 4 heaped teaspoons of the dulce de leche into balls and place one in each ramekin. Divide the remaining fondant mixture between the ramekins, covering the dulce de leche completely.

6 Bake the fondants in the oven for 12 minutes, until the sides are set and the centre is soft to the touch. Leave to cool for 1 minute. To remove the fondant, run a knife around the edge of the ramekin, place a serving plate on top, and turn over. Serve the fondants immediately with **double cream**, if desired.

PLAN AHEAD
You can wrap the fondant mixture in cling film at the end of step 5 and chill up to 2 days ahead, or freeze them up to 1 month ahead. Bring to room temperature before baking.

Dulce de leche

⏱ **25 mins**
plus cooling and chilling 🍴 **MAKES 4**

FONDANT
peanut butter

Peanut butter melts at high temperatures, creating a salty contrast to the interior – rather like a sophisticated chocolate and peanut bar.

1 Grease **four 200ml (7fl oz) ramekins** with **unsalted butter** and place in the fridge to chill. Melt **150g (5½oz) finely chopped good-quality dark chocolate** and **150g (5½oz) unsalted butter** in a heatproof bowl over a small saucepan of simmering water (see Dulce de leche fondant, step 3). Stir and leave to cool.

2 Preheat the oven to 200ºC (400ºF/Gas 6). Whisk **3 large eggs** and **75g (2½oz) caster sugar** in a large bowl, until fluffy and tripled in volume. Whisk in the chocolate mixture until well combined. Sift **1 heaped tbsp plain flour** into the mixture and gently fold it in.

3 Lightly dust the ramekins with **cocoa powder**, shaking off any excess. Half-fill the ramekins with the fondant mixture, spreading it out to form an even base. Shape **4 heaped tsp creamy peanut butter** into balls and place one in each ramekin. Divide the remaining fondant mixture between the ramekins, covering the peanut butter completely.

4 Bake the fondants in the oven for 12 minutes, until the sides are set and the centre is soft to the touch. Leave to cool for 1 minute, before turning them out (see Dulce de leche fondant, step 6). Dust with cocoa powder, if desired, and serve immediately.

PLAN AHEAD
You can wrap the fondant mixture in cling film at the end of step 3 and chill up to 2 days ahead, or freeze them up to 1 month ahead. Bring to room temperature before baking.

Peanut butter

 **50–55 mins**
plus resting and cooling

SERVES 4–6

BREAD AND BUTTER PUDDING *brioche*

Originally conceived as an everyday dessert that took advantage of store-cupboard ingredients, rich and creamy versions of bread and butter pudding are now favourites at dinner parties, restaurants, and pudding bars.

INGREDIENTS

unsalted butter, for greasing

250g (9oz) brioche, cut into 2.5cm (1in) cubes

2 eggs

50g (1¾oz) caster sugar

200ml (7fl oz) whole milk

200ml (7fl oz) double cream

icing sugar, for dusting

chocolate ice cream, to serve (optional)

SPECIAL EQUIPMENT

20 x 25cm (8 x 10in) ovenproof dish

1 Preheat the oven to 180°C (350°F/Gas 4). Grease the ovenproof dish. Spread out the brioche pieces in the dish, pressing down gently to form an even layer.

2 Place the eggs and caster sugar in a bowl and whisk to combine. Add the milk and cream, a little at a time, whisking constantly to combine.

3 Pour the mixture over the brioche, pushing down to help the liquid to absorb. Rest for 5 minutes. Place the dish in a large roasting tin. Pour hot water into the tin.

The hot water should come halfway up the sides of the dish.

4 Bake for 40–45 minutes, until golden brown. Lift the dish out of the tin and leave to cool slightly. Dust with icing sugar. Serve with chocolate ice cream, if desired. You can store the pudding, covered in the fridge, for up to 2 days.

35 mins plus cooling   **MAKES 4**

BREAD AND BUTTER PUDDING
bourbon and pecan

Bourbon lends a warming flavour to these grown-up puddings. The caramelized pecans add a sweet crunch to the texture.

INGREDIENTS
1 tbsp unsalted butter, plus extra for greasing
1 tbsp caster sugar
30g (1oz) pecans
150g (5½oz) brioche, diced into 1cm (½in) cubes
30g (1oz) sultanas
3 eggs
225ml (7¾fl oz) single cream
2 tbsp bourbon
½ tsp vanilla extract
2 heaped tbsp soft light brown sugar
double cream, to serve (optional)

SPECIAL EQUIPMENT
4 x 200ml (7fl oz) ramekins

PLAN AHEAD
You can store the candied pecans in an airtight container up to 1 week ahead.

1 Preheat the oven to 180°C (350°F/Gas 4) and grease the ramekins. Heat the butter, caster sugar, and pecans in a non-stick frying pan over a medium heat. Cook for 5 minutes, stirring frequently, until the caramel is golden and smooth and the pecans are well coated. Place them on a lightly greased plate and leave to cool.

2 Mix the brioche and sultanas in a large bowl. Whisk together the eggs, cream, bourbon, vanilla extract, and brown sugar in a separate bowl and pour over the brioche mixture. Stir well to ensure that the bread is soaked in the cream mixture.

3 Divide the mixture equally between the ramekins, heaping it up in the centre. Pour over any remaining liquid, making sure the ramekins are not overflowing. Bake on the top shelf of the oven for 20 minutes, until they are well risen and golden brown.

4 Remove from the heat and leave them to cool for about 5 minutes. Chop the candied pecans and sprinkle over the puddings. Serve them warm with double cream, if desired. You can store the puddings, covered in the fridge, for up to 2 days.

55 mins plus resting and cooling   **SERVES 4–6**

BREAD AND BUTTER PUDDING pain au chocolat

The perfect way to use up day-old pain au chocolat. Adding white chocolate makes this dessert even more luxurious.

INGREDIENTS
unsalted butter, for greasing
215g (7½oz) chocolate croissants, torn into large chunks
30g (1oz) good-quality white chocolate chips
2 eggs
50g (1¾oz) caster sugar

200ml (7fl oz) whole milk
200ml (7fl oz) double cream
1 tsp vanilla extract
vanilla ice cream or cream, to serve

SPECIAL EQUIPMENT
18 x 23cm (7 x 9in) ovenproof dish

1 Preheat the oven to 180°C (350°F/Gas 4) and lightly grease the ovenproof dish. Place the croissant chunks and chocolate chips in the dish. Toss well to combine and spread the mixture out in an even layer, pressing it down gently to make a packed base.

2 Whisk the eggs and sugar in a large bowl until light. Add the milk, cream, and vanilla extract. Whisk to combine and pour over the base, pushing down lightly to help the liquid to absorb. Leave to rest for 5 minutes.

3 Place the dish in a large roasting tin. Pour hot water into the tin to come halfway up the sides of the dish. Bake for 40–45 minutes, until golden brown. Remove carefully and leave to cool for 5 minutes. Serve warm with vanilla ice cream or cream. You can store the pudding, covered in the fridge, for up to 2 days.

⏱ **50 mins**
plus resting and cooling

🍴 **SERVES 4–6**

BREAD AND BUTTER PUDDING
panettone and marmalade

Bursting with citrus flavours, this dessert is great for serving a crowd. The pudding is cooked at a low temperature, so it is not necessary to use the classic bain-marie method in the oven.

INGREDIENTS
unsalted butter, for greasing

150g (5½oz) marmalade

250g (9oz) panettone, thickly sliced

200ml (7fl oz) whole milk

3 eggs, lightly beaten

3 tbsp double cream

50g (1¾oz) light brown sugar

½ tsp mixed spice

finely grated zest and juice of 1 orange

SPECIAL EQUIPMENT
18 x 23cm (7 x 9in) ovenproof dish

1 Preheat the oven to 160°F (325°F/Gas 3) and grease the ovenproof dish. Spread the marmalade evenly over the panettone slices. Arrange the slices in the dish in a neat layer, making sure they overlap slightly.

2 Pour the milk into a jug. Add the remaining ingredients. Whisk to combine and pour over the panettone, pushing down lightly to help the liquid to absorb. Leave to rest for 15 minutes.

3 Place the dish on a baking sheet and bake for 30 minutes, until golden brown. Remove and leave to cool for 5 minutes. Serve warm, or at room temperature. You can store the pudding, covered in the fridge, for up to 2 days.

🕐 **30 mins**
plus soaking

🍴 **SERVES 6-8**

🌡 Also great
COLD

TAPIOCA PUDDING vanilla

Some associate tapioca pudding with bland flavour and unappealing texture. This grown-up version is the perfect comfort food and anything but bland – it is rich and creamy with a good textural contrast from the tapioca pearls.

INGREDIENTS

750ml (1¼ pints) whole milk

70g (2¼oz) small pearl tapioca

2 large egg yolks

¼ tsp salt

50g (1¾oz) dark brown sugar

50g (1¾oz) caster sugar

1 vanilla pod

30 blackberries, to serve

single cream, to serve

1 Pour 200ml (7fl oz) milk into a heavy-based saucepan. Add the tapioca pearls and stir to mix. Leave the mixture to soak for about 45 minutes.

2 Stir in the remaining milk. Add the egg yolks, salt, and both lots of sugar and whisk well to combine. Split the vanilla pod with a sharp knife, add to the pan, and stir well to mix.

Bring the mixture to the boil over a medium heat, stirring constantly. Reduce the heat to a simmer and cook for 15 minutes, stirring occasionally, until the tapioca pearls are soft and the pudding has thickened slightly.

4

Remove from the heat and discard the vanilla pod. Serve warm with blackberries and a swirl of cream; serve it chilled for a thicker texture. You can store it in an airtight container in the fridge for 2–3 days.

Orange

Chocolate
and banana

🕐 **30 mins**
plus soaking　　🍴 **SERVES 6–8**　　🌡 Also great
COLD

TAPIOCA PUDDING
chocolate and banana

Add grated good-quality dark chocolate to still
warm tapioca to create this marvellously rich
dessert, that is topped with banana slices.

1 Place **200ml (7fl oz) whole milk** in a heavy-based saucepan.
Add **70g (2¼oz) small pearl tapioca**, stir well, and leave to
soak for about 45 minutes.

2 Add **750ml (1¼ pints) whole milk** and **60ml (2fl oz) double
cream**, and mix well. Whisk in **2 large egg yolks, 50g (1¾oz)
caster sugar**, and **¼ tsp salt** until combined. Bring to the boil
over a medium heat, stirring constantly. Then reduce the heat to
a simmer and cook, stirring occasionally, for 15 minutes, or until
the tapioca pearls are soft.

3 Remove from the heat. Stir in **140g (5oz) finely chopped dark
chocolate**, until melted. Then stir in **½ tsp vanilla extract** and
top with **2–3 thinly sliced bananas**. Serve warm, or chill for 2
hours before serving if a thicker texture is preferred. You can store
the pudding in an airtight container in the fridge for 2–3 days.

🕐 **30 mins**
plus soaking　　🍴 **SERVES 6–8**　　🌡 Also great
COLD

TAPIOCA PUDDING
orange

Use both orange zest and juice to give a fresh
flavour to this pudding. Blood oranges, when in
season, can also add a wonderfully deep colour.

1 Place **200ml (7fl oz) whole milk** in a heavy-based saucepan.
Add **70g (2¼oz) small pearl tapioca**, stir well, and leave to
soak for about 45 minutes.

2 Stir in **475ml (15½fl oz) whole milk** and **120ml (4fl oz) double
cream**. Add **2 large egg yolks, ¼ tsp salt, 65g (2¼oz) caster
sugar, grated zest of 1 orange** and **juice of ½ orange**, and mix well.
Bring to the boil over a medium heat, stirring constantly. Then reduce
the heat to a simmer and cook, stirring occasionally, for 15 minutes,
or until the tapioca pearls are soft.

3 Remove from the heat. Stir in **½ tsp vanilla extract** and decorate
with **30g (1oz) roughly chopped unsalted and skinned
pistachios**. Serve warm, or chill for 2 hours before serving if
a thicker texture is preferred. You can store the pudding in an airtight
container in the fridge for 2–3 days.

Lime and
mango

Coconut

🕐 **30 mins**
plus soaking   🍴 **SERVES 6-8**   🌡 Also great
COLD

TAPIOCA PUDDING
coconut

Tapioca is made from cassava plants that are grown
in Asia alongside coconut trees. This explains why
this creamy pairing is so popular in Asian cuisine.

1. Place **200ml (7fl oz) coconut milk** in a heavy-based saucepan.
Add **70g (2¼oz) small pearl tapioca**, stir well, and leave to
soak for about 45 minutes.

2. Add **550ml (18fl oz) coconut milk**, **1 large egg yolk**, **¼ tsp
salt**, and **100g (3½oz) caster sugar**. Whisk well to combine.
Bring the mixture to the boil over a medium heat, stirring constantly.
Then reduce the heat to a simmer and cook, stirring occasionally,
for 15 minutes, or until the tapioca pearls are soft.

3. Remove from the heat. Stir in **¼ tsp vanilla extract** and sprinkle
over **30g (1oz) toasted, desiccated coconut**. Serve warm, or
chill for 2 hours before serving if a thicker texture is preferred. You
can store it in an airtight container in the fridge for 2–3 days.

🕐 **30-35 mins**
plus chilling   🍴 **SERVES 6-8**   🌡 Also great
COLD

TAPIOCA PUDDING
lime and mango

For a very quick tropical-flavoured pudding,
add cooked tapioca pearls to a purée of ripe
mango, lime, and a little condensed milk.

1. Place **1.2 litres (2 pints) water** in a large saucepan, bring to
the boil, and add **100g (3½oz) small pearl tapioca**. Cook for
20–25 minutes, stirring constantly, until the tapioca pearls are soft
and translucent. Remove from the heat, drain, and rinse under
running cold water to halt the cooking process.

2. Drain well again, place the tapioca in a small bowl, and set
aside. Place **2 peeled, stoned, and roughly chopped mangoes**
in a food processor and pulse to a smooth purée. Transfer to a bowl
and add **120ml (4fl oz) condensed milk**, **⅛ tsp salt**, and **juice of
½ lime**. Mix well until smooth.

3. Add the tapioca pearls to the mango pudding and mix until
combined. Decorate with the **zest of ½ lime**, and **½ pineapple,
thinly sliced**. Serve warm, or chill for 2 hours before serving if a
thicker texture is preferred. You can store it in an airtight container
in the fridge for 2–3 days.

INGREDIENTS

45g (1½oz) unsalted butter

100g (3½oz) short-grain rice

50g (1¾oz) dark brown sugar

50g (1¾oz) caster sugar

¾ tsp ground cinnamon

¼ tsp grated nutmeg, plus extra for sprinkling

¼ tsp salt

1 litre (1¾ pints) whole milk

120ml (4fl oz) double cream

1 tsp pure vanilla extract

1 bay leaf

SPECIAL EQUIPMENT

2.5 litre (4⅓ pint) ovenproof dish

🕐 **1 hr 50 mins**   🍴 **SERVES 6-8**   🌡 Also great **COLD**

RICE PUDDING baked

This is a sophisticated dessert of soft, fragrant, and billowy rice cooked in creamy milk. Some people associate rice pudding with nursery food, but when it is cooked to perfection and infused with spices, that couldn't be further from the truth.

1

Preheat the oven to 150°C (300°F/Gas 2). Melt the butter in a saucepan over a medium heat. Add the rice and stir well to coat.

2

Add both lots of sugar, the cinnamon, nutmeg, salt, and 1-2 tablespoons of the milk. Cook, stirring frequently, until the sugar dissolves.

3

Increase the heat and add the remaining ingredients. Bring to a simmer, stirring the mixture occasionally. Remove from the heat. Discard the bay leaf and pour the mixture into the ovenproof dish.

4

Bake for 30 minutes. Then remove, stir, and sprinkle with nutmeg. Bake for a further 1 hour –1 hour 10 minutes. Remove from the heat and serve hot. You can store the pudding in an airtight container in the fridge for 2–3 days.

🕐 **50–55 mins**
plus chilling   🍴 **SERVES 4**   🌡 Also great
COLD

RICE PUDDING
coconut and lime

This sumptuous dessert, delicately flavoured with lime and coconut, makes the perfect finale to a meal inspired by Asian flavours.

1 Lightly crack **2 cardamom pods** and place them in a large saucepan. Add **1 small, halved cinnamon stick** and place the saucepan over a medium heat. Toast lightly for 30–45 seconds, until fragrant.

2 Add **400ml (14fl oz) coconut milk, 200ml (7fl oz) whole milk, 65g (2¼oz) brown sugar**, and **⅛ tsp salt** to the saucepan. Bring the mixture to the boil, stirring until the sugar dissolves. Then reduce the heat to low.

3 Add **150g (5½oz) cooked plain, long-grain rice** and **grated zest of ½ lime** to the saucepan. Cook for 40 minutes, stirring occasionally, until thick. Remove from the heat and take out the cardamom pods and cinnamon stick.

4 Divide the pudding between four ramekins. Decorate with **toasted coconut** and **lime zest** to serve. You can also chill it for 30 minutes and serve cold. You can store the pudding in an airtight container in the fridge for 4–5 days, although it will become very thick.

🕐 **50–55 mins**
plus cooling   🍴 **SERVES 4**   🌡 Also great
COLD

ARROZ con leche

Popular all over South America, arroz con leche is a delicious vanilla-infused sweet rice pudding. The use of three kinds of milk provides the creamy texture.

1 Split **1 vanilla pod** and place both the seeds and the pod in a saucepan. Add **1 small, halved cinnamon stick** and place the saucepan over a medium heat. Toast lightly for 30–45 seconds, until fragrant.

2 Add **350ml (12fl oz) evaporated milk, 240ml (8fl oz) whole milk, 180ml (6fl oz) condensed milk**, and **⅛ tsp salt**. Bring to the boil, stirring frequently. Then reduce the heat to a simmer.

3 Add **150g (5½oz) cooked plain, long-grain rice** to the pan. Cook for 40 minutes, stirring frequently, until thick. Remove from the heat and take out the vanilla pod and cinnamon stick. Leave to cool slightly.

4 Divide the pudding between four ramekins, sprinkle with **ground cinnamon**, and serve warm. You can keep the pudding in an airtight container in the fridge for 4–5 days, although it will become very thick.

Coconut and lime

Arroz con leche

🕐 **30 mins**
plus chilling and cooling 🍴 **SERVES 4–6** 🌡 Also great **COLD**

RICE PUDDING Swedish with berry sauce

Traditionally made at Christmas in Sweden, this cold dessert is served with a warm and sharp berry sauce for a contrast in flavour and texture.

1 Boil **800ml (1½ pints) whole milk**, **150g (5½oz) long-grain rice**, and **50g (1¾oz) caster sugar** in a large, heavy-based saucepan, stirring frequently. Then reduce the heat to a simmer and cook for 15 minutes, stirring frequently, until the rice is soft. Remove, leave to cool, then transfer to a large bowl.

2 Whisk **280ml (9½fl oz) double cream** in a bowl to form soft peaks and fold into the rice. Then fold in **85g (3oz) blanched, toasted, and finely chopped almonds**, **1 tbsp sherry**, and **1 tsp vanilla extract**. Chill the pudding for 3–4 hours.

3 For the sauce, place **50g (1¾oz) caster sugar**, **1 tbsp water**, and **300g (10oz) mixed raspberries, blackberries, and blackcurrants** in a large saucepan. Cook over a low heat for 3–4 minutes, until cooked through. Remove from the heat.

4 Use a hand-held blender to blend the mixture to a purée, then strain it into a small bowl. Serve the chilled pudding with the warm sauce poured over the top. You can store it in an airtight container in the fridge for up to 3 days.

Swedish with berry sauce

🕐 **50 mins**
plus cooling 🍴 **SERVES 4** 🌡 Also great **COLD**

RICE PUDDING Arborio

Rice pudding is traditionally made with a short-grain pudding rice. Italian Arborio rice is starchier and produces an even creamier finish.

1 Lightly crack **4 cardamom pods** and place them in a large saucepan. Add **1 large, halved cinnamon stick** and **4 whole cloves** and place the pan over a medium heat. Toast lightly for 30–45 seconds, until fragrant.

2 Add **1 litre (1¾ pints) whole milk**, **60ml (2fl oz) double cream**, **¼ tsp grated nutmeg**, **80g (2¾oz) dark brown sugar**, and **100g (3½oz) Arborio rice**. Bring to the boil, stirring until the sugar dissolves.

3 Reduce the heat to a low simmer and cook the pudding for 40–45 minutes, stirring frequently, until the rice has cooked through. Remove from the heat and take out the cardamom pods and cinnamon stick.

4 Add **½ tsp vanilla bean paste** or **vanilla extract** and stir to combine. Divide the pudding between four bowls and top each with **5 blackberries**. Serve immediately. You can store it in an airtight container in the fridge for 4–5 days, although it will become very thick.

Arborio

🕐 **1 hr**　🍴 **SERVES 4**　🌡 Also great **COLD**

BAKED APPLES with cinnamon sugar

Of all fruits, apples are the easiest to bake. For a luscious no-fuss dessert, they just need sweetening with sugar, flavouring with a little spice, and a long, gentle bake. Serve with bowls of good-quality ice cream for a winning hot-cold combination.

INGREDIENTS

½ tsp ground cinnamon, plus extra for dusting

4 tbsp light brown sugar

¼ tsp ground allspice

4 dessert apples, such as Braeburn

30g (1oz) unsalted butter

vanilla ice cream, to serve

Preheat the oven to 190°C (375°F/Gas 5). Place the cinnamon, sugar, and allspice in a bowl and mix well to combine.

1

Core each apple, leaving about 2cm (¾in) of the bottom intact. Fill the centre of each apple with a quarter of the sugar mixture.

2

Pour 120ml (4fl oz) water into a shallow baking dish. Place the apples in the dish and top them with equal quantities of the butter.

3

Bake for 40–50 minutes, until tender. Remove from the heat. Top the apples with boules of vanilla ice cream and dust with cinnamon. Serve warm. You can store them in an airtight container in the fridge for 1–2 days.

4

🕐 **50 mins** plus cooling   🍴 **SERVES 6**   🌡️ Also great **COLD**

ROASTED PEACHES
with cardamom cream

Use ripe and juicy peaches for this recipe, as the natural sugars in the juice concentrate as the fruit roasts.

INGREDIENTS
3 large peaches, halved and stoned

3 tbsp dark brown sugar

pinch of salt

2 tbsp unsalted butter, melted

For the cream

240ml (8fl oz) double cream

½ tsp ground cardamom

¼ tsp vanilla extract

3 tbsp icing sugar

SPECIAL EQUIPMENT
1.7 litre (3 pint) baking dish

PLAN AHEAD
You can prepare and store the cream in an airtight container in the fridge up to 1 day ahead.

1 Preheat the oven to 200°C (400°F/Gas 6). Remove any rough fibres from the peaches and place them cut-side up in the baking dish. Whisk the brown sugar, salt, and butter in a small bowl and pour over the peaches.

2 Roast the peaches for 30–35 minutes or longer, depending on their size and ripeness, until tender when tested with a fork and lightly golden on top. Remove from the heat and leave to cool slightly.

3 For the cream, whisk all the ingredients in a large bowl to form medium peaks. Chill the mixture until cold. Serve the roasted peaches warm with the cream. You can store the peaches, in an airtight container in the fridge, for 1–2 days.

🕐 **25 mins** plus cooling   🍴 **SERVES 4**   🌡️ Also great **COLD**

BANANAS FOSTER with orange and pecans

This decadent dessert is a quick and easy flourish at the end of a meal. You can whip it up in minutes with fresh bananas and a few store-cupboard essentials.

INGREDIENTS
50g (1¾oz) pecans, roughly chopped

60g (2oz) unsalted butter

4 heaped tbsp soft dark brown sugar

juice and grated zest of 1 orange

2 large under-ripe bananas, cut into 1cm (½in) pieces

60ml (2fl oz) dark rum

4 slices brioche, thickly cut

4 large scoops good-quality vanilla ice cream

1 Toast the pecans in a large, dry, heavy-based frying pan, over a medium heat for 3–4 minutes. Stir occasionally, until brown in places. Remove from the heat and leave to cool.

2 Place the butter, sugar, and orange juice in a large frying pan. Add the orange zest, reserving a little, and cook over a medium heat, stirring until the sugar dissolves. Increase the heat to high and cook the sauce for a further 2–3 minutes, until it reduces slightly and begins to look glossy.

3 Add the bananas and cook for a further 2–3 minutes, until the sauce reduces and the banana pieces are just tender. Add the pecans and rum, and cook for a further 1 minute. Use a match to carefully light the alcohol – the pan will flare up for 1 minute. Remove from the heat.

4 Lightly toast the brioche slices and cut each into two 7cm (2¾in) rounds. Place two rounds each on four serving plates. Top with a quarter of the banana mixture and one scoop of ice cream. Serve immediately topped with the reserved orange zest.

20 mins plus cooling　　**SERVES 4**　　Also great **COLD**

CARAMELIZED APRICOTS with almonds

Home-made caramel makes a wonderful sauce for sweet and ripe apricots.

INGREDIENTS
4–5 tbsp flaked almonds

2½ tbsp unsalted butter

pinch of salt

4 tbsp dark brown sugar

8 apricots, halved and stoned

whipped cream, to serve

SPECIAL EQUIPMENT
23cm (9in) frying pan

1 Toast the almonds in a dry frying pan over a medium heat, stirring constantly, until lightly coloured and fragrant. Remove from the heat, transfer to a dish, and leave to cool completely.

2 Place the butter, salt, and sugar in the frying pan and cook over a medium heat, until smooth and bubbling. Carefully place the apricots, cut-side down, over the caramel. Increase the heat slightly.

3 Cook the apricots for 4–5 minutes, until the cut sides are caramelized and softened. Remove from the heat and leave to cool slightly. Sprinkle the almonds over the apricots. Serve warm with whipped cream. You can store the apricots, in an airtight container in the fridge, for 1–2 days.

20–25 mins　　**SERVES 4**　　Also great **COLD**

ROASTED FIGS with thyme and red wine

If you are lucky enough to have access to home-grown figs, you may find that they are not as sweet as their shop-bought cousins. Roasting them like this can intensify their sweetness.

INGREDIENTS
3 tbsp red wine

4 tbsp light brown sugar

¼ tsp vanilla extract

¼ tsp lemon juice

grated zest of ½ lemon

2–3 sprigs of thyme

8 fresh figs, halved lengthways

plain yogurt, to serve

SPECIAL EQUIPMENT
1.7 litre (3 pint) baking dish

1 Preheat the oven to 200°C (400°F/Gas 6). Combine the wine, sugar, vanilla extract, and lemon juice and zest in a large bowl. Remove the leaves from the sprigs of thyme, add to the mixture, and mix. Add the figs, and toss well to coat.

2 Place the figs, cut-side down, in a baking dish and pour the wine mixture over. Roast the figs in the oven for 10–15 minutes or longer, depending on their size and ripeness, until they are tender when tested with a fork.

3 Remove and brush the cooking liquid over the figs to glaze. Transfer the figs to serving plates and drizzle over a little of the cooking liquid, if desired. Serve with a spoonful of plain yogurt. You can store the figs and the cooking liquid in an airtight container in the fridge, for 2–3 days.

🕐 **45–55 mins**
plus cooling and chilling

🍴 **SERVES 4**

🌡 Also great
COLD

POACHED PEARS
in red wine

Taking on the rich purple hues of red wine, poached pears are a simple and classic dessert. Here the pears are laced with cinnamon, orange zest, and a little fresh thyme. The flavours deepen the longer the pears are kept in the cooking liquid.

INGREDIENTS
750ml (1¼ pints) red wine
150g (5½oz) caster sugar
1 cinnamon stick
pared zest of 1 orange
1 sprig of thyme
4 just-ripe pears, peeled
whipped cream, to serve

PLAN AHEAD
You can prepare and store the pears and cooking liquid, covered in the fridge, up to 2 days ahead.

1 Place the wine, sugar, cinnamon, orange zest, and thyme in a lidded, heavy-based saucepan. Bring to the boil, stirring until the sugar melts. Then reduce the heat to a low simmer.

2 Slice a disc off the base of each pear to allow it to stand upright. Add them to the pan, making sure they are submerged in the wine. Cover and cook for 20–30 minutes, until the pears are just soft when pierced with a knife.

4 Strain 200ml (7fl oz) of the cooking liquid into a heavy-based saucepan. Bring to the boil, then reduce the heat to a simmer. Cook for 15 minutes, until slightly thickened. Leave to cool until just warm. Place the pears upright on serving plates and pour over a little of the sauce. Serve warm with whipped cream.

3 Remove and cool to room temperature. Transfer the pears and cooking liquid to a large dish and cover with cling film. Chill until needed, or overnight to darken the colour. Bring to room temperature before serving. Then discard the cinnamon, orange zest, and thyme.

🕐 **30–35 mins**
plus steeping and cooling   🍴 **SERVES 4**   🌡 Also great
COLD

PLUMS in tea and star anise

Plums have a rich and deep flavour that intensifies as they cook. Add Earl Grey tea and pungent star anise for an exotic twist.

1 Place **2 Earl Grey teabags**, 30g (1oz) caster sugar, **2 whole star anise**, and **1 cinnamon stick** in a large, lidded heavy-based saucepan. Pour over **500ml (16fl oz) boiling water**, cover, and steep for 10 minutes.

2 Remove the teabags and stir to ensure that the sugar has melted. Add **8 large, just-ripe, halved plums**, cut-side up, and bring to the boil. Then reduce the heat to a low simmer. Cook for 8–10 minutes, until the plums are soft when pierced with a knife.

3 Transfer the plums, cut-side up, to four serving bowls. Set aside to cool. Return the pan to the heat and bring the liquid to the boil. Then reduce the heat to a low simmer and cook for 15 minutes, until the liquid has reduced and thickened slightly.

4 Remove and cool until just warm. Then take out the spices and pour the juice over the plums. Top with **1 scoop softened vanilla ice cream** and serve immediately. You can chill the fruit and liquid for up to 3 days. Bring to room temperature to serve.

🕐 **40 mins**
plus cooling   🍴 **SERVES 4**   🌡 Also great
COLD

APRICOTS with wine and lemon thyme

Perfect to serve when apricots are in season, this simple, fragrant dessert makes the ideal finish to any summertime meal.

1 Place **500ml (16fl oz) dry white wine**, **3 tbsp runny honey**, **1 sprig of lemon thyme**, and **zest and juice of 1 large lemon** in a large, heavy-based, saucepan. Bring to the boil, stirring, until the honey has melted.

2 Remove from the heat. Add **8 large, just-ripe, halved and stoned apricots** to the pan, cut-side up, and bring to the boil over a medium heat. Then reduce the heat to a low simmer and cook for 5 minutes, until the apricots are just soft when pierced with a knife.

3 Transfer the apricots, cut-side up, to four serving bowls. Set aside to cool. Remove the thyme and lemon zest and return the pan to the heat. Bring the liquid to the boil, then reduce the heat to a low simmer.

4 Add **1 tbsp caster sugar** and cook for 20–25 minutes, until the liquid has reduced and thickened. Remove and leave to cool until just warm, then pour over the apricots. Serve with **crème fraîche**. You can chill the fruit and liquid for up to 3 days. Bring to room temperature to serve.

Plums in tea and star anise

⏱ **25–30 mins**
plus cooling

🍴 **SERVES 4–6**

🌡 Also great
COLD

FRUIT COMPOTE with yogurt and pistachios

Even when seasonal fruit is scarce, whip up a fruity dessert using the dried fruit in your store-cupboard. Save any leftovers to serve with breakfast.

1 Heat **500ml (16fl oz) water, 30g (1oz) soft light brown sugar, zest and juice of 1 large orange,** and **1 cinnamon stick** in a heavy-based, lidded saucepan. Stir frequently to dissolve the sugar.

2 Add **400g (14oz) assorted chopped dried fruit** such as cherries, figs, prunes, apricots, and cranberries. Bring to the boil, then reduce the heat to a low simmer. Cook for 20–25 minutes, covered, until the fruit is soft and plump. Remove from the heat and take out the cinnamon stick.

3 Pour the compote into four serving bowls and cool to room temperature. To serve, add **1 tbsp Greek yogurt** to each bowl and top with **30g (1oz) roughly chopped unsalted and skinned pistachios**. You can chill the fruit and liquid for up to 3 days. Bring to room temperature to serve.

Apricots with wine and lemon thyme

Fruit compote with yogurt and pistachios

COLD

Pâtisserie ▪ Trifles and layered cakes
Puddings ▪ Cakes and tortes ▪ Traybakes
and small bakes

INGREDIENTS
4 large egg whites,
    at room temperature

¼ tsp salt

¼ tsp cream of tartar

200g (7oz) caster sugar

2 tsp vanilla extract

350ml (12fl oz) double
    cream

2 tsp icing sugar, plus
    extra for dusting
    (optional)

strawberries and
    raspberries, to
    serve (optional)

SPECIAL EQUIPMENT
piping bag fitted with
    a 1cm (½in) nozzle

PLAN AHEAD
You can store the
unfilled meringues in
an airtight container
up to 1 week ahead.

🕐 **3 hrs 15 mins**
plus cooling

🍴 **MAKES 30**

MERINGUES with cream

Light, crisp, and creamy white in colour, meringues are a
versatile dessert staple. For faultless results, use eggs at room
temperature, a scrupulously clean mixing bowl, and a low and
long cooking time.

1

Preheat the oven to
110°C (225°F/Gas ¼)
and line two baking
sheets with baking
parchment. Set aside.
Whisk the egg whites
and salt in a large
bowl with a hand-held
whisk until foamy.

2

Add the cream of tartar and whisk until soft peaks
form. Then add the caster sugar, a tablespoon at
a time, and whisk after each addition until the
mixture is well combined and forms stiff peaks.

3

Add the vanilla extract to the mixture and fold it in gently with a spatula, so that you lose as little air as possible. Once evenly combined, transfer the mixture to the piping bag.

Pipe 30 even-sized meringues onto each baking sheet. Bake for 3 hours, until crisp. Turn off the heat and leave to cool completely in the oven. Whisk the cream and icing sugar until thick and use to sandwich the meringues. Serve immediately with strawberries, raspberries, and a dusting of icing sugar, if desired.

4

Make sure the meringues are spaced well apart.

🕐 **45 mins**
plus infusing and chilling

🍴 **SERVES 4**

ÎLES flottantes

This French classic features just-poached meringues served over crème anglaise, which is a delicious vanilla custard.

INGREDIENTS

300ml (10fl oz) double
  cream
1 vanilla pod
175g (6oz) caster sugar,
  plus 2 tsp extra
450ml (15fl oz) whole milk
2 tsp cornflour
4 egg yolks

1 tsp pure vanilla
  extract
3 egg whites
2 tbsp grated chocolate,
  to serve

PLAN AHEAD
You can prepare and store the custard, covered in the fridge, up to 2 days ahead.

1 Place the cream, vanilla pod, 2 teaspoons of sugar, and half the milk in a saucepan. Bring to a simmer, then remove from the heat. Leave to infuse for 30 minutes, before removing the vanilla pod.

2 Place the cornflour in a bowl and stir in a little cold milk. Pour the mixture into the infused milk and stir to combine. Bring the mixture to the boil, stirring constantly. Reduce the heat to a simmer, cook for 2 minutes, and remove. Whisk the egg yolks in a separate bowl until smooth.

3 Gradually add the egg yolks to the milk mixture and whisk to combine. Whisk the custard until it is thick enough to coat the back of a spoon, making sure it does not curdle. Stir in the vanilla extract. Pour the custard into a large bowl and cover its surface with dampened cling film. Chill until needed.

4 In a large bowl, whisk the egg whites to stiff peaks. Gradually whisk in the sugar until combined. Boil the remaining milk and 300ml (10fl oz) water in a deep-sided frying pan. Then reduce the heat to a simmer and carefully add 3-4 tablespoons of the mixture to the pan.

5 Cook the meringues in the hot liquid, for 1 minute, turning them over once, until they double in size. Remove with a slotted spoon and drain on a plate lined with kitchen paper. Divide the custard between 4 bowls and top with the meringues. Sprinkle with chocolate to serve immediately.

🕐 **1 hr 50 mins**
plus cooling

🍴 **MAKES 12**

MINI PAVLOVAS tropical fruit

These pavlovas are great if you need to cater for large numbers. Make sure you press small indents in the mixture before baking, so the filling can nestle in place.

INGREDIENTS

250g (9oz) caster sugar
1¾ tsp cornflour
5 egg whites, at
  room temperature
pinch of salt
1 tsp white wine vinegar
¼ tsp vanilla extract
¼ tsp orange blossom
  extract

For the filling
300ml (10fl oz) double
  cream, whipped
5-6 kiwis, halved and
  thinly sliced
3-4 passionfruits, pulped

PLAN AHEAD
You can store the unfilled pavlovas in an airtight container up to 1 week ahead.

1 Preheat the oven to 140°C (275°F/Gas 1). Trace 12 circles, each measuring 7.5cm (3in) in diameter, on a sheet of baking parchment. Flip the sheet over and use it to line a large baking sheet. Combine the sugar and cornflour in a bowl.

2 In a large bowl, whisk the egg whites and salt until you reach soft peaks. Gradually whisk in the sugar mixture to form stiff peaks. Add the white wine vinegar, vanilla extract, and orange blossom extract, folding gently so that you lose as little air as possible.

3 Divide the mixture between the circles on the baking parchment, creating swirls with a palette knife. Make small indents in the centre. Reduce the oven temperature to 120°C (225°F/Gas ¼) and bake for 1 hour, until the pavlovas are hard and hollow when tapped.

4 Turn off the heat and leave the pavlovas in the oven to cool completely before removing them. Top the pavlovas with equal quantities of whipped cream, kiwi, and passionfruit. Serve immediately.

🕐 **1 hr 50 mins**
plus cooling

🍴 **SERVES 6–8**

PAVLOVA chocolate, apple, and pear

Light, airy pavlovas are often associated with summertime, but autumnal fruits can work beautifully with a cocoa-infused meringue base. Added warmth comes from a little sprinkled cardamom and cinnamon in the cream filling.

INGREDIENTS

4 egg whites, at room temperature

pinch of salt

¼ tsp cream of tartar

200g (7oz) caster sugar

½ tsp vanilla extract

2 tbsp cocoa powder, plus extra for dusting

For the filling

¼ tsp cinnamon

1½ tsp icing sugar

¼ tsp cardamom

85g (3oz) green apple, thinly sliced

85g (3oz) pear, thinly sliced

240ml (8fl oz) double cream, whipped

PLAN AHEAD

You can store the unfilled pavlova in an airtight container up to 1 week ahead.

1 Preheat the oven to 140°C (275°F/Gas 1). Line a baking sheet with baking parchment and set aside. Whisk the egg whites and salt in a bowl until foamy. Add the cream of tartar and whisk to form soft peaks. Then gradually add the caster sugar and whisk to form stiff peaks.

2 Add the vanilla extract and cocoa powder and whisk well to combine. Use a palette knife to spread the mixture on the baking sheet to a circle about 5cm (2in) thick and 20cm (8in) wide. Create neat swirls as you spread the mixture and make a small indent in the centre.

3 Reduce the oven temperature to 130°C (250°F/Gas ½) and bake the pavlova for 1 hour and 20 minutes, until it is hard. Turn off the heat and leave it to cool completely in the oven before removing.

4 For the filling, combine the cinnamon, icing sugar, and cardamom in a bowl. Add the fruit, toss to coat, and leave for 5–10 minutes. Spread the whipped cream on the pavlova. Arrange the fruit on top, sprinkle with cocoa powder, and serve immediately.

50-55 mins
plus resting and cooling

MAKES 20

MACARONS buttercream

Light and delicate creations, macarons are tricky to get right. If the humidity or heat in your kitchen is too harsh, or if you do not rest the mixture for long enough, you can get unexpected results. Follow this recipe closely for impressive results.

INGREDIENTS

100g (3½oz) icing sugar

75g (2½oz) ground almonds

2 large egg whites, at room temperature

75g (2½oz) caster sugar

For the filling

60g (2oz) unsalted butter, softened

125g (4½oz) icing sugar

½ tsp vanilla extract

SPECIAL EQUIPMENT

piping bag fitted with a 3cm (1in) plain nozzle

piping bag fitted with a 1cm (½in) plain nozzle

PLAN AHEAD

You can prepare and store the unfilled macaron shells in an airtight container up to 3 days ahead.

1

Preheat the oven to 150°C (300°F/Gas 2). Use the 3cm (1in) nozzle to trace 20 well spaced circles each on two sheets of silicone paper. Turn the sheets over and place on two baking sheets.

2

Pulse the icing sugar and almonds in a food processor to a fine powder. Whisk the egg whites in a large bowl to form soft peaks. Then whisk in the caster sugar, a little at a time, until the mixture is stiff and well combined, but still glossy.

3

Gently fold the almond and sugar mixture into the egg mixture, gradually, so that you lose as little air as possible. Take care not to overmix. Place the piping bag with the 3cm (1¼in) nozzle in a glass and carefully transfer the macaron mixture into it.

The mixture should be shiny, with a thick, ribbon-like consistency.

4

Using the traced guidelines, pipe the macaron mixture into the centre of each circle, holding the piping bag vertically. Keep the circles even in volume, as the mixture will spread very slightly. Lightly bang the baking sheets on a work surface. Leave to rest at room temperature for 30 minutes.

KNOW-HOW It is important to bang the trays, as it levels any peaks that may stay when baked. You could also dampen the end of your finger and push peaks down gently.

5

Bake on the top shelf of the oven for 20–25 minutes, until the surface of the shells are set but delicate. Remove and leave to rest on the baking sheets for 15–20 minutes. Then transfer to a wire rack to cool completely.

6

For the filling, beat the ingredients in a bowl until soft and creamy. Place the second piping bag in a glass, and spoon the filling in. Pipe a small amount of the filling onto the flat side of 10 macaron shells and gently sandwich them with the remaining shells. Serve immediately. You can store filled macarons for 2–3 days in an airtight container.

🕐 **50–55 mins**
plus resting and cooling   🍴 **MAKES 20**

MACARONS raspberry

Pretty as a picture, these macarons are stuffed with fresh raspberries and mascarpone and look fantastic served on a dessert platter.

1 Preheat the oven to 150°C (300°F/Gas 2). Trace 20 circles each on two sheets of silicone paper. Turn them over, use to line two baking sheets, and set aside. Pulse **75g (2½oz) ground almonds** and **100g (3½oz) icing sugar** in a food processor, to a fine powder. Sieve to discard large lumps and set aside.

2 Whisk **2 large egg whites** with a hand-held whisk in a large bowl to form stiff peaks. Add **75g (2½oz) caster sugar**, a little at a time, whisking well after each addition until the mixture is stiff and glossy. Add **¼ tsp red food colouring paste**, and whisk until you achieve the desired shade of pink.

3 Use a silicone spatula to gently fold half the dry ingredients into the egg white mixture, until combined. Add the remaining dry ingredients and mix until you reach a shiny mixture with a thick, ribbon-like consistency. Transfer the mixture to a **piping bag** fitted with a **1cm (½in) plain nozzle**.

4 Pipe the mixture in the centre of each traced circle. Lightly bang the sheets on a work surface, and leave to rest for 30 minutes. Bake in the oven for 20–25 minutes, until the surface is firm. Rest on the baking sheets for 10 minutes, then transfer to a wire rack to cool completely.

5 Beat **150g (5½oz) mascarpone, 2 tbsp double cream**, and **2 tbsp icing sugar** in a bowl and transfer to a piping bag. Halve **30 raspberries** lengthways. Pipe a little of the cream filling onto 10 shells and top with 3 raspberry slices, arranged cut-side down in a star shape. Pipe the filling onto the remaining shells and place on top of the raspberries. Serve immediately.

🕐 **50–55 mins**
plus resting, cooling, and chilling   🍴 **MAKES 20**

MACARONS pistachio

It is important to use raw, unsalted pistachios for this melt-in-the-mouth recipe – rub off the skin with a clean kitchen towel before grinding them.

1 Preheat the oven to 150°C (300°F/Gas 2). Prepare two baking sheets (see Raspberry macarons, step 1) and set aside. Pulse **40g (1¼oz) unsalted and skinned whole pistachios** in a food processor to a coarse powder. Add **100g (3½oz) icing sugar** and **25g (scant 1oz) ground almonds**, and pulse to a very fine powder. Sieve to discard large lumps and set aside.

2 Whisk **2 large egg whites** with a hand-held whisk in a large bowl to form stiff peaks. Add **75g (2½oz) caster sugar**, a little at a time, whisking after each addition until the mixture is stiff and glossy. Add **¼ tsp green food colouring paste**, and whisk until you achieve the desired shade.

3 Use a silicone spatula to fold the dry ingredients into the egg white mixture in two stages (see Raspberry macarons, step 3). Transfer the mixture to a **piping bag** fitted with a **1cm (½in) plain nozzle**. Pipe, rest, and bake the macaron shells (see Raspberry macarons, step 4). Rest the baked shells on the baking sheets for 10 minutes, then transfer to a wire rack to cool.

4 Melt **125g (4½oz) finely chopped good-quality white chocolate, 3 tbsp double cream**, and **1 tsp unsalted butter** in a heatproof bowl over a saucepan of simmering water, making sure it does not touch the bowl. Beat with a wooden spoon, until thick and shiny. Transfer to a piping bag and chill until cool, but not stiff.

5 To serve, pipe a little of the chocolate ganache onto 10 shells and sandwich with the remaining shells. You can store the macarons in an airtight container in the fridge for up to 1 day.

Raspberry

Pistachio

🕐 **50–55 mins**
plus resting, cooling, and chilling

🍴 **MAKES 20**

MACARONS chocolate

A ganache is one of the basic recipes all dessert enthusiasts should have at their fingertips – here it makes a perfect filling for dark chocolate macarons.

1 Preheat the oven to 150°C (300°F/Gas 2). Prepare two baking sheets (see Raspberry macarons, step 1) and set aside. Pulse **50g (1¾oz) ground almonds**, **25g (scant 1oz) cocoa powder**, and **100g (3½oz) icing sugar** in a food processor until well combined.

2 Whisk **2 large egg whites** with a hand-held whisk in a large bowl to form stiff peaks. Add **75g (2½oz) caster sugar**, a little at a time, whisking after each addition until the mixture is stiff and glossy. Use a silicone spatula to fold the dry ingredients into the egg white mixture in two stages (see Raspberry macarons, step 3).

3 Transfer the mixture to a **piping bag** fitted with a **1cm (½in) plain nozzle**. Pipe, rest, and bake the macaron shells (see Raspberry macarons, step 4). Rest the baked shells on the baking sheets for 10 minutes, then transfer to a wire rack to cool.

4 Heat **90ml (3fl oz) double cream** in a heavy-based saucepan until hot, but not boiling. Remove from the heat and add **100g (3½oz) finely chopped good-quality dark chocolate**. Leave to melt, then combine with a wooden spoon. Transfer to a piping bag and chill until cool, but not stiff.

5 To serve, pipe a little of the chocolate ganache onto 10 shells and sandwich with the remaining shells. You can store the macarons in an airtight container in the fridge for up to 1 day.

Chocolate

Simple alternatives

This array of macaron recipes adapts the classic recipe on pages 104–105. Make sure you use food colouring paste, as liquid varieties may loosen the mixture.

Rosewater and raspberry Add ¼ tsp red food colouring paste to the macaron mixture (see p105, step 3) and combine well. For the filling, combine 60g (2oz) crushed raspberries, 125g (4½oz) mascarpone, and ¼ tsp rosewater.

Orange flower Add ¼ tsp orange food colouring paste to the macaron mixture (see p105, step 3). Add 1 tsp finely grated orange zest and 1 tsp orange flower water to the buttercream filling (see p105, step 6).

Mocha Add 1 tbsp instant coffee powder to the ground almonds and sugar before pulsing (see p105, step 2). Sandwich the macaron shells with the chocolate ganache filling (see Chocolate macarons, steps 4–5).

Hazelnut Replace 25g (scant 1oz) of the ground almonds with skinned and finely ground hazelnuts (see p105, step 2). Sandwich with the buttercream filling (see p105, step 6), and roll the edges of the filled macarons in very finely chopped hazelnuts.

Lime and dark chocolate Add ¼ tsp green food colouring paste to the macaron mixture (see p105, step 3) and 1 tsp finely grated lime zest to the chocolate ganache filling (see Chocolate macarons, steps 4–5).

Tangerine Add 1 tsp grated tangerine zest to the ground almonds and sugar (see p105, step 2). Add ¼ tsp orange food colouring paste to the macaron mixture (see p105, step 3). Add 1 tsp grated tangerine zest to the buttercream filling (see p105, step 6).

Lavender Add ¼ tsp purple food colouring to the macaron mixture (see p105, step 3). Add ¼ tsp finely chopped culinary lavender to the buttercream filling (see p105, step 6).

Chocolate orange Make the chocolate macaron shells (see Chocolate macarons, steps 1–4). For the filling, add 1 tsp finely grated orange zest to the buttercream filling (see p105, step 6).

45 mins
plus cooling and chilling

MAKES 26–30

TRUFFLES dark chocolate

In their simplest form, truffles are a mixture of good-quality chocolate and cream. It is difficult to achieve a chocolatier-style finish, but this simple method of dipping, dusting, and brushing gives them an attractive and appetizing look.

INGREDIENTS

175ml (5¾fl oz) double cream

350g (12oz) good-quality dark chocolate, finely grated

2–3 tbsp cocoa powder

SPECIAL EQUIPMENT

2 disposable piping bags

1

Heat the cream in a saucepan over a medium heat until hot, but not boiling. Place 225g (8oz) of the chocolate in a heatproof bowl, pour over the cream, and leave it to melt. Then whisk the mixture until smooth and glossy. Leave to cool for 30 minutes.

2

Spoon the ganache into the piping bags and snip off the ends. Line a large baking sheet with greaseproof paper. Pipe walnut-sized balls of the ganache onto the sheet, spaced well apart. Chill for 30 minutes, until hardened.

3

Roll each ball gently between your palms, until smooth. Place the truffles back on the sheet and chill for a further 30 minutes.

4

Melt the remaining chocolate in a heatproof bowl over a pan of simmering water, making sure it does not touch the water. Stir until smooth. Place the cocoa powder in a small bowl.

5

Place a truffle on a spoon and dip it into the melted chocolate. Remove, allow any excess to drip back into the bowl, and place gently in the bowl of cocoa powder to coat. Transfer the coated truffle to a clean, lined baking sheet.

6

Repeat for the remaining truffles. Gently brush off any excess cocoa powder and chill for at least 1 hour, before serving. You can store the truffles in an airtight container in the fridge for up to 1 week.

Chocolate, chilli, and cinnamon

Pistachio and white chocolate

🕐 **50 mins**
plus cooling and chilling

🍴 **MAKES 26–30**

TRUFFLES chocolate, chilli, and cinnamon

Mixing chilli and cinnamon is an unusual but inspired idea, as it brings a gentle heat to the truffles. For a pronounced warmth, you could increase the quantity of both spices by ¼ teaspoon.

1 Heat **180ml (6fl oz) double cream** in a saucepan over a medium heat until hot, but not boiling. Place **225g (8oz) finely grated good-quality dark chocolate** in a heatproof bowl, pour the cream over the top, and leave to melt. Whisk the mixture until smooth and glossy. Stir in ½ **tsp ground cinnamon** and ½ **tsp ground cayenne pepper**. Leave the ganache to cool for 30 minutes.

2 Line a baking sheet with greaseproof paper. Spoon the ganache into **2 piping bags** and snip off the ends. Pipe small, walnut-sized balls of the ganache onto the baking sheet, spaced apart. Chill for 30 minutes, until hardened. Roll each ball gently between your palms, until smooth, place back on the sheet and chill for a further 30 minutes.

3 Line a baking sheet with greaseproof paper. Melt **115g (4oz) finely grated good-quality dark chocolate** in a small, heatproof bowl over a saucepan of barely simmering water, making sure it does not touch the water.

4 Place a truffle on a spoon and carefully dip it into the melted chocolate to coat. Remove, allow any excess to drip back into the bowl, and place gently onto the lined sheet. Then repeat for the remaining truffles.

5 Melt **50g (1¾oz) finely grated good-quality white chocolate** in a small heatproof bowl (see step 3), then leave to cool slightly. Use a teaspoon to drizzle the chocolate over the truffles in a zigzag design. Chill them for at least 1 hour and then serve. You can store the truffles in an airtight container in the fridge for up to 1 week.

🕐 **45 mins**
plus cooling and chilling   🍴 **MAKES 26–30**

TRUFFLES pistachio and white chocolate

These creamy treats are a delight to eat and to look at. A specialist baking ingredient, pistachio paste provides a wonderfully intense flavour and smooth texture.

1 Heat **180ml (6fl oz) double cream** and then use it to melt **225g (8oz) finely grated good-quality dark chocolate** (see Chocolate, chilli, and cinnamon truffles, step 1). Whisk the mixture until smooth and glossy. Stir in **2 tbsp pistachio paste**, and leave to cool for 30 minutes.

2 Line a baking sheet with greaseproof paper. Spoon the ganache into **2 piping bags**, pipe it onto the baking sheet, and leave to chill for 30 minutes (see Chocolate, chilli, and cinnamon truffles, step 2). Roll each ball gently between your palms, until smooth. Place the truffles back on the sheet and chill for a further 30 minutes.

3 Melt **165g (5¾oz) finely grated good-quality white chocolate** in a small, heatproof bowl over a saucepan of barely simmering water, making sure it does not touch the water. Line a baking sheet with greaseproof paper. Coat the truffles with the chocolate (see Chocolate, chilli, and cinnamon truffles, step 4), then place them gently onto the lined sheet.

4 Sprinkle over **30g (1oz) finely ground unsalted and skinned pistachios**. Chill for at least 1 hour before serving. You can store the truffles in an airtight container in the fridge for up to 1 week.

🕐 **45 mins**
plus cooling and chilling   🍴 **MAKES 26–30**

TRUFFLES raspberry and sea salt

Freeze-dried raspberries bring bright colour and a concentrated raspberry flavour to these truffles. They also complement dark chocolate very well.

1 Heat **180ml (6fl oz) double cream** and use it to melt **225g (8oz) finely grated good-quality dark chocolate** (see Chocolate, chilli, and cinnamon truffles, step 1). Whisk the mixture until smooth and glossy. Stir in **2 tbsp freeze-dried raspberries** and **½ tsp raspberry extract**. Cool for 30 minutes.

2 Line a baking sheet with greaseproof paper. Spoon the ganache into **2 piping bags**, pipe it onto the baking sheet, and leave to chill for 30 minutes (see Chocolate, chilli, and cinnamon truffles, step 2). Roll each ball gently between your palms, until smooth. Place the truffles back on the sheet and chill for a further 30 minutes.

3 Melt **115g (4oz) finely grated good-quality dark chocolate** (see Chocolate, chilli, and cinnamon truffles, step 3). Line a baking sheet with greaseproof paper. Coat the truffles with the chocolate (see Chocolate, chilli, and cinnamon truffles, step 4), then place gently onto the lined sheet. Repeat for the remaining truffles.

4 Sprinkle half the truffles with **1 tsp sea salt flakes**. Sprinkle the remaining truffles with **1 tbsp freeze-dried raspberries**. Chill them for at least 1 hour before serving. You can store the truffles in an airtight container in the fridge for up to 1 week.

Raspberry and sea salt

1 hr 20 mins
plus cooling and chilling

MAKES 4

MILLEFEUILLES
vanilla

This French dessert is perfection in pastry form. To get ultra-thin, golden brown layers, sandwich the pastry between two baking sheets halfway through cooking – this presses out any bubbles.

INGREDIENTS

250g (9oz) plain flour, plus extra for dusting

250g (9oz) unsalted butter, chilled and grated

½ tsp fine salt

1 egg, beaten to glaze

150g (5½oz) icing sugar

1 heaped tsp cocoa powder

For the crème pâtissière

375ml (13fl oz) whole milk

45g (1½oz) cornflour

60g (2oz) caster sugar

3 large egg yolks, at room temperature

PLAN AHEAD

You can prepare and store the crème pâtissière, covered in the fridge, up to 1 day ahead. Whisk it well before use.

1 Sift the flour into a large bowl. Stir in the butter with a round-bladed knife and add the salt. Rub the mixture together until it resembles breadcrumbs. Add 5–6 tablespoons of iced water and bring the mixture together to form a dough. Wrap the dough in cling film and chill for 20 minutes.

Fold the pastry into thirds, roll, and repeat three times.

2 On a floured surface, roll out the dough to a large, 5mm (¼in) thick rectangle. Fold over one-third of the dough. Fold the other third over the top, then flip it over and roll. Repeat three times. Wrap in cling film and chill for 20 minutes. Preheat the oven to 190°C (375°F/Gas 5).

The slices should be 7.5cm (3in) wide and 15cm (6in) long.

3 Roll out the pastry on a lightly floured surface to a thin rectangle, about 30 x 42cm (12 x 16½in). Cut the pastry into 12 smaller, even-sized slices. Trim the edges and transfer them to two large baking sheets sprinkled with a little water. Brush them lightly with the beaten egg.

4 Bake on the top shelf of the oven for 7–10 minutes, until the pastry slices are puffed up and lightly golden. Place a baking sheet on top of the slices and press down carefully. Leaving the sheet on top, bake for a further 7–10 minutes, until the pastry slices are flat, crisp, and golden brown. Leave to cool.

The crème pâtissière thickens as you whisk it on the heat.

5 For the crème pâtissière, heat three-quarters of the milk for 3–5 minutes. Whisk the remaining ingredients in a heatproof bowl. Whisk in the hot milk until the sugar dissolves. Place in a clean pan and whisk over a low heat for 4–5 minutes. Pour into a bowl and cool. Cover and chill.

6 Combine the icing sugar with a little water to form a smooth paste. In a separate bowl, combine 1 tablespoon of the paste with the cocoa powder until smooth, adding a little water if needed. Spread an even layer of the icing over four pastry slices.

You may need to beat the cooled crème pâtissière a little before using it.

7 Drizzle thin horizontal lines of the cocoa frosting over the icing and drag a skewer through to create a feathered pattern. Work quickly to decorate the icing before it sets. Set the four pastry slices aside to dry.

8 Spread the remaining eight pastry slices with equal amounts of the crème pâtissière. Carefully stack two slices together to form four millefeuilles, pressing down gently to keep them in place. Place one frosted pastry slice over each millefeuilles and serve immediately.

1 hr 10 mins
plus cooling and chilling

MAKES 4

MILLEFEUILLES
pear and hazelnut

This is a great way to use extra poached pears. If poached in red wine (see Poached pears, pp94–95), fold them into the cream at the last minute, to make the best of the vivid colour contrast.

INGREDIENTS
120ml (4fl oz) white wine

2 tbsp caster sugar

½ tsp vanilla extract

2 pears, peeled, cored, and diced into 1cm (½in) pieces

2 sheets ready-rolled, all-butter puff pastry, about 20 x 30cm (8 x 12in)

flour, for dusting

1 egg, lightly beaten

50g (1¾oz) blanched hazelnuts, chopped finely

100g (3½oz) mascarpone cheese

100ml (3½fl oz) whipping cream, whisked to form soft peaks

1 tbsp icing sugar, plus extra for dusting

PLAN AHEAD
You can cook, strain, and store the pears in an airtight container in the fridge up to 3 days ahead.

1 Heat the wine, caster sugar, vanilla extract, and 120ml (4fl oz) water in a saucepan over a medium heat, until the sugar dissolves. Bring to the boil, then reduce the heat to a low simmer.

2 Add the pears to the liquid and cook them for 15–20 minutes, until soft. Drain and discard the liquid. Place the pears in a bowl and leave to cool completely before chilling. Preheat the oven to 190°C (375°F/Gas 5).

3 Unroll the pastry sheets on a lightly floured surface. Cut each sheet into six 12cm (5in) long and 6cm (2½in) wide slices. Trim the edges, place them on baking sheets, and brush with the beaten egg.

4 Sprinkle four pastry slices with a few hazelnuts and press down gently. Bake on the top shelf of the oven for 5–7 minutes, until lightly golden and puffed up. Then press them down gently with a baking sheet, and leave it on top. Bake for a further 7–10 minutes, until flat, crisp, and golden. Leave to cool completely on a wire rack.

5 For the filling, beat the mascarpone in a bowl until light and fluffy. Fold in the whipped cream, poached pears, icing sugar, and the remaining hazelnuts until evenly combined.

6 Spread one-eighth of the filling over each of the plain pastry slices. Stack two slices together to form four millefeuilles, pressing down gently to keep them in place. Top each millefeuille with a nut-topped slice, dust with icing sugar, and serve immediately.

30 mins
plus cooling and chilling

MAKES 4

MILHOJAS

Popular in South America, these crisp pastries are sandwiched with another favourite of the region – dulce de leche.

INGREDIENTS
100ml (3½fl oz) dulce de leche (see p76)

150ml (5fl oz) double cream

2 egg yolks

plain flour, for dusting

2 sheets ready-rolled, all-butter puff pastry, about 20 x 30cm (8 x 12in)

1 egg, beaten to glaze

icing sugar, for dusting

PLAN AHEAD
You can prepare and store the filling in an airtight container in the fridge up to 3 days ahead.

1 Whisk the dulce de leche and cream in a small, heavy-based saucepan. Heat the mixture over a low heat until hot, stirring constantly to ensure that it does not burn. Whisk the egg yolks in a small heatproof bowl.

2 Gently pour the hot cream mixture over the egg yolks, whisking constantly to combine. Pour the custard back into the saucepan and heat gently, stirring constantly, until it thickens. Pour it into a shallow bowl. Cool completely, cover the surface with cling film, and chill for 2 hours.

3 Preheat the oven to 190°C (375°F/Gas 5). Unroll the pastry sheets on a lightly floured surface. Cut each into six slices, trim the edges, and spread out on a baking sheet (see Pear and hazelnut millefeuille, step 3). Brush them with the beaten egg.

4 Score diagonal stripes on the slices, taking care not to cut through. Bake all the slices until flat, crisp, and golden (see Pear and hazelnut millefeuilles, step 4). Place on a wire rack to cool completely.

5 Spread one-eighth of the filling over eight pastry slices. Stack them to form four millefeuilles (see Pear and hazelnut millefeuilles, step 6). Top with the remaining slices, dust with icing sugar, and serve immediately.

🕐 **2 hrs 30 mins**
plus cooling and chilling

🍴 **SERVES 8**

MILLEFEUILLE summer fruit

A large millefeuille is a great dessert to serve at a party – it looks fantastic and is far simpler to make than several smaller pastries. Use whichever berries are in season, or for a quick fix, fill with good-quality tinned fruit, diced into small pieces.

INGREDIENTS

2 x 375g packet ready-made puff pastry

400g (14oz) mixed berries, such as blueberries, raspberries, and hulled and diced strawberries

icing sugar, for dusting

For the cream filling

375ml (13fl oz) whole milk

4 egg yolks

60g (2oz) caster sugar

4 tbsp plain flour, sifted, plus extra for dusting

250ml (9fl oz) double cream

1 For the filling, bring the milk to the boil in a large saucepan over a medium heat. Leave to cool. Whisk the egg yolks and caster sugar in a heatproof bowl for 2–3 minutes, until thick. Whisk in the flour until combined, then gradually whisk in the milk until smooth.

2 Bring the mixture to the boil in a clean pan, whisking, until thickened. Then reduce the heat to low and whisk for a further 2 minutes. Remove and whisk until smooth, if needed. Transfer to a bowl and cool completely. Cover with cling film and chill for 1 hour.

3 Preheat the oven to 200°C (400°F/Gas 6). Sprinkle two large baking sheets with water. On a floured surface, roll out the pastry sheets to two rectangles slightly larger than the baking sheets and about 3mm (⅛in) thick. Transfer to the baking sheets, press down, and chill for 15 minutes.

4 Prick both sheets of pastry with a fork and bake for 15–20 minutes, until just beginning to brown. Then press them down with another two baking sheets and bake for a further 10 minutes, until well browned.

5 While the pastry sheets are still warm, trim the edges and cut out three 5 x 25cm (6 x 10in) strips. Leave to cool. Whisk the cream until stiff and fold it into the filling. Spread half the cream filling over two of the pastry strips. Scatter over half of the fruit.

6 Add another layer of pastry, filling, and fruit. Top with the last pastry strip and press down gently. Dust generously with icing sugar and serve. You can store the millefeuille in the fridge for up to 6 hours.

32 mins plus cooling   **SERVES 4**

PROFITEROLES classic

Freshly prepared profiteroles should be golden, light, bursting with thick cream, and drenched in a dark-chocolate ganache. Make sure that once cooked, you prick the choux buns to allow the steam to escape – this ensures a crisp, delicate pastry.

INGREDIENTS
60g (2oz) plain flour
50g (1¾oz) unsalted butter
2 eggs, beaten

For the filling and topping
400ml (14fl oz) double cream
200g (7oz) good-quality dark chocolate, broken into pieces
2 tbsp golden syrup
25g (scant 1oz) unsalted butter

SPECIAL EQUIPMENT
piping bag with a 1cm (½in) plain nozzle
piping bag with a 5mm (¼in) star nozzle

PLAN AHEAD
You can store the unfilled buns in an airtight container up to 2 days ahead, or freeze them up to 12 weeks ahead.

1

Preheat the oven to 220°C (425°F/Gas 7). Line two large baking sheets with baking parchment. Sift the flour into a large bowl, holding the sieve high to help to aerate it.

2

Melt the butter and 150ml (5fl oz) water in a saucepan over a gentle heat. Bring to the boil and remove from the heat. Add the flour and beat the mixture until it is smooth and forms a ball. Leave to cool for 10 minutes.

3

Gradually add the eggs, beating well after each addition to form a stiff, smooth, and shiny batter. Spoon the batter into the piping bag fitted with the plain nozzle.

4

Use a knife to make a hole in each bun – this allows steam to escape.

Pipe 16 walnut-sized rounds of the batter onto the baking sheets. Bake for 20 minutes, until risen and golden. Remove and make a hole on one side of each bun. Return to the oven for 2 minutes to crisp up. Transfer them to a wire rack to cool completely.

5

Whisk 300ml (10fl oz) of the cream in a large bowl to form soft peaks. Gently heat the chocolate, golden syrup, butter, and remaining cream in a pan, stirring, until melted and smooth.

6

Spoon the whipped cream into the piping bag with the star nozzle and pipe into the buns. Place them on a serving plate, drizzle the chocolate sauce over the top, and serve immediately.

🕐 **2 hrs 40 mins**
plus chilling and cooling

🍴 **SERVES 8**

PARIS-BREST

This praline and choux pastry dessert is complex, but worthy of a special occasion. To simplify the recipe, make the filling the day before you bake the pastry.

INGREDIENTS

3 large egg yolks

270ml (9½fl oz) whole milk

2 tbsp cornflour

⅛ tsp salt

150g (5½oz) caster sugar

15g (½oz) unsalted butter

1½ tsp vanilla extract

125g (4½oz) hazelnuts, skinned

1 tsp powdered gelatine

230ml (8fl oz) double cream, beaten to form stiff peaks

icing sugar, for dusting

For the pastry

125g (4½oz) plain flour

¼ tsp salt

4 tbsp semi-skimmed milk

115g (4oz) unsalted butter

4 large eggs, lightly beaten, plus 1 large egg, lightly beaten, for glazing

30g (1oz) flaked almonds

SPECIAL EQUIPMENT

piping bag fitted with a 2cm (¾in) plain round nozzle

PLAN AHEAD

You can store the unfilled ring in an airtight container up to 1 day ahead. You may wish to crisp it up in a medium oven for 5 minutes before you fill it. You can prepare the filling and store it in an airtight container in the fridge up to 1 day ahead.

1 Whisk the egg yolks and half the milk in a heatproof bowl. Whisk in the cornflour, until smooth. Combine the remaining milk, salt, and 60g (2oz) caster sugar in a saucepan and bring to the boil. Remove from the heat and whisk it into the egg yolk mixture, until combined. Strain the mixture into a clean pan and bring to the boil over a medium heat, stirring, until thick. Cook for 30 seconds, pour it into a bowl, and stir in the butter and vanilla extract. Cover with cling film and chill for 1 hour.

2 In a separate pan, boil the remaining caster sugar and 2 tablespoons of water over a gentle heat. Cook for 7 minutes, until golden. Spread the nuts on a lined baking tray, pour over the caramel, and leave to cool. Then crush and pulse the brittle to fine crumbs in a food processor, and stir into the crème pâtissière. Whisk the gelatine and 1 tablespoon water in a pan and leave for 3–4 minutes to thicken. Cook it over a low heat for 20–30 seconds, then fold it into the crème pâtissière along with the whipped cream. Chill for at least 1 hour.

3 Preheat the oven to 220°C (425°F/Gas 7). Draw a 20cm (8in) circle on the baking parchment, flip it over, and use it to line a baking sheet. For the pastry, combine the flour and salt in a bowl. In a pan, gently boil the milk, butter, and 230ml (8fl oz) water. Remove from the heat and whisk in the flour mixture until smooth. Whisk the dough for a further 1–2 minutes until shiny, smooth, and pulling away from the edges. Stir in half the beaten eggs until smooth. Then stir in the remaining beaten eggs, until combined.

4 Spoon one-third of the mixture into the piping bag and pipe a large 2.5cm (1in) thick ring along the inside of the traced circle on the parchment. Add a third more of the dough to the bag and pipe another ring along the outer edge of the first, touching it. Pipe a third ring with the rest of the dough, along the point at which the two rings meet. Brush the top with the beaten egg and sprinkle over the almonds. Bake for 15 minutes.

5 Reduce the heat to 190°C (375°F/Gas 5) and bake for 25 minutes. Remove from the oven and turn off the heat. Cut a few slits on top of the pastry and place it back in the oven for 20 minutes, leaving the oven door ajar. Remove and place on a wire rack to cool completely. Then use a serrated knife to slice the wreath in half lengthways and pipe the filling on the bottom half. Top with the other half, dust with icing sugar, and serve immediately. Best served on the same day.

🕐 **55 mins–1 hr**
plus cooling   🍴 **SERVES 4**

ÉCLAIRS chocolate

These lovely pastries are also members of the choux family. You could fill them with crème pâtissière (see pp112–15).

INGREDIENTS
50g (1¾oz)
  unsalted butter
80g (2¾oz) plain
  flour, sifted
2 eggs, lightly beaten
250ml (9fl oz)
  double cream
  or whipping cream
100g (3½oz) good-quality
  dark chocolate, broken
  into pieces

SPECIAL EQUIPMENT
piping bag fitted with a
  1.5cm (¾in) plain nozzle

PLAN AHEAD
You can store the éclair buns in an airtight container up to 2 days ahead, or freeze them up to 12 weeks ahead.

1 Preheat the oven to 200°C (400°F/Gas 6). Melt the butter in a pan with 150ml (5fl oz) cold water. Bring to the boil, then remove from the heat and stir in the flour. Beat with a wooden spoon until well combined.

2 Gradually add the eggs to the flour and butter mixture, whisking constantly to combine. Continue whisking until the mixture is shiny and smooth (see Paris-brest, step 3). Transfer to the piping bag.

3 Line two baking sheets with baking parchment. Pipe 8 lengths of pastry, each about 12cm (5in) long, onto the sheets, using a wet knife to cut each length of pastry. Bake for 20–25 minutes, until golden brown. Remove and cut a slit down the side of each bun.

4 Return the buns to the oven for a further 5 minutes, until cooked through. Then remove and leave to cool completely. Whisk the cream in a bowl with a hand-held whisk to form soft peaks and spoon it into each éclair.

5 Melt the chocolate in a heatproof bowl over a pan of simmering water, making sure it does not touch the water. Spoon it over the top of each éclair and leave to set. Serve immediately. Best served on the same day.

🕐 **1 hr 25–30 mins**
plus cooling   🍴 **SERVES 4**

PROFITEROLES salted caramel

Sweet and salty, crisp and creamy – this recipe provides a riot of flavour and texture. Place the buns in the centre of the table, pour over the topping, and ask your guests to help themselves.

INGREDIENTS
12–15 unfilled profiterole
  buns (see p119, steps 1–4)

For the caramel
100g (3½oz) caster sugar
350ml (12fl oz) double
  cream
1 tbsp unsalted butter
¾ tsp vanilla extract
¼ tsp salt

For the topping
100ml (3½fl oz) double
  cream
200g (7oz) good-quality
  dark chocolate, broken
  into pieces
25g (scant 1oz) unsalted
  butter
2 tbsp golden syrup
pinch of salt

SPECIAL EQUIPMENT
piping bag fitted with a
  5mm (¼in) round nozzle

1 For the caramel, place the sugar and 2 tablespoons of water in a saucepan. Bring to the boil over a medium-high heat. As the caramel is cooking, dip a pastry brush in a little water and brush down the sides of the saucepan to prevent crystallization.

2 Cook the sugar for about 5 minutes, until patches of colour appear. Swirl the pan to ensure it cooks evenly. Remove from the heat once the caramel reaches a medium-amber colour. Slowly add 120ml (4fl oz) cream and the butter, vanilla, and salt to the pan and combine well with a wooden spoon.

3 Place back on a medium-low heat to melt any parts that may have hardened, transfer to a bowl, and cool to room temperature. In a separate bowl, beat the remaining cream to form soft peaks, then fold in the caramel, beating until stiff peaks form. Place the salted caramel cream in the piping bag and fill each profiterole bun with cream.

4 For the topping, melt all the ingredients in a heatproof bowl over a saucepan of gently simmering water, making sure it does not touch the water. Remove from the heat and leave to cool for 1–2 minutes. Then drizzle the topping over the profiteroles and serve immediately. Best served on the same day.

TARTE au citron

There are two types of lemon tarts – those filled with cooked curd, and French-style tarts that are filled to the brim with lemon custard and baked in the oven. This custard-style tart is light, delicate, and very lemony.

🕐 **1 hr 30 mins**
plus chilling and cooling

🍴 **SERVES 8**

🌡 Also great
HOT

INGREDIENTS
200g (7oz) plain flour, plus extra for dusting
30g (1oz) caster sugar
100g (3½oz) unsalted butter, chilled and diced
1 egg, beaten
single cream, to serve
raspberries, to serve

For the filling
200ml (7fl oz) double cream
200g (7oz) caster sugar

juice and zest of 2 lemons
4 eggs, plus 1 egg yolk

SPECIAL EQUIPMENT
23cm (9in) loose-bottomed fluted tart tin
baking beans

PLAN AHEAD
You can store the blind-baked tart case in an airtight container up to 3 days ahead.

Combine the flour and sugar in a bowl. Rub in the butter until the mixture resembles breadcrumbs. Add the egg and bring together to form a dough, adding a little iced water if it seems dry. Knead it briefly on a floured surface, until smooth. Wrap in cling film and chill for 1 hour.

1

Preheat the oven to 180°C (350°F/Gas 4). On a floured surface, roll out the pastry to a large circle, 3mm (⅛in) thick. Use it to line the tin, leaving an overhang of 2cm (¾in). Knead the pastry briefly if it crumbles. Prick the pastry, line with greaseproof paper, and fill with baking beans.

3

Place the tart case on a baking sheet and bake for 20–25 minutes. Then remove the beans and paper and bake the case for a further 5 minutes, until golden. Trim the tart case. For the filling, whisk all the ingredients in a bowl until well combined.

KNOW-HOW It is important to trim the overhang while the tart case is still warm, as the pastry hardens as it cools, making it difficult to cut.

4

Place the tart case on a baking tray, pour in the filling, and slide it into the oven. Bake for 40–45 minutes, until just set. Remove from the heat, turn out of the tin, and cool to room temperature. Serve with single cream and raspberries. You can store the tart, covered in the fridge, for up to 2 days.

TART lime and coconut

Substitute coconut milk for cream and lime for lemon and you're left with an exciting take on the French classic.

INGREDIENTS

175g (6oz) plain flour,
plus extra for dusting

25g (scant 1oz) caster
sugar

100g (3½oz) unsalted
butter, softened

1 egg yolk, beaten with
2 tbsp water

icing sugar, for dusting

For the filling

200ml (7fl oz) thick
coconut milk or
coconut cream

225g (8oz) caster sugar

5 eggs

grated zest of 2 limes

juice of 4 limes

SPECIAL EQUIPMENT

23cm (9in) loose-bottomed
fluted tart tin

baking beans

PLAN AHEAD

You can store the blind-baked tart case in an airtight container up to 3 days ahead.

1 Combine the flour and caster sugar in a bowl. Rub in the butter until the mixture resembles fine breadcrumbs. Add the beaten egg yolk and bring together to form a soft dough, adding a little water if it seems dry. Wrap in cling film and chill for 30 minutes.

2 Preheat the oven to 180°C (350°F/Gas 4). On a floured surface, roll out the pastry to a large circle, 5mm (¼in) thick. Use it to line the tart tin, leaving a 1cm (½in) overhang. Prick the pastry, line with greaseproof paper, and fill with baking beans.

3 Place the tin on a baking sheet. Blind bake the tart for 20 minutes. Then remove the beans and paper and bake for a further 5 minutes if the centre looks uncooked. Trim the pastry while it is still warm and set aside.

4 For the filling, whisk all the ingredients in a large bowl until well combined. Pour into a jug and leave to rest for 5 minutes. Then place the tart case on a baking sheet, on an oven rack. Pour the filling in evenly.

5 Carefully slide the rack into the oven and bake for 20–25 minutes, until the filling is just set. Remove and leave to cool completely, before turning the tart out of the tin. Dust with icing sugar and serve cold. You can store the tart, covered in the fridge, for up to 2 days.

🕐 **1 hr 30 mins**
plus chilling and cooling

🍴 **SERVES 6**

🌡 Also great
HOT

TART brown sugar

Also known as sugar cream pie, this North American classic has very few
ingredients, and as such makes a great last-minute dessert. The filling has
a rich, toffee-like flavour and soft texture.

INGREDIENTS
200g (7oz) plain flour,
  plus extra for dusting
30g (1oz) caster sugar
115g (4oz) unsalted butter,
  chilled and diced
1 egg yolk, beaten with
  2 tbsp iced water
whipped cream, to serve

For the filling
125g (4½oz) soft light
  brown sugar, plus extra
  for dusting
2 tbsp plain flour
400ml (14fl oz) double
  cream
1 tsp vanilla extract
pinch of salt

SPECIAL EQUIPMENT
23cm (9in) loose-bottomed
  fluted tart tin
baking beans

PLAN AHEAD
You can store the blind-
baked tart case in an
airtight container up
to 3 days ahead.

1 Combine the flour and caster sugar in a bowl. Rub in the butter, add the egg yolk, and make the dough (see Lime and coconut tart, step 1). Knead it briefly on a floured surface until smooth and even. Wrap it in cling film and chill for 1 hour.

2 Preheat the oven to 180°C (350°F/Gas 4). On a floured surface, roll out the pastry to a large circle, 2mm (⅛in) thick. Use it to line the tin, leaving a 1cm (½in) overhang. Make sure the pastry has no cracks, pinching out any that appear. Prick the pastry, line with greaseproof paper, and fill with baking beans.

3 Blind bake the tart case for 20–25 minutes (see Lime and coconut tart, step 3). Trim the overhang and place on a baking tray. For the filling, whisk the brown sugar and flour in a bowl. Then whisk in the cream, vanilla extract, and salt, until combined, and pour into a large jug.

4 Place the baking tray on an oven rack. Pour the filling into the tart case and slide the rack into the oven, and bake for 40 minutes, until just set. Remove and cool to room temperature, then turn the tart out of the tin. Sprinkle with brown sugar, and serve with whipped cream. You can store the tart, covered in the fridge, for up to 2 days.

1 hr
plus chilling   **MAKES 4**

TARTLETS raspberry and crème pâtissière

These tartlets look stunning enough to have come from a pâtisserie, but are incredibly simple to make at home. The pastry cases and crème pâtissière are easy to make ahead, so you can assemble the tarts at the last minute.

INGREDIENTS

175g (6oz) plain flour, plus extra for dusting

30g (1oz) caster sugar

100g (3½oz) unsalted butter, chilled and diced

1 egg, beaten with 1 tbsp iced water

single cream, to serve, (optional)

For the crème pâtissière

250ml (9fl oz) whole milk

2 egg yolks

50g (1¾oz) caster sugar

15g (½oz) cornflour

1 tsp vanilla extract

For the topping

3 tbsp apricot jam, sieved

250g (9oz) raspberries

SPECIAL EQUIPMENT

4 x 10cm (4in) loose-bottomed tart tins

baking beans

PLAN AHEAD

You can prepare and store the crème pâtissière in an airtight container in the fridge up to 2 days ahead. You can wrap and store the blind-baked pastry cases in the fridge up to 3 days ahead.

Preheat the oven to 180°C (350°F/Gas 4). Combine the flour and sugar in a bowl. Stir in the butter until the mixture resembles fine breadcrumbs. Add the beaten egg and bring together to form a dough, adding a little extra iced water if it seems too dry. Knead it briefly, wrap in cling film, and chill for 30 minutes.

1

Divide the pastry into four equal portions. On a lightly floured surface, roll out each portion to a 3mm (⅛in) circle and use to line the tartlet cases, leaving an overhang of at least 1cm (½in).

2

Trim any excess pastry once it is in the tartlet cases.

Prick the cases, line with greaseproof paper, and fill with baking beans. Bake the cases for 15 minutes. Then remove the beans and paper, and bake for 5–10 minutes, until crisp. Remove from the heat and trim the overhang. Cool them completely in the tins, before turning them out.

3

For the crème pâtissière, heat the milk in a small, heavy-based saucepan until hot, but not boiling. In a heatproof bowl, whisk the egg yolks, sugar, cornflour, and vanilla extract, and little by little, pour in the hot milk.

Whisk the mixture constantly until the sugar dissolves.

4

5

Pour the custard into a clean saucepan. Cook over a medium heat for 2–3 minutes, stirring until just thickened. Reduce the heat to low and cook for a further 2–3 minutes, whisking constantly. Transfer to a bowl, cover with cling film, and chill until cold.

Heat the jam and 1 tablespoon water in a saucepan over a low heat, stirring until smooth. Remove and leave to cool. Divide the crème pâtissière between the cases, beating it gently if it is thick. Top each with the raspberries, then add a little of the apricot glaze. Chill for 1 hour. Serve with cream, if desired. Best served on the same day.

6

🕐 **1 hr 20 mins**
plus chilling and cooling 🍴 **MAKES 6**

TARTLETS mocha

The filling in these little tarts is intense and chocolatey – perfect in small doses.

1 Combine **125g (4½oz) plain flour**, **30g (1oz) caster sugar**, and **30g (1oz) good-quality cocoa powder** in a bowl. Rub in **100g (3½oz) chilled and diced unsalted butter**, until the mixture resembles breadcrumbs.

2 Add **3 tbsp cooled strong black coffee** to the bowl. Bring together to form a dough, adding a little chilled water if it seems dry. Knead it briefly until smooth, wrap in cling film, and chill for 30 minutes. Preheat the oven to 180°C (350°F/Gas 4).

3 On a lightly floured surface, divide and roll out the pastry to four rounds, each 3mm (⅛in) thick. Use them to line **six 10cm (4in) loose-bottomed tart tins**, leaving a 1cm (½in) overhang. Prick the bottom of the pastry.

4 Line the cases with greaseproof paper and fill with **baking beans**. Place them on a baking sheet and bake for 15 minutes. If they look uncooked, remove the beans and paper, and bake for a further 5 minutes. Remove, trim the pastry, and leave to cool. Reduce the temperature to 160°C (325°F/Gas 3).

5 Heat **300ml (10fl oz) double cream** in a heavy-based saucepan until steaming. Remove and stir in **250g (9oz) chopped good-quality dark chocolate**, until melted. Beat until smooth, transfer to a bowl, and leave to cool. Gradually whisk in **2 eggs** and stir in **1 tsp vanilla extract**.

6 Pour the filling into the tartlet cases. Bake for 20 minutes, until just set. Leave to cool in the tins. Then remove and serve immediately. Best served on the same day.

PLAN AHEAD
You can store the blind-baked pastry cases in an airtight container in the freezer up to 3 months ahead.

🕐 **35–45 mins**
plus infusing and cooling 🍴 **MAKES 6**

TARTLETS custard

You can freeze shop-bought filo pastry, making it a great standby for tartlet cases.

1 Preheat the oven to 190°C (375°F/Gas 5). Heat **225ml (7¾fl oz) whole milk**, **150ml (5fl oz) double cream**, and **6 crushed cardamom pods** in a heavy-based saucepan until steaming. Remove from the heat and leave to infuse. Melt **25g (scant 1oz) unsalted butter** in a saucepan over a medium heat.

2 Roll out **3 sheets of filo pastry** and cover with a kitchen towel. On a floured surface, spread out one pastry sheet and brush it with a little of the melted butter. Cover with another pastry sheet, brush with butter, and top with the final pastry sheet. Cut the pastry into six equal-sized pieces.

3 Grease a **deep six-hole, 6cm (2½in) wide muffin tin**. Use the pastry pieces to line the moulds, pushing them into the sides until they stick up in places. Brush the pastry edges with any remaining butter and cover the tin with a damp kitchen towel.

4 Reheat the milk mixture over a gentle heat, but do not boil. Whisk **2 eggs** and **30g (1oz) caster sugar** in a large bowl. Strain the milk mixture into the egg mixture, discarding the cardamom. Whisk the custard until smooth, transfer to a jug, and pour evenly into the tart cases.

5 Bake the tartlets for 15–20 minutes, until they are crisp and just set in the centre. Cool in the tin for 10 minutes, then remove and leave to cool completely. Serve immediately. Best served on the same day.

Custard

Mocha

🕐 **55 mins**
plus chilling and cooling　　🍴 **MAKES 6**

TARTLETS banana and Nutella

These tartlets are a sure-fire hit with children and adults alike. Serve them with cream or vanilla ice cream.

1 Combine **175g (6oz) plain flour** and **25g (scant 1oz) caster sugar** in a bowl. Rub in **100g (3½oz) softened, unsalted butter** until the mixture resembles breadcrumbs. Beat **1 egg yolk** with **2 tbsp water** in a bowl. Add to the flour mixture, bring together to form a dough, then wrap and chill the dough for 30 minutes (see Mocha tartlets, step 2).

2 Preheat the oven to 180°C (350°F/Gas 4). On a lightly floured surface, roll out the pastry into six rounds, each 3mm (⅛in) thick. Use them to line **six 10cm (4in) loose-bottomed tart tins**, leaving a 1cm (½in) overhang. Prick the bottom of the pastry.

3 Line with greaseproof paper, and fill with **baking beans**. Blind-bake the pastry cases (see Mocha tartlets, steps 3–4). Remove, trim the pastry, and leave to cool. Increase the temperature to 200°C (400°F/Gas 6).

4 Combine **10g (¼oz) desiccated coconut**, **25g (scant 1oz) plain flour**, and **25g (scant 1oz) soft light brown sugar** in a bowl. Rub in **25g (scant 1oz) softened, unsalted butter**, until the mixture resembles coarse breadcrumbs.

5 Line the pastry cases with **2–3 bananas, cut into 1cm (½in) rounds**. Spread **1 tbsp Nutella** over the bananas in each tartlet and sprinkle over the coconut topping loosely. Bake for 15 minutes, until lightly brown on top. Leave to cool in the tins, then remove and serve.

PLAN AHEAD
You can store the blind-baked pastry cases in an airtight container in the freezer up to 3 months ahead.

Banana and Nutella

Simple alternatives

Raspberries and crème pâtissière make the ultimate summer filling for a tartlet (see pp126–27), but there are many fabulous ingredient swaps you can try.

Summer berry Follow the method for the classic tartlets and top them with a mixture of raspberries, blueberries, and hulled and diced strawberries.

Strawberry Replace the raspberries with 250g (9oz) strawberries, chopped into thick slices or halved if small.

Chocolate and kiwi Add 15g (½oz) cocoa powder to the crème pâtissière mixture (p127, step 4). Replace the raspberries with 4 thinly sliced kiwis.

Peach In place of the raspberries, use 3 thinly sliced peaches and arrange them over the crème pâtissière in a circular pattern.

Caramelized apricot Use 4 ripe halved, stoned, and thinly sliced apricots in place of the raspberries. Use a small kitchen blowtorch to caramelize the glaze for a few seconds just before serving.

Blueberry A layer of ripe blueberries is an easy substitute for the raspberries. Use 250g (9oz) blueberries and a raspberry or blueberry jam to glaze the topping.

Coconut and mango Follow the classic recipe, but add 2 tsp desiccated coconut to the crème pâtissière (see p127, step 4). Top the tartlets with 2 thinly sliced mangoes instead of the raspberries.

🕐 **1 hr 25 mins**
plus chilling and cooling

🍽 **SERVES 8**

🌡 Also great
HOT

LINZERTORTE almond and raspberry

A speciality of Vienna, linzertorte is sure to delight. It consists of a flaky almond pastry case that is filled with a tart-yet-sweet raspberry reduction and topped with a decorative lattice topping.

INGREDIENTS
125g (4½oz) plain flour, plus extra for dusting
pinch of ground cloves
½ tsp ground cinnamon
175g (6oz) ground almonds
125g (4½oz) unsalted butter, softened and diced, plus extra for greasing
1 egg yolk
100g (3½oz) caster sugar
¼ tsp salt
finely grated zest of 1 lemon
juice of ½ lemon
1–2 tbsp icing sugar, for dusting

For the filling
125g (4½oz) caster sugar
375g (13oz) raspberries

SPECIAL EQUIPMENT
23cm (9in) loose-bottomed tart tin
fluted pastry wheel

PLAN AHEAD
You can prepare and store the dough, covered in cling film, in the fridge up to 2 days ahead. Bring the pastry to room temperature before rolling out.

 Sift the flour into a large bowl. Add the cloves, cinnamon, and almonds. Mix well to combine, then make a well in the centre. Combine the butter, egg yolk, caster sugar, salt, and lemon zest and juice in a separate bowl.

2 Pour the wet mixture into the well in the centre of the dry ingredients. Use a wooden spoon to mix well. Then bring the mixture together to form a dough.

Be careful not to overwork the dough, kneading it until just smooth.

Cook the filling until the sugar dissolves and the raspberries burst.

3 On a lightly floured surface, shape the dough into a ball and knead for 1–2 minutes, until well combined and smooth. Wrap it in cling film and chill for 1–2 hours.

4 Preheat the oven to 190°C (375°F/Gas 5). Grease the tin and set aside. For the filling, cook the ingredients in a large saucepan over a medium heat for 10–12 minutes, until thickened. Remove and leave to cool.

5 Strain half of the raspberry mixture into a bowl, using the back of a wooden spoon to press the fruit pulp through. Then pour the remaining raspberry mixture into the bowl, and mix well.

6 On a lightly floured surface, roll out two-thirds of the pastry to a 28cm (11in) round and use to line the tin. Trim and reserve any overhanging pastry. Spread the filling in the pastry case evenly.

Use the overhang to line the edge of the pastry shell.

7 Roll out the remaining pastry to a 15 x 30cm (6 x 12in) rectangle. Use a fluted wheel to cut 12 x 1cm (5 x ½in) strips and create a lattice top over the filling, trimming the strips to the correct length as you go. Chill for 15 minutes.

8 Bake for 15 minutes. Then reduce the temperature to 180°C (350°F/Gas 4), and bake for a further 25–30 minutes. Cool the tart in the tin for 5–10 minutes. Then remove and cool for 30 minutes. Dust with icing sugar and serve. You can store the tart in an airtight container for up to 2 days.

⏱ **1 hr 20 mins**
plus chilling and cooling

🍴 **SERVES 8**

🌡 Also great
HOT

CROSTATA di marmellata

This classic Italian recipe is a large jam tart with a beautifully latticed top. Replace the apricot jam with any variety you wish.

INGREDIENTS

175g (6oz) plain flour, plus extra for dusting

100g (3½oz) unsalted butter, chilled and diced

50g (1¾oz) caster sugar

1 egg yolk

2 tbsp whole milk, plus extra if needed

½ tsp vanilla extract

450g (1lb) good-quality apricot or cherry jam

1 egg, beaten to glaze

SPECIAL EQUIPMENT

23cm (9in) loose-bottomed tart tin

baking beans

PLAN AHEAD

You can store the blind-baked pastry case in an airtight container in the freezer up to 1 month ahead.

1 Place the flour in a bowl and rub in the butter until the mixture resembles fine breadcrumbs. Stir in the sugar. Beat the egg yolk, milk, and vanilla extract in a separate bowl and add to the dry ingredients. Bring the mixture together to form a dough, adding more milk if it seems dry. Wrap in cling film and chill for 1 hour.

2 Preheat the oven to 180°C (350°F/Gas 4). On a floured surface, roll out the pastry to a 3mm (⅛in) thick circle. If it crumbles, knead it gently and roll out again. Line the tin with the pastry, leaving an overhang of 2cm (¾in). Roll the trimmings, re-wrap, and chill for later.

3 Prick the pastry base, line with greaseproof paper, and fill with the baking beans. Place it on a baking sheet and bake for 20 minutes. If the centre looks uncooked, remove the beans and paper, and bake for a further 5 minutes. Remove from the heat and trim the overhang. Increase the oven temperature to 200°C (400°F/Gas 6).

4 Spread the jam in the pastry case in a 1–2cm (½–¾in) thick layer. Roll out the reserved pastry to a 3mm (⅛in) thick square just larger than the tart. Cut out 12 x 1cm (½in) wide strips and create a lattice top over the filling.

5 Brush the pastry top and edges with the beaten egg and bake for 20–25 minutes, until golden brown. Remove and cool for 10 minutes in the tin. Turn the tart out and cool completely before serving. You can store it in an airtight container in the fridge for up to 2 days.

⏱ **2 hrs 10 mins**
plus chilling

🍴 **SERVES 8**

🌡 Also great
HOT

JALOUSIE apple

The French word "jalousie" translates as a louvred shutter, and refers to the beautiful decorative slashes in the pastry.

INGREDIENTS

250g (9oz) plain flour, plus extra for dusting

1 tsp salt

250g (9oz) unsalted butter, chilled and coarsely grated

1 tsp lemon juice

2.5cm (1in) piece of fresh root ginger, finely chopped

100g (3½oz) caster sugar

1 egg white, beaten, to glaze

For the filling

15g (½oz) unsalted butter

1kg (2¼lb) tart dessert apples, peeled, cored, and diced

1 Sift the flour and salt into a bowl. Rub in the butter until it resembles breadcrumbs. Add the lemon juice and 90–100ml (3–3½fl oz) water and bring together to form a dough. Knead it on a floured surface, flatten slightly, and place in a plastic bag. Chill for 20 minutes.

2 On a floured surface, roll out the pastry to a long rectangle, short sides 25cm (10in). Fold over one-third of the dough, then fold the other third over the top. Flip it over and roll out to a similar size as the original rectangle, making sure the joins are sealed. Repeat the folding, turning, and rolling. Chill for 20 minutes.

3 Roll, fold, and turn the pastry twice more, then chill for 20 minutes. Melt the butter in a saucepan over a low heat. Add the apples, ginger, and the sugar, reserving 2 tablespoons. Sauté for 15–20 minutes, until the apples are tender and caramelized. Leave to cool.

4 Roll out the pastry on a floured surface to 28 x 33cm (11 x 13in). Halve lengthways. Fold one of the halves in half again, and slash the fold at 5mm (¼in) gaps, leaving the edge intact. Place the other half on a non-stick baking sheet, and spread over the filling. Open up the cut pastry and place over the filling.

5 Chill for 15 minutes and preheat the oven to 220°C (425°F/Gas 7). Bake for 20–25 minutes. Brush with the egg white and sprinkle over the remaining sugar. Return to the oven and continue baking for 10–15 minutes. Remove and cool completely before serving. Best served on the same day.

🕐 **50 mins**
plus chilling and cooling

🍴 **MAKES 12**

🌡 Also great
HOT

LATTICE-TOPPED TARTS mincemeat

The perfect sweet treat around Christmas time, mincemeat tarts benefit from a lattice pastry top – it looks very attractive and keeps them light. Serve with custard, if desired.

INGREDIENTS

200g (7oz) plain flour, plus extra for dusting

30g (1oz) caster sugar

100g (3½oz) unsalted butter, chilled and diced

grated zest of 1 orange

1 egg, beaten, plus 1 egg extra, for glazing

For the filling

300g (10oz) good-quality mincemeat

1 tbsp brandy

zest of 1 orange

1 small dessert apple, peeled and roughly grated

30g (1oz) almonds, roughly chopped

SPECIAL EQUIPMENT

12-hole shallow bun tin

7cm (2¾in) fluted pastry cutter

PLAN AHEAD

You can prepare and chill the unbaked pies in the tin 1–2 days ahead. Add 5–10 minutes to the baking time.

1 For the filling, combine all the ingredients in a large airtight container. Cover and chill for at least 12 hours, or preferably overnight.

2 Place the flour and sugar in a bowl. Rub in the butter until the mixture resembles breadcrumbs. Add the orange zest and egg and bring together to form a smooth dough. Wrap in cling film, and chill for 30 minutes.

3 Preheat the oven to 180°C (350°F/Gas 4). On a floured surface, roll out the pastry to a large circle, 3mm (⅛in) thick. Cut out 12 rounds with the pastry cutter and use to line the tin. Divide the filling between them, patting it down slightly.

4 Roll out the pastry off-cuts and cut out 36 strips, each at least 12cm (5in) long and 1cm (½in) wide. Cut the strips in half to get a total of 72 strips. Brush the edges of the tarts with the beaten egg and use the strips to create a lattice top over each tart.

5 Brush the tarts with a little egg glaze and bake for 20 minutes, until golden brown. Cool in the tin for 5 minutes, before turning out. Place on a wire rack to cool completely before serving. You can store the tarts, in an airtight container, up to 3 days ahead.

1 hr 20 mins
plus chilling and cooling

SERVES 8

MERINGUE PIE lemon

The meringue topping on a classic meringue pie is softer and more delicate than a traditional meringue, to contrast with the flaky pastry. If you like a crispier texture, leave the pie in the oven for an additional 15 minutes, watching the colour carefully.

INGREDIENTS
110g (3¾oz) unsalted butter, chilled and grated, plus extra for greasing
150g (5½oz) plain flour, plus extra for dusting
1 tbsp caster sugar
½ tsp salt
1 tsp apple cider vinegar, whisked with 4 tbsp chilled water

For the filling
¼ tsp salt
30g (1oz) cornflour
3 tbsp plain flour
200g (7oz) caster sugar
5 large egg yolks, beaten
15g (½oz) unsalted butter
grated zest of 2 lemons
120ml (4fl oz) lemon juice

For the meringue
4 egg whites
⅛ tsp salt
¼ tsp cream of tartar
100g (3½oz) caster sugar
1 tbsp cornflour

SPECIAL EQUIPMENT
23cm (9in) fluted tart dish or tin, about 5cm (2in) deep
baking beans

PLAN AHEAD
You can store the blind-baked pastry case in an airtight container in the fridge 2–3 days ahead.

Grease the dish. Combine the flour, sugar, salt, and butter in a large bowl. Sprinkle the vinegar mixture over the top and use two forks to fluff the mixture until it forms clumps. Add a little cold water if it seems dry. Knead the dough, wrap it in cling film, and chill for 30 minutes.

Knead the dough very gently until it just comes together.

1

Preheat the oven to 190°C (375°F/Gas 5). On a floured surface, roll out the pastry to a 30cm (12in) circle, 3mm (⅛in) thick. Use to line the dish, leaving an overhang of 1cm (½in). Prick the pastry and chill for 30 minutes. Then line it with greaseproof paper, fill with baking beans, and bake for 25 minutes. Remove the beans and paper, and return to the oven, until golden. Leave to cool.

Remove the beans and paper and bake the pastry for 6-10 minutes, until golden.

2

3

Reduce the temperature to 180°C (350°F/Gas 4). For the filling, mix the dry ingredients in a saucepan. Whisk in 300ml (10fl oz) water gradually, until smooth. Cook for 5-6 minutes over a medium heat, stirring, until thick. Bring to the boil, then reduce the heat. Cook for 1 minute, then whisk a little mixture into the yolks.

The mixture may clump at first, but will come together towards the end.

4

Stir a little more hot mixture into the yolk mixture, then pour the yolk mixture into the pan. Bring to the boil over a medium-low heat, stirring frequently. Reduce the heat and cook for 1 minute. Remove from the heat and whisk in the remaining filling ingredients, until combined. Cover and keep warm.

5

For the meringue, whisk the egg whites and salt in a bowl until foamy. Then whisk in the cream of tartar to form soft peaks. Combine the sugar and cornflour in a small bowl and gradually whisk into the egg white mixture to form stiff, glossy peaks.

Pour the filling into the pastry case. Spoon the meringue in a circle around the inside edge of the pie, then top the whole pie. Bake for 15 minutes, until lightly browned. Cool completely on a wire rack before serving. Best served on the same day.

6

MERINGUE PIE
chocolate

Using both milk chocolate and dark chocolate in this filling gives an added complexity to its rich flavour.

INGREDIENTS

3 large egg yolks

75ml (2½fl oz) condensed milk

500ml (16fl oz) whole milk

30g (1oz) cornflour

¼ tsp salt

¾ tsp vanilla extract

15g (½oz) unsalted butter, diced

125g (4½oz) good-quality very dark chocolate, finely chopped

85g (3oz) good-quality milk chocolate, finely chopped

1 sweet shortcrust pastry case (see p137, steps 1–2)

For the meringue

100g (3½oz) caster sugar

1 tbsp cornflour

4 egg whites

⅛ tsp salt

¼ tsp cream of tartar

SPECIAL EQUIPMENT

23cm (9in) fluted tart tin, about 5cm (2in) deep

1 Preheat the oven to 180°C (350°F/Gas 4). Whisk the egg yolks, condensed milk, and 250ml (9fl oz) whole milk in a bowl. Whisk the cornflour, salt, and remaining milk in a lidded saucepan, until smooth. Cook over a medium heat for 4–5 minutes, until steaming. Remove and whisk a small amount into the yolk mixture to combine.

2 Stir a little more of the hot mixture into the yolk mixture. Pour the yolk mixture into the pan. Cook over a medium–low heat, stirring constantly, until thick. Bring to the boil, then reduce the heat and cook for 30 seconds. Remove from the heat and whisk in the vanilla extract, butter, and both lots of chocolate, until fully incorporated. Cover to keep warm.

3 For the meringue, combine the sugar and cornflour in a bowl. In a separate bowl, whisk the eggs whites and salt until foamy. Whisk in the cream of tartar to form soft peaks. Add the sugar mixture to the egg white mixture, a tablespoon at a time, whisking well after each addition. Whisk the mixture until it is glossy and forms stiff peaks.

4 Pour the chocolate filling into the pastry case. Spoon the meringue in a circle around the inside edge of the pie, then top the whole pie. Bake for 15 minutes, until the meringue is lightly browned. Place on a wire rack to cool completely. Then chill for at least 5 hours, until the filling has set, before serving. Best served on the same day.

🕐 **1 hr 40 mins** plus cooling   🍴 **SERVES 8**

MERINGUE PIE *grapefruit*

Grapefruit can offset the sweetness of meringue with a welcome tartness – however, if you find normal grapefruit a little too tart, try a sweeter pink variety instead.

INGREDIENTS
5 large egg yolks

¼ tsp salt

30g (1oz) cornflour

3 tbsp plain flour

150g (5½oz) caster sugar

15g (½oz) unsalted butter

½ tsp lemon zest

1 tbsp grated grapefruit zest

1 tbsp lemon juice

120ml (4fl oz) grapefruit juice

1 sweet shortcrust pastry case (see p137, steps 1–2)

For the meringue
4 egg whites

⅛ tsp salt

¼ tsp cream of tartar

1 tbsp cornflour

100g (3½oz) caster sugar

SPECIAL EQUIPMENT
23cm (9in) fluted tart tin, about 5cm (2in) deep

1. Preheat the oven to 180°C (350°F/Gas 4). Whisk the egg yolks in a heatproof bowl. Combine the salt, cornflour, flour, and sugar in a lidded saucepan.

2. Pour over 50ml (1½fl oz) water, and whisk until smooth. Stir 250ml (9fl oz) water into the cornflour mixture. Bring to the boil over a medium heat, stirring, until thick.

3. Reduce the heat to medium–low, and cook for 1 minute. Remove from the heat and pour a small amount into the yolk mixture. Whisk well to combine, then stir a little more of the hot mixture into the yolk mixture. Pour the yolk mixture into the pan.

4. Bring to the boil over a medium–low heat, stirring frequently. Reduce the heat to low and cook for 1 minute. Remove and whisk in the butter and both lots of zest.

5. Whisk in the lemon juice and grapefruit juice until fully incorporated. Cover the yolk mixture and keep warm. Prepare the meringue (see Chocolate meringue pie, step 3).

6. Pour the grapefruit filling into the pastry case. Top with the meringue (see Chocolate meringue pie, step 4). Bake for 10 minutes, until lightly browned. Cool the pie completely on a wire rack, before serving. Best served on the same day.

🕐 **1 hr 30 mins**
plus chilling and cooling

🍴 **SERVES 8**

PIE banana cream

Banana and custard are old-fashioned favourites
that work fabulously when combined in a crisp and
buttery pastry case. Smother the pie with billowy
whipped cream for a truly decadent dessert.

INGREDIENTS

150g (5½oz) plain flour,
  plus extra for dusting

1 tbsp caster sugar

½ tsp salt

115g (4oz) unsalted butter,
  chilled and diced

1 tsp apple cider vinegar

2–4 bananas, sliced,
  plus extra for topping

For the filling

100g (3½oz) caster sugar

½ tsp salt

3 tbsp cornflour

500ml (16fl oz) whole milk

3 large egg yolks

15g (½oz) unsalted butter

1 tsp vanilla extract

For the topping

180ml (6fl oz) double
  cream

2 tsp icing sugar

SPECIAL EQUIPMENT

23cm (9in) pie dish, about
  5cm (2in) deep

baking beans

PLAN AHEAD

You can prepare and
store the pastry, covered
in the fridge, up to 2 days
ahead. You can store the
blind-baked pastry case
in an airtight container
up to 2 days ahead.

Rub in the butter with the flour mixture, until it resembles breadcrumbs.

1 Place the flour, caster sugar, and salt in a large bowl and mix well to combine. Then rub in the butter with your fingertips until the mixture resembles breadcrumbs. Place the vinegar in a separate bowl. Pour over 120ml (4fl oz) cold water and mix well to combine.

2 Gradually add 4 tablespoons of the liquid mixture to the flour mixture, using two forks to fluff and stir them together until clumps form. Add a little more of the liquid mixture if it seems too dry, making sure you do not add too much, as it can toughen the pastry.

Work the dough until the texture is just smooth.

Use the rolling pin to transfer the pastry to the pie dish.

3 On a lightly floured work surface, turn out the mixture and knead it gently for 3–6 minutes to form a dough. Cover the dough with cling film and chill in the fridge for about 30 minutes, or preferably overnight.

4 On a floured surface, roll out the pastry to a 30–33cm (12–13in) circle, about 3mm (⅛in) thick. Use the circle to line the pie dish, leaving a 1cm (½in) overhang. Crimp the edges of the pastry and chill the pastry for 30 minutes. Preheat the oven to 190°C (375°F/Gas 5).

5 Prick the pastry base, line with greaseproof paper, and fill with baking beans. Bake for 25 minutes, until the edges are slightly brown. Then remove the beans and paper, and bake for a further 6–10 minutes, until the pastry case is golden brown. Remove and leave to cool.

6 For the filling, combine the caster sugar, salt, and cornflour in a saucepan. Add the milk, gradually, whisking until smooth. Heat the mixture over a medium-high heat until steaming. Remove and whisk 2 tablespoons of the mixture with the egg yolks in a small bowl.

7 Pour the egg and milk mixture back into the pan and bring to the boil over a medium heat. Stir well and remove from the heat. Whisk in the butter and vanilla extract until well combined. Transfer to a large bowl, cover with cling film, and chill for 30 minutes.

8 Layer half the banana slices in the pastry case. Top with the filling, cover with cling film, and chill for 2 hours. Beat the double cream and icing sugar to form stiff peaks. Top the pie with the remaining bananas and the cream, and serve. You can store the pie, covered, for up to 3 days in the fridge.

Pro piping

For pâtisserie-style decorative results, give your pies a piped cream topping. All you need is a large piping bag and a variety of tips.

Circular rosettes To decorate a Banana cream pie (see pp140–43), pipe medium-sized rosettes around the edge of the pie, and follow with central circle of smaller rosettes. Insert upright slices of banana between each rosette. Serve immediately.

Stars Use a medium open-star tip to pipe stars tightly over your cream pie. For an even finish, start at the outside edge of the pie, and pipe concentric circles of stars, working towards the centre of the pie. Serve immediately.

Shells Top the Mascarpone and berry cream pie (see opposite), with cream and berries. Whisk 200ml (7fl oz) double cream with 1 tsp icing sugar, and pipe large shells of the mixture over the pie using an open-star tip. Allow the cream to fan as you drag and drop each shell. Decorate with berries.

Roses Use a large drop flower tip to pipe large roses. Start with the centre of each rose and pipe in an anti-clockwise direction, applying an even pressure. Pipe a ring of roses around the edge of the pie, finishing with one in the centre. For the Coconut cream pie (see right), sprinkle with coconut.

🕐 **1 hr 30 mins**
plus chilling and setting

🍴 **SERVES 8**

CREAM PIE coconut cream

Three types of coconut are used to maximize the flavour of this pie. Using coconut milk as the custard base is an easy way to impart extra flavour to the filling.

INGREDIENTS

115g (4oz) unsalted butter, chilled and diced, plus extra for greasing

150g (5½oz) plain flour, plus extra for dusting

1 tbsp caster sugar

½ tsp salt

1 tsp apple cider vinegar

For the filling

3 large egg yolks

150g (5½oz) caster sugar

½ tsp salt

30g (1oz) cornflour

500ml (16fl oz) coconut milk

120ml (4fl oz) whole milk

1 tbsp unsalted butter

¼ tsp vanilla extract

85g (3oz) desiccated coconut

For the topping

4 tbsp desiccated coconut

200ml (7fl oz) double cream

1 tsp sugar

SPECIAL EQUIPMENT

23cm (9in) round pie dish, about 5cm (2in) deep

baking beans

PLAN AHEAD

You can store the blind-baked pastry case in an airtight container up to 3 days ahead.

1 Grease the pie dish and set aside. Combine the flour, sugar, and salt in a bowl. Rub in the butter and mix until the mixture resembles breadcrumbs. Combine the vinegar with 120ml (4fl oz) cold water in a separate bowl and gradually add 4 tablespoons of it to the flour mixture.

2 Use two forks to fluff the flour mixture to form shaggy crumbs, adding more water if it is dry. On a floured surface, knead the dough gently until just smooth. Wrap it in cling film and chill for 30 minutes.

3 Roll out the pastry on a floured surface to a 28cm (11in) circle, at least 3mm (⅛in) thick. Use to line the pie dish, leaving a 2cm (¾in) overhang. Crimp the edges and chill the pastry case for 30 minutes. Preheat the oven to 190°C (375°F/Gas 5).

4 Prick the pastry, line with greaseproof paper, and fill with baking beans. Bake for 25 minutes, until the edges are slightly brown. Then remove the beans and paper, and bake for a further 6–10 minutes, until golden brown. Remove and leave to cool.

5 For the filling, place the egg yolks in a heatproof bowl. Combine the sugar, salt, and cornflour in a large saucepan. Slowly whisk in both lots of milk until smooth and well combined. Cook the mixture over a medium heat until steaming. Remove from the heat.

6 Pour a little of the milk mixture into the egg yolks, whisking constantly until combined. Add the egg mixture to the pan, whisking continuously to combine. Cook over a medium heat until thick. Then bring to the boil, stir well, and remove from the heat.

7 Add the butter, vanilla extract, and desiccated coconut to the cream filling. Mix well and pour the filling into the pastry case. Cover in cling film and chill for 2–3 hours, until set.

8 For the topping, toast the coconut in a frying pan over a medium heat until lightly brown. Beat the cream and sugar in a bowl to form stiff peaks. Top the pie with the cream and sprinkle over the toasted coconut, and serve. You can store the pie, covered in the fridge, for 1–2 days.

⏱ **30 mins** plus chilling   🍴 **SERVES 8**

CREAM PIE
chocolate and cinnamon

Adding a little cinnamon to the chocolate gives a warm and spicy flavour to this pie, and contrasts well with the cream topping.

INGREDIENTS

15g (½oz) unsalted butter, plus extra for greasing

270g (9½oz) sweet pastry (see Coconut cream pie, steps 1–2)

3 large egg yolks

100g (3½oz) light brown sugar

½ tsp salt

30g (1oz) cornflour

620ml (20fl oz) whole milk

1 tsp ground cinnamon, plus extra for dusting

½ tsp vanilla extract

¼ tsp almond extract

140g (5oz) good-quality dark chocolate, finely chopped

85g (3oz) good-quality milk chocolate, finely chopped

For the topping

200ml (7fl oz) double cream

2 tsp icing sugar

SPECIAL EQUIPMENT

23cm (9in) round pie dish
baking beans

1 Preheat the oven to 190°C (375°F/Gas 5) and grease the pie dish. Roll out the pastry, use to line the pie dish, and blind bake it (see Coconut cream pie, steps 3–4). Beat the egg yolks in a heatproof bowl and set aside.

2 Combine the brown sugar, salt, and cornflour in a saucepan. Slowly whisk in the milk until smooth and cook over a medium heat until steaming. Remove from the heat and pour a little of the milk mixture into the egg yolks, whisking constantly until combined.

3 Pour the egg mixture into the pan. Cook over a medium heat, whisking constantly, until thick. Then bring to the boil, stir well, and remove from the heat.

4 Add the butter, cinnamon, vanilla extract, almond extract, and both lots of chocolate to the cream filling. Mix well and pour into the pastry case. Wrap the pie in cling film and chill for 5–6 hours, until set.

5 For the topping, beat the ingredients in a bowl to form stiff peaks and spoon over the filling. Dust lightly with cinnamon and serve. You can store the pie, covered in the fridge, for 2–3 days.

⏱ **30 mins** plus chilling and setting   🍴 **SERVES 8**

CREAM PIE
mascarpone and berry

Mix mascarpone with citrus-infused whipped cream to make a quick and easy filling for a pie. If you use a ready-baked pie crust, it can be rustled up in minutes.

INGREDIENTS

270g (9½oz) sweet pastry (see Coconut cream pie, steps 1–2)

350g (12oz) mascarpone cheese

200ml (7fl oz) whipping cream

80g (2¾oz) caster sugar, plus 2 tbsp extra

¼ tsp salt

¾ tsp vanilla extract

grated zest of 2 lemons

125g (4½oz) blueberries

125g (4½oz) blackberries

SPECIAL EQUIPMENT

23cm (9in) round pie dish
baking beans

1 Preheat the oven to 190°C (375°F/Gas 5). Roll out the pastry, use to line the pie dish, and blind bake it (see Coconut cream pie, steps 3–4). Place the mascarpone in a bowl and fold gently to soften. In a separate bowl, whisk the cream, sugar, salt, and vanilla extract to form stiff peaks.

2 Add in a small amount of the cream mixture to the mascarpone and mix well. Fold in the remaining cream mixture until well combined. Fold in the lemon zest until evenly incorporated.

3 Pour the filling into the pastry case. Top with the blueberries and blackberries. Wrap the pie with cling film and chill for at least 1 hour, until set. Serve chilled. You can store the pie, covered in the fridge, for up to 2 days.

INGREDIENTS
85g (3oz) unsalted butter, melted, plus extra for greasing
300g (10oz) Oreos, finely crushed

For the filling
115g (4oz) unsalted butter
30g (1oz) good-quality very dark chocolate
85g (3oz) good-quality dark chocolate
3 tbsp plain flour
1 tsp instant espresso powder
pinch of salt
150g (5½oz) dark brown sugar
50g (1¾oz) caster sugar
½ tsp vanilla extract
3 large eggs

For the topping
200ml (7fl oz) double cream
1½ tsp icing sugar
4 tbsp chopped pecans

SPECIAL EQUIPMENT
23cm (9in) pie dish, about 5cm (2in) deep

PLAN AHEAD
You can prepare and store the unfilled biscuit base in an airtight container in the fridge up to 1 week ahead.

45–50 mins
plus chilling and cooling

SERVES 10

MUD PIE Mississippi

A chocolate lover's delight, this traditional American dessert is a crowd-pleasing dessert whatever the occasion – especially if children are involved. Serve the pie in small slices, as it is rich and a little goes a long way.

Grease the pie dish. Place the butter and biscuit crumbs in a large bowl. Mix well to combine.

1

2

Spread the mixture evenly in the pie dish, pressing it firmly into the bottom and sides to form a smooth base. Chill for 45 minutes, until firm.

3

Preheat the oven to 190°C (375°F/Gas 5). For the filling, melt the butter and both lots of chocolate in a saucepan over a medium–low heat. Remove from the heat. Add the flour, espresso powder, salt, and both lots of sugar. Whisk until well combined.

4

Gradually whisk the vanilla extract and the eggs into the chocolate mixture, until combined and smooth. Pour the filling into the biscuit base.

5

Bake the pie for 30–35 minutes, until the filling is just set. Remove from the heat. Leave to cool for 1–2 hours, until the filling sinks a little.

For the topping, whisk the cream and icing sugar in a bowl to form soft peaks and spread over the pie. Sprinkle the pecans over, and serve. You can store the pie, covered in the fridge, for up to 2 days.

6

🕐 **15–20 mins** plus chilling   🍴 **SERVES 10**

MUD PIE peanut butter

Dark chocolate, peanut butter, and whipped cream combine together to make an intense filling for this rich, sweet dessert. If peanut butter cups are not available, try a handful of chopped salted peanuts.

1 Grease a **23cm (9in) pie dish, about 5cm (2in) deep**. Combine **300g (10oz) finely crushed Oreos** and **85g (3oz) melted, unsalted butter** in a bowl and spread the mixture evenly in the dish. Press it into the bottom and sides to form a smooth base and chill for 45 minutes, until firm.

2 For the filling, beat **225g (8oz) cream cheese**, **300g (10oz) creamy peanut butter**, and **100g (3½oz) icing sugar** in a bowl until combined. Stir in **4 tbsp double cream**, and mix until smooth. In a separate bowl, whisk **120ml (4fl oz) double cream** to form stiff peaks.

3 Gradually fold the cream into the peanut butter mixture, until well combined. Pour the filling over the biscuit base evenly. For the topping, beat **200ml (7fl oz) double cream**, **½ tsp vanilla extract**, **2 tsp caster sugar**, and a **pinch of salt** in a bowl to form stiff peaks.

4 Spread the topping over the filling. Top with **3 large crushed peanut butter cups** and cover with cling film. Chill for at least 1 hour, until firm, before serving. You can store the pie, covered in the fridge, for 3–4 days.

PLAN AHEAD
You can prepare and store the unfilled biscuit base in an airtight container in the fridge 2–3 days ahead.

Peanut butter

🕐 **35 mins**
plus cooling and chilling

🍴 **SERVES 10**

MUD PIE mocha

Chocolate and coffee are a classic flavour pairing. This recipe combines the best of both ingredients to produce a rich pie. Instant coffee can be used instead of espresso powder – simply double the amount.

1 Grease a **23cm (9in) pie dish**, about 5cm (2in) deep. Combine **300g (10oz) finely crushed Oreos** and **85g (3oz) melted, unsalted butter** in a large bowl. Spread in the dish and chill for 45 minutes (see Peanut butter mud pie, step 1).

2 Melt and combine **175g (6oz) finely chopped dark chocolate**, **60g (2oz) unsalted butter**, **3 tbsp water**, and **1 tbsp instant espresso powder** in a heatproof bowl over a saucepan of simmering water, making sure it does not touch the water. Leave to cool.

3 Beat **240ml (8fl oz) whipping cream**, **½ tsp vanilla extract**, **⅛ tsp salt**, and **2 tbsp caster sugar** in a bowl to form stiff peaks. Chill until needed. Whisk **3 large egg yolks** and **2 tbsp caster sugar** in a separate heatproof bowl.

4 Place the bowl of whisked egg yolks over a pan of simmering water, making sure it does not touch the water. Whisk the mixture vigorously for 3 minutes, until it turns pale and almost triples in volume. Remove and cool for 1–2 minutes, then add it to the chocolate mixture and combine well.

5 Gradually fold the chilled cream mixture into the chocolate mixture, until it is evenly incorporated and no streaks remain. Pour the filling over the biscuit base and cover with cling film. Chill for 2–3 hours, until set.

6 For the topping, beat **230ml (8fl oz) double cream** and **1 tbsp caster sugar** in a large bowl to form stiff peaks. Spread it over the pie and sprinkle over some **grated chocolate** to serve. You can store the pie, covered in the fridge, for up to 2 days.

PLAN AHEAD

You can prepare and store the unfilled biscuit base in an airtight container in the fridge 2–3 days ahead.

Mocha

INGREDIENTS
175g (6oz) digestive
  biscuits, crushed
75g (2½oz) unsalted
  butter, melted

For the filling
1 large egg, plus 1 yolk
1 tbsp grated lime zest,
  plus extra to decorate
400g can condensed
  milk
230ml (8fl oz) lime juice
pinch of salt

For the topping
200ml (7fl oz) double
  cream
2 tsp icing sugar

SPECIAL EQUIPMENT
23cm (9in) pie dish, about
  5cm (2in) deep

PLAN AHEAD
You can store the blind-
baked biscuit base in an
airtight container in the
fridge up to 1 day ahead.

40–45 mins
plus cooling

SERVES 8

PIE key lime

This dessert takes its name from the small limes that grow
in the Florida Keys, where the recipe originated – although it
is now popular throughout the United States. A biscuit crust
is a simple and easy alternative to a pastry crust.

1

Preheat the oven to
180°C (350°F/Gas 4).
Pulse the biscuits in
a food processor to
a fine powder and
place in a bowl. Add
the butter and mix
well to combine.

Spread the mixture in the pie dish,
pressing it evenly into the bottom
and sides for a firm base. Bake the
biscuit base for 8–10 minutes, until
golden. Set aside to cool.

2

3

For the filling, whisk the egg, yolk, and lime zest in a bowl for 2 minutes. Then whisk in the milk, lime juice, and salt until smooth. Pour the filling mixture over the base. Bake the pie for 25–30 minutes, until the filling is set.

4

Remove from the heat and leave to cool completely. Chill for 1–2 hours. For the topping, beat the cream and sugar in a bowl to form stiff peaks. Spread it over the filling and decorate with lime zest to serve. You can store the pie, covered in the fridge, for up to 2 days.

PIE peach and soured cream

Using soured cream in this pie filling gives it a rich, tangy flavour that complements the sweet peaches.

INGREDIENTS

175g (6oz) digestive
  biscuits, finely crushed
75g (2½oz) unsalted
  butter, melted

For the filling

350g (12oz) peaches,
  stoned and sliced
115g (4oz) caster sugar
225g (8oz) soured cream
½ tsp vanilla extract
¼ tsp salt
grated zest of 1 lemon

1 large egg
1 tbsp plain flour

SPECIAL EQUIPMENT

23cm (9in) pie dish, about
  5cm (2in) deep

PLAN AHEAD

You can store the blind-baked biscuit base in an airtight container in the fridge up to 1 day ahead.

1 Preheat the oven to 180°C (350°F/Gas 4). Combine the biscuits and butter in a large bowl. Spread the mixture in the pie dish and bake in the oven (see Orange pie, step 1). Set aside to cool.

2 For the filling, combine the peaches and 1 tablespoon of the sugar in a large bowl and leave to macerate. In a separate bowl, place the soured cream, vanilla extract, salt, lemon zest, and remaining sugar. Whisk well until the sugar dissolves.

3 Whisk in the egg, then stir in the flour and whisk well to combine. Use a slotted spoon to transfer the peaches to the cream mixture and fold them in until evenly combined.

4 Pour the filling evenly into the biscuit base. Bake the pie for 30–35 minutes, until the filling is set. Remove from the heat and cool to room temperature, before serving. You can store the pie in an airtight container in the fridge for up to 1 day.

PIE orange

Sweet orange juice and zest bring a bright flavour to this pie. Swap in blood oranges for a bolder colour and deeper flavour.

INGREDIENTS

175g (6oz) digestive
  biscuits, finely crushed
75g (2½oz) unsalted
  butter, melted

For the filling

1 large egg, plus 1 yolk
grated zest of 1 orange,
  plus extra to decorate
400g can condensed
  milk
200ml (7fl oz) orange juice
4 tbsp lemon juice
pinch of salt

For the topping

180ml (6fl oz) double cream
2 tsp icing sugar

SPECIAL EQUIPMENT

23cm (9in) pie dish, about
  5cm (2in) deep

PLAN AHEAD

You can store the blind-baked biscuit base in an airtight container in the fridge up to 1 day ahead.

1 Preheat the oven to 180°C (350°F/Gas 4). Combine the biscuits and butter in a large bowl. Spread the mixture evenly in the pie dish, pressing it down into the bottom and sides to form a smooth base. Bake for 8–10 minutes, until golden. Set aside to cool.

2 For the filling, whisk the egg, yolk, and orange zest for 2 minutes in a large bowl. Whisk in the milk until well combined. Then whisk in the orange juice, lemon juice, and salt until smooth.

3 Pour the filling evenly into the biscuit base. Bake the pie for 15–20 minutes, until the centre is set. Remove from the heat and cool to room temperature. Then chill the pie for 1–2 hours.

4 For the topping, beat the cream and sugar in a large bowl to form stiff peaks. Spread the mixture in the centre of the filling and decorate with orange zest to serve. You can store the pie in an airtight container in the fridge for up to 1 day.

20 mins plus chilling **SERVES 8–10**

PIE banoffee

This modern classic is incredibly rich and sweet, just as it should be. It is great for a party, as a little goes a long way. Allow the chilled caramel and pie base to rest out of the fridge in advance of serving, so that it can soften.

INGREDIENTS

250g (9oz) digestive biscuits, crushed

100g (3½oz) unsalted butter, melted and cooled

For the caramel

50g (1¾oz) unsalted butter

50g (1¾oz) soft light brown sugar

400g can condensed milk

For the topping

2 large, ripe bananas, sliced into 5mm (¼ in) thick rounds

250ml (9fl oz) double cream, whipped

30g (1oz) good-quality dark chocolate, to decorate

SPECIAL EQUIPMENT

23cm (9in) round springform cake tin

PLAN AHEAD

You can store the blind-baked biscuit base in an airtight container in the fridge up to 1 day ahead.

1 Line the tin with baking parchment. Combine the biscuits and butter in a large bowl until well combined. Spread the mixture evenly in the pie dish, pressing it down firmly to form a smooth base. Cover and chill.

2 For the caramel, melt the butter and sugar in a small, heavy-based saucepan over a medium heat. Stir in the milk and bring to the boil. Then reduce the heat to a simmer and cook for 2–3 minutes, stirring constantly, until thick and golden.

3 Pour the caramel evenly over the biscuit base. Chill for 30 minutes, until set. Transfer to a large serving plate 30 minutes before serving. Cover the caramel with a layer of the bananas, and spread the cream evenly over the top.

4 Shave half the chocolate to form short ribbons. Grate the remaining chocolate and sprinkle both forms of chocolate over the pie. Serve immediately. You can store it in an airtight container in the fridge for up to 2 days.

35 mins
plus chilling and cooling

SERVES 6-8

TRIFLE summer fruit

A well-prepared trifle is a wonderful thing – soft and gently yielding with a creamy texture and subtle flavours. It is best to use frozen berries for this recipe, as they are softer than fresh ones and can complement the texture of the trifle.

INGREDIENTS

1 tbsp butter, melted, for brushing

20g (¾oz) plain flour, plus extra for dusting

2 eggs, separated

60g (2oz) caster sugar

200g (7oz) frozen mixed berries, thawed

150ml (5fl oz) double cream, whipped to soft peaks

1 heaped tbsp finely chopped unsalted and skinned pistachios

For the custard

250ml (9fl oz) single cream
250ml (9fl oz) whole milk

4 egg yolks

50g (1¾oz) caster sugar

1 tsp vanilla extract

1 tbsp cornflour

SPECIAL EQUIPMENT

20 x 30cm (8 x 12in) Swiss roll tin

23cm (9in) deep-sided glass bowl

PLAN AHEAD

You can prepare and store the custard, covered in cling film, in the fridge up to 2 days ahead.

1

Preheat the oven to 220°C (425°F/Gas 7). Line the tin with baking parchment, brush it lightly with butter, and chill for 5 minutes. Then dust the sheet lightly with flour and tip off any excess.

2

Whisk the egg yolks and 40g (1½oz) sugar in a bowl with a hand-held whisk, until light and fluffy. Whisk the egg whites in a large bowl to form stiff peaks, then whisk in the remaining sugar until glossy. Fold the egg yolk mixture and flour into the egg white mixture, until combined.

Pour the batter into the tin to form a thin, even layer. Bake for 7–10 minutes, until it is risen, and an inserted toothpick comes out clean. Cool in the tin for 2 minutes, before turning out. Place on a wire rack to cool completely, then cut into small pieces.

3

4

For the custard, heat the cream and milk in a heavy-based saucepan until hot, but not boiling. Whisk the remaining ingredients in a heatproof bowl until smooth. Gradually whisk in the cream mixture until the sugar dissolves.

Pour the mixture into a clean, heavy-based pan and bring to the boil over a medium heat, stirring constantly. Reduce the heat to a simmer and cook for 3–4 minutes, stirring until it is thick enough to coat the back of the spoon. Pour the custard into a dish and cover its surface with cling film. Chill for 1 hour.

6

Spread out the fruit in an even layer.

Line the bowl with cake pieces. Top with the fruit, pouring over any juices. Spread the custard over, and then the cream. Sprinkle over the pistachios. Chill for 4 hours before serving. You can store the trifle in the fridge for up to 1 day.

5

10 mins plus chilling    **MAKES 4**

MINI TRIFLES peach, lemon, and Amaretti

This quick and easy recipe requires simple store-cupboard ingredients, making it the ideal choice for last-minute entertaining. Use any jam jars you have to hand.

INGREDIENTS

150g (5½oz) good-quality lemon curd

250g (9oz) good-quality ready-made custard

150g (5½oz) Amaretti biscuits, plus extra to decorate

400g can peaches in natural juice, drained and roughly chopped

100ml (3½fl oz) double cream, whipped to form soft peaks

SPECIAL EQUIPMENT

4 x 320ml (11fl oz) wide-mouthed jars

1 Whisk the lemon curd with 1 tablespoon of the custard in a bowl until combined. Then fold in the remaining custard until well combined and smooth.

2 Line the bottom of the jam jars with the biscuits, breaking them a little to fill any gaps if necessary. Spread a thin layer of the peaches over the biscuits.

3 Top the peaches with a layer of the custard mixture. Repeat the process to get another layer each of the biscuits, peaches, and custard.

4 Top the trifles with a layer of the whipped cream and chill them for at least 4 hours. Then top with some biscuit crumbs and serve immediately. Best served on the same day.

---

 20 mins plus cooling and chilling   **SERVES 6–8**

TRIFLE sherry and raspberry

Tangy raspberries, flaked almonds, and home-made custard give this sherry trifle a modern make-over.

INGREDIENTS

115g (4oz) sponge fingers

4 tbsp sherry

175g (6oz) raspberries

150ml (5½fl oz) double cream, whipped to form soft peaks

1 heaped tbsp flaked almonds, toasted

For the custard

4 egg yolks

30g (1oz) caster sugar

1 tsp vanilla extract

1 tbsp cornflour

250ml (9fl oz) whole milk

250ml (9fl oz) single cream

SPECIAL EQUIPMENT

23cm (9in) deep-sided glass bowl

PLAN AHEAD

You can prepare and store the custard, covered in the fridge, up to 2 days ahead.

1 For the custard, whisk the egg yolks, sugar, vanilla extract, and cornflour in a large bowl until well combined and smooth. Heat the milk and cream in a heavy-based saucepan until hot, but not boiling.

2 Gradually pour the milk mixture over the egg yolk mixture, whisking constantly, until the sugar dissolves. Pour the custard mixture into a clean pan. Bring to the boil over a medium heat, stirring constantly.

3 Cook the custard over a low simmer for 3–4 minutes, stirring constantly, until it is thick enough to coat the back of a spoon. Remove from the heat and pour into a shallow dish. Cover the surface of the custard with cling film, leave to cool completely, then chill for 1 hour.

4 Cut one-third of the sponge fingers in half. Set them around the sides of the bowl, finished sides facing outwards. Fill the centre of the sponge ring with the remaining sponge fingers, breaking and pushing them down to form a firm, single layer.

5 Sprinkle the sherry over the sponge layer and scatter over the raspberries. Beat the custard gently until smooth and spread it out over the raspberries in an even layer. Top with the whipped cream and sprinkle over the almonds. Chill for 4 hours before serving. You can store the trifle in the fridge for up to 1 day.

35 mins
plus cooling and chilling

SERVES 6-8

TRIFLE black forest

This is a grown-up version of a traditional trifle. It celebrates the well-loved flavour combination of chocolate and cherries, using both chocolate sponge and creamy chocolate custard to enhance the richness.

INGREDIENTS

1 tbsp melted butter

35g (1¼oz) cocoa powder, plus extra for dusting

5 eggs, separated

150g (5½oz) caster sugar, plus 1 tbsp extra

1 tbsp plain flour

300g (10oz) frozen black cherries

4 tbsp Kirsch

200ml (7fl oz) double cream, whipped to form soft peaks

shaved or grated dark chocolate, to decorate

For the custard

4 egg yolks

30g (1oz) caster sugar

2 tbsp cocoa powder

1 tbsp cornflour

250ml (9fl oz) whole milk

250ml (9fl oz) single cream

SPECIAL EQUIPMENT

30 x 37cm (12 x 15in) Swiss roll tin

23cm (9in) deep-sided glass bowl

PLAN AHEAD

You can prepare and store the custard, covered in the fridge, up to 2 days ahead.

1 Preheat the oven to 220°C (425°F/Gas 7). Line the tin with baking parchment and brush lightly with the butter. Chill for 5 minutes. Then dust it with 1 teaspoon of cocoa powder, tipping off any excess.

2 Whisk the egg yolks with 100g (3½oz) of the sugar in a bowl until light and fluffy. In a separate bowl, whisk the egg whites to form stiff peaks, then whisk in the remaining sugar until glossy.

3 Sift the cocoa powder and flour into a bowl. Gently fold the cocoa mixture and egg white mixture into the egg yolk mixture, in batches, so that you lose as little air as possible. Pour the batter into the tin evenly.

4 Bake the sponge for 7-10 minutes, until it is well risen and an inserted toothpick comes out clean. Remove from the heat and cool in the tin for 2 minutes, before transferring to a wire rack to cool completely.

5 For the custard, whisk the egg yolks, sugar, cocoa powder, and cornflour in a large bowl, until smooth.

Heat the milk and cream in a heavy-based saucepan and gradually pour over the egg yolk mixture (see Sherry and raspberry trifle, steps 1-2).

6 Pour the custard mixture into a clean pan and bring to the boil. Then reduce the heat and cook for 3-4 minutes, stirring, until thick (see Sherry and raspberry trifle, steps 2-3). Transfer to a shallow bowl, cover, cool, then chill (see Sherry and raspberry trifle, steps 2-3).

7 Combine the cherries and 1 tablespoon of sugar in a bowl. Leave to thaw, then chop into pieces and reserve the liquid. Cut the sponge into pieces and spread half of it in a single layer in the bowl. Sprinkle over half of the Kirsch and top with a single layer of the cherries.

8 Spread over half of the cold custard and half of the whipped cream. Repeat to add another layer each of the sponge, Kirsch, cherries, custard, and cream. Sprinkle with the chocolate and chill for at least 4 hours before serving. You can store it in the fridge for up to 1 day.

🕐 **1 hr 5 mins**
plus cooling and chilling

🍴 **MAKES 6**

CAKE CUPS red velvet and blueberry

Modern mini trifles, cake cups are fun to make, look great, and taste divine. These cups offer layers of delicate sponge, fluffy icing, and juicy berry compote in every mouthful. For best results, use 160ml (5½fl oz) jars with wide openings.

INGREDIENTS

115g (4oz) self-raising flour

1½ tsp baking powder

3 eggs

175g (6oz) unsalted butter, softened

175g (6oz) caster sugar

4 tbsp whole milk

60g (2oz) cocoa powder

1 tbsp red food colouring paste

1 tsp vanilla extract

For the icing

60g (2oz) cream cheese, at room temperature

60g (2oz) unsalted butter, at room temperature

240g (8¾oz) icing sugar

1 tbsp whole milk

1 tsp vanilla extract

For the compote

200g (7oz) blueberries

2 tbsp caster sugar

For decorating

40 blueberries

2 tbsp violet crystals

2 tbsp freeze-dried raspberries

2 tbsp finely chopped unsalted and skinned pistachios

SPECIAL EQUIPMENT

23 x 33cm (9 x 13in) Swiss roll tin

5cm (2in) round cutter

6 x 160ml (5½fl oz) glass jars, each 5 x 7.5cm (2 x 3in)

disposable piping bag

PLAN AHEAD

You can store the sponge in an airtight container up to 2 days ahead. You can prepare and store the compote in an airtight container in the fridge up to 3 days ahead.

1

Preheat the oven to 180ºC (350ºF/Gas 4). Line the tin with greaseproof paper. Sift the flour and baking powder into a bowl, and add the eggs, butter, sugar, and milk.

2

Whisk the ingredients until smooth and combined. Then fold in the cocoa powder, food colouring, and vanilla extract.

Fold it all in until no streaks remain.

3

Pour the mixture evenly into the tin and bake for 20 minutes. Remove and leave to cool in the tin. Then use the cutter to cut out 18 rounds and place one in each jar.

4

For the icing, beat all the ingredients together until light and creamy. Transfer to a piping bag, snipping off the end.

A piping bag gives you a precise finish.

5

For the compote, place the blueberries, sugar, and 1 tablespoon water in a lidded, heavy-based saucepan over a low heat. Cook, covered, for 5 minutes. Then uncover and cook for a further 5 minutes, until thick. Cool completely. Pipe a little of the icing on top of each cake round.

Smooth out the icing to create an even layer.

6

Top the icing with 2 teaspoons of the compote. Repeat the process until you reach the third layer of cake. Pipe over some icing, cover, and chill for 1–4 hours. To serve, decorate the cake cups with the blueberries and flavourings.

🕐 **1 hr 25 mins** plus cooling   🍴 **MAKES 6**

CUPS fruity meringue

Deconstructed mini pavlovas, these melt in the mouth. You could use shop-bought meringues.

1 Preheat the oven to 150ºC (300ºF/Gas 2). Line a baking sheet with greaseproof paper. Whisk **1 egg white** in a bowl to form soft peaks. Gradually beat in **75g (2½oz) caster sugar** until the mixture is thick, glossy, and forms stiff peaks.

2 Spread the mixture out in a 1cm (½in) layer on the baking sheet. Bake the meringue for 1 hour, until hard. Remove from the heat and cool completely, then break it into small pieces.

3 Whisk **100ml (3½fl oz) double cream** in a bowl until smooth. Fold in **100ml (3½fl oz) Greek yogurt** and set aside. Dice **3 ripe kiwi**, and chop **200g can drained peaches** into thin slices. Set aside one-third of each fruit.

4 Place a layer of meringue in **six 160ml (5½fl oz) glass jars**. Top with one layer each of the kiwi, cream, and peach. Then add another layer of meringue, top with cream, and decorate with the reserved fruit. Serve immediately.

PLAN AHEAD
You can bake and store the meringue in an airtight container up to 5 days ahead.

🕐 **40–50 mins** plus cooling and chilling   🍴 **MAKES 6**

CAKE CUPS lemon and fig

Pretty and full of fresh flavours, these cups could make the perfect finale to a Mediterranean meal.

1 Preheat the oven to 180ºC (350ºF/Gas 4). Line a **23 x 33cm (9 x 13in) cake tin** with baking parchment. Sift **175g (6oz) self-raising flour** and **1½ tsp baking powder** into a large bowl. Add **175g (6oz) soft unsalted butter**, **175g (6oz) caster sugar**, **3 eggs**, and **4 tbsp whole milk**. Whisk for 2 minutes.

2 Stir in the **juice and zest of 1 lemon** and **1 tbsp poppy seeds**. Pour the mixture into the tin, and spread it out evenly. Bake for 20 minutes. Remove and cool completely in the tin. Then use a **5cm (2in) cutter** to cut out 18 rounds. Place one round each in **six 160ml (5½fl oz) glass jars**.

3 Place **200ml (7fl oz) whipped double cream** in a bowl and fold in **1 tsp rose water**. Top each cake round with 1 tbsp of the mixture and smooth it out. Thinly slice **5 large ripe figs** and layer on top. Repeat until you reach the third layer of cake. Finish with a layer of cream and chill for 1–4 hours. Decorate with **pomegranate seeds** and serve immediately.

PLAN AHEAD
You can bake and store the sponge in an airtight container up to 5 days ahead.

Lemon and fig

Fruity meringue

🕐 **10 mins**   🍴 **MAKES 6**

CUPS quick granola

These easy and nutritious layered desserts are the perfect choice for health-conscious guests.

1 Whisk **300g (10oz) full-fat Greek yogurt** in a large bowl until smooth and set aside. Place **2 tsp good-quality ready-made granola** in each of **six 160ml (5½fl oz) glass jars**. Spread it out in an even layer.

2 Top the granola with 2 tsp of the whipped yogurt and spread it out to form an even, thin layer. Halve **150g (5½oz) raspberries**, vertically, and layer over the yogurt.

3 Repeat to add two more layers of granola, yogurt, and raspberries. Finish with another layer of granola and decorate with **1 tbsp mixed dried fruit**, such as sultanas, raisins, and apricot. Serve immediately.

Quick granola

🕐 **1 hr 10 mins**
plus cooling and chilling   🍴 **MAKES 6**

CAKE CUPS black forest

With cherries, chocolate sponge, and mascarpone, these cake cups are like mini black forest gâteaux.

1 Preheat the oven to 180ºC (350ºF/Gas 4). Line a **23 x 33cm (9 x 13in) cake tin** with baking parchment. Sift **115g (4oz) self-raising flour**, **60g (2oz) cocoa powder**, and **1½ tsp baking powder** into a large bowl.

2 Add **175g (6oz) soft unsalted butter**, **175g (6oz) caster sugar**, **3 eggs**, and **4 tbsp whole milk**. Whisk until smooth and pour into the tin evenly. Bake for 15–20 minutes. Remove and cool completely in the tin. Use a **5cm (2in) cutter** to cut out 18 rounds.

3 Place **150g (5½oz) chopped cherries** and **3 tbsp raspberry liqueur** in a bowl and leave to macerate. Whisk **150g (5½oz) mascarpone** in a separate bowl until fluffy. Then whisk in **150ml (5fl oz) double cream**.

4 Place one cake round each in **six 160ml (5½fl oz) glass jars**. Top with 2 tsp mascarpone and a layer of cherries. Repeat until you have 3 layers of cake. Top with the cream and chill for 1–4 hours. Serve immediately, sprinkled with **grated dark chocolate** and chopped cherries.

PLAN AHEAD
You can store the sponge in an airtight container up to 2 days ahead.

Black forest

🕐 **35 mins**
plus chilling   🍴 **SERVES 12**

ICEBOX CAKE raspberry and white chocolate

This is an easy American recipe that layers Graham crackers, fruit, and cream. Although these biscuits are available internationally, you could use digestives instead – simply follow the directions for the Chocolate and almond icebox cake (see p164).

INGREDIENTS
900ml (1½ pints) double cream
85g (3oz) icing sugar
juice of ½ lemon
grated zest of 2 lemons
24 Graham crackers
85g (3oz) white chocolate, finely grated
675g (1½lb) raspberries

1 Whisk the cream, sugar, and lemon juice and zest in a large bowl to form stiff peaks.

2 Place six crackers on a large serving dish. Spread over one-quarter of the cream evenly.

3

Sprinkle one-quarter of the chocolate over the cream. Halve 500g (1lb 2oz) of the raspberries. Layer one-third of the fruit over the chocolate.

4

Repeat to add three more layers of each ingredient, using the reserved whole raspberries for the top. Cover with cling film and chill for 3–4 hours, or until the biscuits have softened. Serve chilled. You can store the cake, covered in the fridge, for 1–2 days.

⏱ **20 mins**
plus chilling 🍴 **SERVES 12**

ICEBOX CAKE chocolate and almond

A quick and simple alternative to a chilled cheesecake, this rich dessert can feed a large crowd. During chilling, the digestive biscuits soften into the chocolate mousse, making it easy to cut the cake into portions without it shattering.

INGREDIENTS

900ml (1½ pints) double cream

30g (1oz) cocoa powder

pinch of salt

120ml (4fl oz) golden syrup

28 digestive biscuits

50g (1¾oz) flaked almonds

60g (2oz) good-quality dark chocolate, finely chopped

115g (4oz) strawberries, hulled and halved, to serve

SPECIAL EQUIPMENT

23cm (9in) springform cake tin

1 Whisk the cream in a bowl until slightly thick. Sift over the cocoa powder and salt and stir in the golden syrup. Whisk the mixture to form stiff peaks. Line the bottom of the tin with seven biscuits.

2 Spread one-quarter of the cream mixture over the biscuit layer and sprinkle evenly with one-quarter of the almonds. Repeat to form three more layers each of biscuits, cream, and almonds. Cover with cling film and chill for 3–4 hours, until the biscuits have softened.

3 Gently melt the chocolate in a small heatproof bowl over a saucepan of gently simmering water, making sure it does not touch the water. Stir until smooth and remove from the heat. Leave to cool.

4 Place the tin on a serving plate and carefully remove the sides. Drizzle the chocolate over the cake, top with the strawberries, and serve. You can store the cake, covered with cling film, in the fridge for 1–2 days.

🕐 **1 hr 5 mins**
plus resting, cooling, and chilling

🍴 **SERVES 8–10**

CHARLOTTE CAKE strawberry

With a set strawberry filling and light sponge base, Charlotte cake was invented by the great pastry chef Marie-Antoine Carême in the 1800s. He named it after Princess Charlotte.

INGREDIENTS

900g (2lb) strawberries, hulled and halved, plus extra to serve

50g (1¾oz) caster sugar

7g (1 heaped tsp) powdered gelatine

400ml (14fl oz) double cream

250g (9oz) mascarpone cheese, at room temperature

1½ tsp vanilla extract

¼ tsp salt

60g (2oz) icing sugar, sifted (optional)

300g (10oz) sponge fingers

SPECIAL EQUIPMENT

23cm (9in) springform cake tin

1 Heat the strawberries and caster sugar in a saucepan over a low heat for 10–12 minutes, until the fruit is soft and has released its juices. Remove from the heat and blend the mixture with a hand-held blender to form a smooth purée.

2 Transfer the fruit purée to a large bowl set over an ice bath. Stir until cool. Combine 90g (3¼oz) of the purée with the gelatine in a small saucepan and leave to rest for 3–4 minutes, until thick. Then gently warm the mixture over a low heat, until no longer firm.

3 Stir the gelatine mixture into the cooled purée and combine well. Whisk the cream, mascarpone, vanilla extract, and salt in a bowl to form stiff peaks. Gradually fold it into the fruit and gelatine mixture, until combined. Stir in the icing sugar to taste, if needed.

4 Cut about 2.5cm (1in) from the edges of 28 sponge fingers. Line the bottom of the pan with whole sponge fingers. Place the trimmed sponge fingers along the sides of the tin, cut-side down, pouring in a little of the cream mixture to help secure them.

5 Pour the remaining cream mixture into the sponge case, cover with cling film, and chill overnight. Then place the tin on a serving plate and carefully remove the sides. Decorate with strawberries and serve. You can store the cake, covered with cling film, in the fridge for up to 2 days.

🕐 **30 mins**
plus cooling and chilling

🍴 **SERVES 8**

TIRAMISU classic

This beloved Italian dessert is a fairly recent invention dating back to the 1960s. It is classically a light, layered dessert of coffee-flavoured sponge fingers and mascarpone, but coffee liqueur and Marsala wine are also popular additions.

INGREDIENTS

2 tbsp instant espresso powder

2 tsp caster sugar

120ml (4fl oz) Marsala wine

For the filling

6 large egg yolks

135g (5oz) icing sugar, sifted

85ml (2¾fl oz) Marsala wine

2 tsp vanilla extract

450g (1lb) mascarpone cheese, at room temperature

500ml (16fl oz) double cream, chilled

400g (14oz) sponge fingers

unsweetened cocoa powder, for dusting

SPECIAL EQUIPMENT

33 x 23 x 5cm (13 x 9 x 2in) tin or dish

1 Boil 500ml (16fl oz) water in a kettle and cool for 5 minutes. Then combine the water with the espresso powder, caster sugar, and Marsala in a bowl. Leave to infuse. For the filling, whisk the egg yolks and icing sugar in a heatproof bowl for 2–3 minutes, until thick and pale in colour.

2 Place the bowl over a saucepan of gently simmering water, making sure it does not touch the water. Add the Marsala in a steady stream, whisking constantly to combine. Whisk the mixture for 5 minutes, until thick and ribbon-like in texture. Remove from the heat, cover, and cool. Stir in the vanilla extract.

3 Place the mascarpone in a large bowl and fold gently with a spatula to soften the cheese. Then add the cooled egg yolk and Marsala mixture. Whisk gently until well combined and smooth.

4 In a separate bowl, whisk the double cream to form stiff peaks. Fold a little of the cream into the mascarpone mixture and mix well. Then gently fold in the rest and mix until it is well combined.

Start with a little of the whipped cream, then add the rest.

5 Dip half of the sponge fingers into the coffee mixture, briefly on each side, and use them to line the bottom of the serving dish. Cover with half of the cream filling and sift some cocoa powder on top.

6 Add another layer of sponge fingers and filling. Sprinkle generously with cocoa powder, wrap in cling film, and chill for 4–6 hours. Remove the tiramisu from the fridge 15 minutes before serving. You can store it, covered in the fridge, for 1–2 days.

Beer

Cherry mocha

TIRAMISU beer

Give this Italian classic a modern twist with a rich, dark stout such as Guinness, which works well with traditional flavours.

1. Combine **2 tsp caster sugar** and **240ml (8fl oz) stout beer** in a bowl and set aside. Whisk **250ml (9fl oz) whipping cream**, **1 tsp instant espresso powder**, and **a pinch of salt** in a large bowl to form stiff peaks.

2. Use a spatula to combine **450g (1lb) mascarpone cheese**, **2½ tsp vanilla extract**, and **115g (4oz) sifted icing sugar** in a large bowl. Fold in the cream and coffee mixture, a little at a time, until evenly combined.

3. Briefly dip **200g (7oz) sponge fingers** in the beer mixture on each side, and use to line the bottom of an **18 x 23cm (7 x 9in) dish**. Cover with half of the cream mixture filling and sprinkle over some **unsweetened cocoa powder**.

4. Add another layer of the sponge fingers and filling. Dust the top generously with more cocoa powder, wrap with cling film, and chill for at least 4–6 hours. Remove from the fridge 15 minutes before serving. You can store it, covered in the fridge, for up to 2 days.

TIRAMISU cherry mocha

Dark chocolate and cherries are often paired together in desserts, such as Black Forest gâteau. The cherries give welcome contrast to the rich and creamy filling.

1. Boil **500ml (16fl oz) water** in a kettle and leave to cool for 5 minutes. Then combine the water with **2 tbsp instant espresso powder**, **4 tsp caster sugar**, and **1½ tbsp unsweetened cocoa powder** in a small bowl and leave to cool. In a large bowl, whisk **500ml (16fl oz) whipping cream**, **1 tsp instant espresso powder**, and **a pinch of salt** to form stiff peaks.

2. In a separate bowl, combine **450g (1lb) mascarpone cheese**, **2 tsp pure vanilla extract**, **3 tbsp cocoa powder**, and **115g (4oz) sifted icing sugar**. Fold in the cream and coffee mixture, a little at a time, until evenly combined.

3. Briefly dip **200g (7oz) sponge fingers** in the coffee mixture on each side. Use them to line the bottom of an **18 x 23cm (7 x 9in) dish**. Cover with half of the cream mixture and scatter over half of **350g (12oz) pitted and quartered black cherries**.

4. Sift over some **cocoa powder** and add another layer of the sponge fingers, filling, and cherries. Dust, wrap, and chill (see Beer tiramisu, step 4). Remove from the fridge 15 minutes before serving. You can store it, covered in the fridge, for up to 2 days.

⏱ **30 mins**
plus chilling   🍴 **SERVES 6**

TIRAMISU Amaretto

Amaretto, an almond-based liqueur, is often used in Italian desserts. In this recipe, it helps to distribute the coffee flavour.

1 Boil **500ml (16fl oz) water** in a kettle and cool for 5 minutes. Combine the water with **2 tbsp instant espresso powder**, **2 tsp caster sugar**, and **120ml (4fl oz) Amaretto** in a bowl and leave to cool. Whisk **6 egg yolks** and **135g (5oz) caster sugar** in a heatproof bowl until thick and pale yellow in colour.

2 Place the bowl of egg yolks over a saucepan of simmering water, making sure it does not touch the water. Add **2 tbsp Amaretto** and whisk the mixture vigorously for 5–6 minutes, until it is thick and forms ribbons when the whisk is lifted. Remove, cover, and cool to room temperature. Then stir in **1 tsp vanilla extract**.

3 In a large bowl, whisk **240ml (8fl oz) chilled whipping cream** to form stiff peaks and chill until needed. In a separate bowl, fold and soften **450g (1lb) mascarpone cheese** with a spatula. Add the egg yolk mixture and whisk to combine. Then gradually add the whipped cream and whisk well to combine.

4 Briefly dip **200g (7oz) sponge fingers** in the coffee mixture on each side. Use them to line the bottom of an **18 x 23cm (7 x 9in) dish**. Cover with half of the cream mixture and sift some **unsweetened cocoa powder** over the top.

5 Add another layer of the sponge fingers and filling. Dust, wrap, and chill (see Beer tiramisu, step 4). Remove from the fridge 15 minutes before serving. You can store the tiramisu, covered in the fridge, for up to 2 days.

Amaretto

🕐 **1 hr**
plus cooling, chilling, and resting

🍴 **MAKES 6**

CRÈME BRÛLÉE classic

Every home-cook needs to know how to make the perfect crème brûlée. For a contrast of texture and flavour, you could serve these caramelized custards with delicate biscuits, such as these Maple pecan sablés (see p262).

INGREDIENTS

5 egg yolks

75g (2½oz) caster sugar, plus 3 tbsp extra

1 tsp vanilla extract

500ml (16fl oz) double cream

sablés, to serve (optional)

SPECIAL EQUIPMENT

6 x 150ml (5fl oz) ramekins

small kitchen blowtorch

PLAN AHEAD

You can prepare and store the uncaramelized custard in the fridge up to 3 days ahead.

1 Preheat the oven to 160°C (325°F/Gas 3). Whisk the egg yolks, sugar, and vanilla extract in a large bowl until combined. Heat the cream in a small saucepan over a low heat until it is hot, but not boiling.

Remove the cream from the heat and pour it into the egg yolk mixture. Whisk until the sugar dissolves. Place the ramekins in a roasting tin and pour the custard mixture into them evenly.

2

3

Carefully pour hot water into the tin to come halfway up the sides of the ramekins. Bake for 30–40 minutes, until just set, but slightly wobbly in the centre. Remove from the heat and cool to room temperature. Then cover with cling film and chill for 2 hours.

4

Sprinkle ½ tablespoon sugar over each custard and gently spread it out with the back of a spoon. Melt the sugar with the blowtorch, sweeping the flame over it gently. Leave the crème brûlées to rest for at least 5 minutes before serving with sablés, if desired.

🕐 **1 hr**
plus cooling, chilling, and resting   🍴 **MAKES 6**

CRÈME BRÛLÉE
white chocolate

Creamy white chocolate gives a subtle flavour to these custards. Use good-quality white chocolate, which is not oversweet.

1 Preheat the oven to 160°C (325°F/Gas 3). Whisk **4 egg yolks**, **60g (2oz) caster sugar**, and **1 tsp vanilla extract** in a large bowl until well combined. Heat **400ml (14fl oz) double cream** in a large saucepan over a low heat until hot, but not boiling.

2 Remove from the heat and add **100g (3½oz) finely chopped good-quality white chocolate**. Stir until the chocolate melts, and then pour into the egg yolk mixture, whisking well to combine. Place **six 150ml (5fl oz) ramekins** in a roasting tin.

3 Pour the custard into the ramekins. Carefully pour hot water into the tin to come halfway up the sides of the ramekins, making sure it does not splash. Bake for 30–40 minutes, until just set, but wobbly in the centre. Cool for 5 minutes, then cover with cling film, and chill for 2 hours.

4 Sprinkle **½ tbsp caster sugar** over each custard and gently spread it out with the back of a spoon. Use a **kitchen blowtorch** to caramelize the sugar, sweeping it over gently. Leave to rest for 5 minutes before serving.

PLAN AHEAD
You can prepare and store the uncaramelized custard in the fridge up to 3 days ahead.

White chocolate

Lavender

🕐 **1 hr 10 mins**
plus cooling, chilling, and resting   🍴 **MAKES 6**

CRÈME BRÛLÉE
lavender

Gently steeping dried lavender in double cream gives the most beautifully fragrant flavour to the finished dish.

1 Preheat the oven to 160°C (325°F/Gas 3). Heat **500ml (16fl oz) double cream** and **1 tbsp dried culinary lavender** in a large saucepan over a low heat until hot, but not boiling. Remove from the heat, cover, and leave to steep for 15 minutes.

2 Whisk **5 egg yolks** and **75g (2½oz) caster sugar** in a large bowl until well combined. Strain the infused cream into the egg yolk mixture and whisk well to combine. Discard the lavender. Place **six 150ml (5fl oz) ramekins** in a roasting tin.

3 Pour the custard into the ramekins and carefully pour hot water into the tin (see White chocolate crème brûlée, step 3). Bake for 30–40 minutes, until just set, but wobbly in the centre. Cool, cover, and chill for 2 hours (see White chocolate crème brûlée, step 3).

4 Spread **½ tbsp caster sugar** over each custard and use a **kitchen blowtorch** to caramelize (see White chocolate crème brûlée, step 4). Leave to rest for 5 minutes before serving.

PLAN AHEAD
You can prepare and store the uncaramelized custard in the fridge up to 3 days ahead.

CRÈME BRÛLÉE
Earl Grey

Earl Grey tea's strong flavour is mixed with the gentle flavours of this custard base, imparting its characteristic citrus–floral notes.

1 Preheat the oven to 160ºC (325ºF/Gas 3). Heat **500ml (16fl oz) double cream** in a large saucepan over a low heat until hot, but not boiling. Remove from the heat and add **4 Earl Grey teabags**. Cover and leave to steep for 10 minutes.

2 Whisk **5 egg yolks** and **75g (2½oz) caster sugar** in a large bowl. Strain the infused cream into the egg yolk mixture, pressing down on the teabags to extract the flavour. Discard the teabags. Whisk the mixture well to combine. Place **six 150ml (5fl oz) ramekins** in a roasting tin.

3 Pour the custard into the ramekins and carefully pour hot water into the tin (see White chocolate crème brûlée, step 3). Bake for 30–40 minutes, until just set, but wobbly in the centre. Cool, cover, and chill for 2 hours (see White chocolate crème brûlée, step 3).

4 Spread ½ **tbsp soft light brown sugar** over each custard and gently spread it out with the back of a spoon. Use a **kitchen blowtorch** to caramelize (see White chocolate crème brûlée, step 4). Leave to rest for 5 minutes before serving.

PLAN AHEAD
You can prepare and store the uncaramelized custard in the fridge up to 3 days ahead.

Earl Grey

Crèma Catalana

CRÈMA CATALANA

This recipe originates from Catalonia, Spain. It is incredibly simple to make – you don't need to bake it in the oven or in a bain-marie.

1 Cut the **zest of 1 small lemon** into strips. Place it with **500ml (16fl oz) whole milk** and **1 cinnamon stick** in a heavy-based saucepan. Cook over a low heat until hot, but not boiling. Remove from the heat, cover, and leave to steep for 15 minutes.

2 Whisk **4 egg yolks**, **75g (2½oz) caster sugar**, and **1½ tbsp cornflour** in a large bowl until combined. Strain the infused milk into the egg yolk mixture and whisk until the sugar has melted. Discard the cinnamon stick and lemon zest. Return the custard to the pan.

3 Cook over a gentle heat, stirring, until the custard begins to thicken. Then reduce the heat to low and cook for 2 minutes, whisking constantly. Pour it into **six 150ml (5fl oz) ramekins**. Leave to cool completely, then cover with cling film, and chill for at least 3 hours.

4 Spread ½ **tbsp caster sugar** over each custard and use a **kitchen blowtorch** to caramelize (see White chocolate crème brûlée, step 4). Chill the crème brûlée for about 10 minutes before serving.

PLAN AHEAD
You can prepare and store the uncaramelized custard in the fridge up to 3 days ahead.

20 mins plus chilling · **SERVES 4**

VANILLA PUDDING
with raspberries

This simple pudding is nothing more than a smooth and silky chilled vanilla custard. Serve it with raspberries for a sweet-sharp flavour contrast. You could also prepare the pudding and chill it in individual glasses, or layer it with seasonal fruit.

INGREDIENTS

100g (3½oz) caster sugar

3 tbsp cornflour

3 large egg yolks

½ tsp salt

500ml (16fl oz) whole milk

15g (½oz) unsalted butter

3 tsp vanilla extract

30-40 raspberries, to serve

1

Place the sugar, cornflour, egg yolks, and salt in a large bowl. Pour in half the milk and whisk until well combined and smooth.

2

Heat the remaining milk in a saucepan over a medium-low heat, until steaming. Pour half the hot milk into the yolk mixture, in a steady stream, whisking constantly to combine. Then pour the yolk and milk mixture back into the pan and mix well to combine.

3

Increase the heat to medium and bring to the boil, stirring constantly. Reduce the heat to a simmer and cook for a further 1 minute, stirring, until the mixture has thickened. Remove and strain through a fine sieve into a large bowl.

4

Whisk in the butter and vanilla extract until evenly combined. Cover with cling film, making sure it touches the top of the pudding. Chill for at least 3-4 hours. Serve it with raspberries. You can store the pudding in an airtight container in the fridge for 2-3 days.

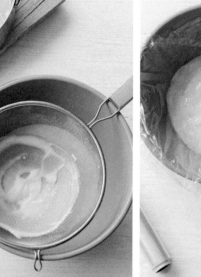

Covering the surface of the pudding with cling film prevents a skin from forming.

20 mins
plus chilling

SERVES 8–10

VANILLA PUDDING banana

Banana pudding, similar in style to a British trifle, is a classic dessert of the American South, although you can now find it all over the United States. It is very quick to prepare and guaranteed to impress.

INGREDIENTS

6 large egg yolks

60g (2oz) cornflour

1 tsp salt

175g (6oz) caster sugar

1 litre (1¾ pints) whole milk

20g (¾oz) butter

½ tsp vanilla extract

2½ tsp banana extract

For the topping

250ml (9fl oz) whipping cream

150g (5½oz) sponge fingers

4 bananas, thinly sliced

1 Whisk the egg yolks, cornflour, salt, sugar, and 250ml (9fl oz) milk in a large bowl until smooth. Heat the remaining milk in a saucepan over a medium-low heat until steaming. Pour half the hot milk into the egg yolk mixture in a steady stream, whisking constantly to combine.

2 Pour the milk and egg yolk mixture back into the pan. Increase the heat to medium and bring to the boil, stirring constantly to prevent the mixture from sticking to the bottom of the pan. Reduce the heat and cook for a further 1 minute, stirring, until it thickens.

3 Remove from the heat and strain the pudding through a fine sieve into a large bowl. Add the butter, vanilla extract, and banana extract, and whisk until smooth. Cover with cling film, making sure it touches the surface of the pudding to prevent a skin from forming. Chill for 3–4 hours.

4 For the topping, place the cream in a large bowl and beat to form stiff peaks. Use half the sponge fingers to line the bottom of a large serving bowl. Cover with half the pudding and top with a layer of the bananas.

5 Repeat to add one more layer of sponge fingers and pudding. Top with the remaining bananas, then add the whipped cream. Cover with cling film and chill for at least 1 hour before serving. You can store the pudding in the fridge for 1–2 days.

🕐 **15 mins**   🍴 **SERVES 4**   🌡️ Also great **HOT**

VANILLA PUDDING *zabaglione*

Whisk this Marsala-infused Italian dessert until it is light and frothy. The prolonged whisking of the egg yolks over the indirect heat of a bain-marie ensures they are cooked through with a silky texture.

INGREDIENTS

3 large egg yolks
3 tbsp caster sugar
60ml (2fl oz) Marsala wine
¼ tsp vanilla extract
berries or other soft
    fruit, to serve

1 Whisk the egg yolks and sugar in a large heatproof bowl with a hand-held whisk for 3 minutes, until well combined and pale yellow in colour. Place the bowl over a saucepan of gently simmering water, making sure it does not touch the water.

2 Pour the Marsala wine and vanilla extract into the bowl, in a steady stream, whisking constantly to bring the mixture together. Whisk the mixture for a further 8–10 minutes, until it turns pale, triples in volume, and forms ribbons when the whisk is lifted.

3 Remove from the heat. Serve immediately, or at room temperature over berries, or other soft fruit. Serve the pudding on the same day, as it will start to separate if chilled.

40 mins
plus chilling

MAKES 6

CRÈME CARAMEL classic

Making crème caramel is not as tricky as you may think. For best results, it is very important that you cook them gently in a bain-marie in the oven – this helps them to set without splitting.

INGREDIENTS
225g (8oz) caster sugar
2 eggs, plus 2 egg yolks
1 tsp vanilla extract
500ml (16fl oz) whole milk

SPECIAL EQUIPMENT
6 x 150ml (5fl oz) ramekins

Preheat the oven to 180°C (350°F/Gas 4). Place 150g (5½oz) of the sugar and 2 tablespoons of water in a small, heavy-based saucepan. Cook over a medium heat, without stirring, until the sugar dissolves and turns golden brown. Swirl the pan gently and occasionally, to cook the sugar evenly.

1

2

Remove and distribute the caramel equally between the ramekins, swirling them to coat the bottom and a little way up the sides.

3

In a large heatproof bowl, whisk the eggs, egg yolks, vanilla extract, and the remaining sugar until well combined.

4

Place the milk in a saucepan over a low heat, until hot, but not boiling. Pour it over the egg mixture and whisk well. Chill the custard for 30 minutes.

5

Place the ramekins in a roasting tin and pour the custard into them evenly. Pour enough hot water into the tin to come halfway up the sides of the ramekins. Bake for 25–30 minutes, until the custard is just set, but still wobbly in the middle.

Remove and transfer the ramekins to a baking tray to cool. Then chill them for 2 hours. To serve, run a knife around the insides of the ramekins and turn out onto serving plates, scraping all the caramel on top. You can store them, covered with cling film, in the fridge for up to 2 days. Bring to room temperature before serving.

6

55 mins
plus cooling and chilling   **MAKES 4**

CRÈME CARAMEL orange flower

Orange flower water is quickly becoming a popular ingredient in recipes for sweet treats. Its perfume-like fragrance is strong and heady, so a little goes a long way.

INGREDIENTS
225g (8oz) caster sugar
2 whole eggs, plus
  2 egg yolks
2 tsp orange flower water
500ml (16fl oz) whole milk

SPECIAL EQUIPMENT
4 x 200ml (7fl oz)
  ovenproof ramekins

1 Preheat the oven to 180°C (350°F/Gas 4). Cook 150g (5½oz) of the sugar in a heavy-based saucepan over a medium heat, until the sugar dissolves and turns golden. Swirl the pan gently and occasionally to ensure that the sugar cooks evenly.

2 Remove from the heat and distribute the caramel equally between the ramekins, swirling them to coat the bottom and a little way up the sides. In a large bowl, whisk the eggs, egg yolks, orange flower water, and remaining sugar, until combined.

3 Heat the milk in a saucepan over a low heat, until hot, but not boiling. Whisk the hot milk into the egg mixture until well combined. Chill the custard for 30 minutes. Then pour into the ramekins.

4 Place the ramekins in a roasting tin. Pour enough hot water into the tin to come halfway up the sides of the ramekins. Bake for 35–40 minutes, until just set, but wobbling in the middle. Remove from the heat.

5 Cool to room temperature before chilling for 6 hours, or overnight. To serve, run a sharp knife around the insides of the ramekins and turn them out onto plates. Spoon the caramel on top.

1 hr 15 mins
plus cooling and chilling   **SERVES 6**

FLAN vanilla

Versions of this dessert hail from Spain, Mexico, and South America. This creamy variety is perfect for serving a crowd.

INGREDIENTS
unsalted butter,
  for greasing
200g (7oz) caster sugar
3 eggs
340ml (11¾fl oz)
  evaporated milk

160ml (5½fl oz) double
  cream
1 tsp vanilla extract

SPECIAL EQUIPMENT
20cm (8in) deep-sided
  cake tin

1 Preheat the oven to 180°C (350°F/Gas 4). Grease the tin and set aside. Cook 150g (5½oz) of the sugar in a heavy-based saucepan over a medium heat, until the sugar dissolves and turns golden. Swirl the pan gently and occasionally to ensure that the sugar cooks evenly.

2 Remove from the heat and spread the caramel in the cake tin, swirling it to coat the bottom and a little way up the sides. In a large bowl, whisk the eggs and remaining sugar, until combined.

3 Add the evaporated milk, cream, and vanilla extract to the egg mixture and whisk until incorporated. Pour the custard into the cake tin in an even layer, cover with foil, and place in a roasting tin.

4 Pour enough hot water into the roasting tin to come halfway up the sides of the cake tin. Bake in the oven for 1 hour, until just set, but still wobbling in the middle. Remove from the heat.

5 Cool to room temperature before chilling for 6 hours, or overnight. To serve the flan, run a sharp knife around its sides to loosen it. Turn it out onto a large serving dish and spoon the caramel on top.

50 mins
plus cooling and chilling

MAKES 4

CRÈME CARAMEL coconut

This delicately flavoured dessert makes the perfect end to an Asian feast. Easy to prepare in advance, you could serve it with a tropical fruit garnish.

INGREDIENTS

225g (8oz) caster sugar

2 whole eggs, plus
 2 egg yolks

400ml (14fl oz) coconut
 milk

100ml (3½fl oz) whole milk

SPECIAL EQUIPMENT

4 x 200ml (7fl oz)
 ovenproof ramekins

1 Preheat the oven to 180°C (350°F/Gas 4). Cook 150g (5½oz) of the sugar in a heavy-based saucepan over a medium heat, until the sugar dissolves and turns golden. Swirl the pan gently and occasionally to ensure that the sugar cooks evenly.

2 Remove from the heat and distribute the caramel between the ramekins (see Orange flower crème caramel, step 2). In a large bowl, whisk the eggs, egg yolks, and remaining sugar, until well combined.

3 Heat both lots of milk in a saucepan over a low heat, until hot, but not boiling. Add the hot milk mixture to the egg mixture and whisk until well combined. Chill the custard for 30 minutes.

4 Pour the custard into the ramekins and place them in a roasting tin. Pour hot water into the tin (see, Orange flower crème caramel, step 4). Bake for 30–40 minutes, until just set, but still wobbling in the middle. Remove from the heat.

5 Cool to room temperature before chilling for 6 hours, or overnight. To serve, run a sharp knife around the insides of the ramekins and turn them out onto plates. Spoon the caramel on top.

40 mins
plus chilling and cooling

MAKES 6

MOUSSE chocolate

This light and fluffy mousse is very simple to prepare, and endlessly adaptable. Depending on your preference, you can make it with dark or milk chocolate, and you could even flavour it with a splash of your favourite liqueur.

INGREDIENTS
120ml (4fl oz) whipping cream
1 tsp instant espresso powder
175g (6oz) good-quality dark chocolate, chopped
60g (2oz) unsalted butter
3 large eggs, separated
50g (1¾oz) caster sugar
pinch of salt
¼ tsp cream of tartar
chocolate shavings, to decorate

SPECIAL EQUIPMENT
6 x 200ml (7fl oz) cups

1 Whisk the cream in a bowl to form stiff peaks and chill until needed. Combine the espresso powder with 2 tablespoons of hot water in a small bowl. Place the chocolate and butter in a large heatproof bowl. Pour the coffee mixture over and stir to mix.

Stir until the chocolate has melted and is smooth.

2 Melt the chocolate mixture over a saucepan of gently simmering water, making sure it does not touch the water. Stir well, remove from the heat, and leave to cool.

3 Whisk the egg yolks and 2 tablespoons of sugar with a hand-held whisk in a heatproof bowl, until smooth. Then whisk the mixture over a pan of simmering water for 2–3 minutes, until thick and pale. Leave to rest for 2 minutes, then combine with the chocolate mixture.

4 Whisk the egg whites and salt in a separate bowl until fluffy. Add the cream of tartar and whisk to form soft peaks. Then gradually whisk in the remaining sugar to form stiff peaks.

5 Stir a little of the egg white mixture into the chocolate mixture to lighten the texture. Then fold in the chilled cream and the remaining egg white mixture.

Fold gently until no streaks remain.

6 Divide the mixture evenly between the cups and chill for 2–3 hours, until set. You can keep the mousse, covered in the fridge, for up to 2 days. Remove from the fridge 10–15 minutes before serving and sprinkle over the chocolate shavings.

🕐 **30 mins**
plus chilling and setting   🍴 **MAKES 6**

MOUSSE Kahlua-coffee

This is a wonderfully smooth chocolate and coffee combination. Although Kahlua is used here, you could try any coffee liqueur.

1 Melt **60g (2oz) unsalted butter**, **175g (6oz) finely chopped good-quality dark chocolate**, and **2½ tbsp Kahlua** in a heatproof bowl over a saucepan of simmering water, making sure it does not touch the water. Stir well, remove from the heat, and leave to cool. Whisk **120g (4fl oz) whipping cream** in a bowl to form stiff peaks, and chill until needed.

2 Whisk **3 large egg yolks** and **25g (scant 1oz) caster sugar** in a separate heatproof bowl until smooth. Place the bowl over a pan of simmering water, as before. Whisk vigorously, adding **60ml (2fl oz) strong coffee** in a steady stream. Whisk for 3 minutes until the mixture is pale and has tripled in volume.

3 Remove from the heat, rest for 1 minute, then combine with the chocolate mixture. Whisk the **3 large egg whites** and a **pinch of salt** in a bowl until frothy. Add **¼ tsp cream of tartar** and whisk to form soft peaks. Then add **25g (scant 1oz) caster sugar** and whisk to form stiff peaks.

4 Gradually fold the egg white mixture and the whipped cream into the chocolate mixture, until no streaks remain. Pour it into **six 175ml (5¾fl oz) glasses** and chill for 2–3 hours, until set. You can keep the mousse, covered in the fridge, for 2–3 days. Remove from the fridge 10–15 minutes before serving and top with a little **whipped cream** and **grated dark chocolate**.

🕐 **35 mins**
plus chilling and setting   🍴 **MAKES 6**

MOUSSE butterscotch

This rich and silky mousse does not require whisked egg whites to give it volume. Instead, butterscotch and cream provide the airy texture.

1 Melt **175g (6oz) butterscotch chips**, **60g (2oz) unsalted butter**, and **2 tbsp double cream** in a heatproof bowl over a saucepan of simmering water, making sure it does not touch the water. Stir well, remove from the heat, and leave to cool.

2 Whisk **350ml (12fl oz) double cream** in a bowl to form stiff peaks. Chill until needed. In a heatproof bowl, whisk **3 large egg yolks** and **2 tbsp caster sugar**. Place the bowl over a pan of simmering water, as before. Whisk vigorously for 3 minutes, until the mixture is pale and has tripled in volume.

3 Gradually fold the egg yolk mixture and whipped cream into the butterscotch mixture until no streaks remain. Pour the mixture into **six 120ml (4fl oz) glasses** and chill for 2–3 hours, until set. Cook **150g (5½oz) caster sugar** in a heavy-based saucepan over a medium heat for 5 minutes.

4 Stir the sugar gently to form a light-coloured caramel. Pour onto a lined baking sheet and leave to cool completely, before breaking the caramel into small pieces. You can keep the mousse, covered in the fridge, for 2–3 days. Remove from the fridge 10–15 minutes before serving and top with the caramel.

Kahlua-coffee

Butterscotch

25 mins
plus chilling, setting, and drying

MAKES 6

MOUSSE chocolate and mint

Evoke the flavour of after-dinner mints with this mousse. Add a flourish and additional flavour by decorating with frosted mint leaves.

1 Melt **175g (6oz) finely chopped dark chocolate**, **3 tbsp whipping cream**, and a **pinch of salt** in a heatproof bowl over a saucepan of simmering water, making sure it does not touch the water. Stir well, remove from the heat, and leave to cool. Whisk **200ml (7fl oz) whipping cream** in a bowl to form stiff peaks, and chill until needed.

2 In a separate bowl, whisk **2 egg whites** and a **pinch of salt** to form soft peaks. Add **2 tbsp caster sugar**, one tablespoon at a time, and whisk to form stiff peaks. Then gently stir in **½ tsp mint extract** until combined.

3 Mix a little of the egg whites into the chocolate mixture to lighten it. Then gently fold in the rest along with the whipped cream until no streaks remain. Pour the mixture into **six 200ml (7fl oz) glasses** and chill for 2–3 hours, until set.

4 Brush **9 mint leaves** with **1 lightly beaten egg white**. Dip them in **caster sugar** and leave to dry on baking parchment for 1 hour. You can keep the mousse, covered in the fridge, for 2–3 days. Remove from the fridge 10–15 minutes before serving and top with the crystallized mint leaves.

40 mins
plus chilling and setting

MAKES 6

MOUSSE strawberry lemonade

The flavour of lemon juice is quite distinct in this mousse, making it a little tart – just like pink lemonade.

1 Place **450g (1lb) hulled and quartered strawberries**, **75ml (2½fl oz) fresh lemon juice**, **100g (3½oz) caster sugar**, and a **pinch of salt** in a saucepan. Simmer over a low heat for 8–10 minutes unt il the strawberries have softened. Remove from the heat and use a hand-held blender to blend until smooth.

2 Strain the purée and pour it back into the pan. Simmer the purée over a medium-low heat for 5 minutes, then transfer to a heatproof bowl set over an ice bath and stir until cold. Transfer 60g (2oz) of the fruit purée to a small saucepan and stir in **1 tsp powdered gelatine**. Leave to thicken for 3–4 minutes.

3 Use a hand-held whisk to whisk **240ml (8fl oz) double cream** and **1 tsp vanilla extract** in a bowl to form stiff peaks. Heat the gelatine mixture over a low heat until no longer firm. Add it to the reserved fruit purée and mix to combine. Then gradually fold in the whipped cream, until no streaks remain.

4 Pour the mixture into **six 175ml (5¾fl oz) glasses** and chill for 2–3 hours until set. You can keep the mousse, covered in the fridge, for 2–3 days. Remove from the fridge 10–15 minutes before serving and top with **halved strawberries** and **lemon zest curls**.

Chocolate and mint

Strawberry lemonade

20 mins
plus infusing, cooling, setting, and chilling

MAKES 4

PANNA COTTA
vanilla with raspberry coulis

Translated from Italian, panna cotta means "cooked cream". Sweetened cream and milk are gently heated then set with gelatine, providing a soft and delicate dessert that makes a perfect foil for the raspberry coulis.

INGREDIENTS
375ml (13fl oz) whipping cream
250ml (9fl oz) whole milk
1 vanilla pod, split lengthways
7g (1 heaped tsp) powdered gelatine
100g (3½oz) caster sugar
1 tbsp sunflower oil, for greasing

For the coulis
200g (7oz) frozen raspberries
45g (1½oz) caster sugar

SPECIAL EQUIPMENT
4 x 150ml (5fl oz) dariole moulds or ramekins

1

Heat the cream, 200ml (7fl oz) milk, and vanilla pod in a heavy-based saucepan over a low heat, until steaming. Whisk the gelatine and reserved milk in a small bowl, then leave it to rest for about 5 minutes.

2

Remove from the heat, take out the vanilla pod, and scrape the seeds into the pan. Place the sugar in a heatproof bowl and pour the cream mixture over the top, whisking until the sugar dissolves. Whisk in the gelatine mixture.

3

Return the mixture to the pan and heat gently, stirring, for 2–3 minutes to ensure that the gelatine has dissolved. Do not boil or the gelatine will not set. Remove from the heat.

4

Lightly grease the moulds and pour in the hot cream mixture evenly. Leave them to cool to room temperature. Cover with cling film and chill for 4–6 hours, until set.

5

For the coulis, cook the raspberries, sugar, and 3 tablespoons of water in a pan over a low heat for 2–3 minutes, until the fruit has broken down. Remove from the heat and purée the mixture with a hand-held blender. Push through a sieve and chill until cold.

6

Carefully dip each mould in a bowl of hot water, run a knife around the edge, and invert onto a plate. Pour the coulis over to serve. You can store the panna cottas and coulis separately, covered in the fridge, for up to 2 days.

🕐 **20 mins**
plus cooling and chilling   🍴 **MAKES 4**

PANNA COTTA green tea

Vanilla panna cotta makes the perfect base for the delicate fragrance of green tea. Decorate with matcha powder to enhance the flavours further.

1. Place **50ml (1½fl oz) whole milk** in a bowl, whisk in **7g (1 heaped tsp) powdered gelatine**, and leave to rest for 5 minutes. Meanwhile, place **200ml (7fl oz) whole milk**, **375ml (13fl oz) whipping cream**, and **3 good-quality green teabags** in a heavy-based saucepan over a low heat. Heat for 5 minutes, until steaming, but not boiling.

2. Remove the pan from the heat and take out the teabags, squeezing them to extract extra flavour, if desired. Place **100g (3½oz) caster sugar** in a heatproof bowl. Pour in the hot milk mixture and whisk well until the sugar dissolves. Then whisk in the gelatine mixture until combined.

3. Return the mixture to the pan and heat gently, stirring, for 3–4 minutes to ensure that the gelatine has dissolved. Do not boil or the gelatine will not set. Remove from the heat. Use **1 tbsp sunflower oil** to lightly grease **four 150ml (5fl oz) ramekins**, and pour in the hot mixture evenly.

4. Leave them to cool to room temperature. Chill for 4–6 hours, or until set. Carefully dip the ramekins in a bowl of hot water, run a knife around the edges, and invert onto individual serving plates. Sprinkle with **matcha powder** and serve immediately. You can store the panna cottas, covered in the fridge, for up to 2 days.

🕐 **15 mins**
plus cooling and chilling   🍴 **MAKES 4**

PANNA COTTA lavender

Lavender has a heady perfume that lends a fabulously floral flavour to this dessert. Make sure you use culinary lavender.

1. Place **50ml (1½fl oz) whole milk** in a bowl, whisk in **7g (1 heaped tsp) powdered gelatine**, and leave to rest for 5 minutes. Meanwhile, place **200ml (7fl oz) whole milk**, **375ml (13fl oz) whipping cream**, and **1 tbsp dried culinary lavender flowers** in a heavy-based saucepan over a low heat. Heat for 5 minutes, until steaming, but not boiling.

2. Place **100g (3½oz) caster sugar** in a heatproof bowl. Strain the hot milk mixture into the bowl and whisk well until the sugar dissolves. Then whisk in the gelatine mixture until combined. Return the mixture to the pan and heat until the gelatine has dissolved (see Green tea panna cotta, step 3).

3. Remove from the heat. Use **1 tbsp sunflower oil** to lightly grease **four 150ml (5fl oz) ramekins**, and pour in the hot mixture evenly. Cool to room temperature, then chill for 4–6 hours, until set.

4. Carefully turn out the panna cottas onto individual serving plates (see Green tea panna cotta, step 4). Serve immediately with sablés, if desired (see pp260–61). You can store the panna cottas, covered in the fridge, for up to 2 days.

Lavender

Green tea

Yogurt and
pistachio

Orange flower
and pomegranate

🕐 **15 mins**
plus cooling and chilling 🍴 **MAKES 4**

PANNA COTTA
orange flower
and pomegranate

Orange flower water has a strong scent, so use
it sparingly. A sprinkle of fresh pomegranate
seeds enhances the Middle Eastern flavour.

1 Whisk **50ml (1½fl oz) whole milk** and **7g (1 heaped tsp)
powdered gelatine** in a bowl and leave to rest for 5 minutes.
Meanwhile, place **200ml (7fl oz) whole milk**, **375ml (13fl oz)
whipping cream**, **1½ tbsp orange flower water**, and **1 tsp
finely grated orange zest** in a heavy-based saucepan over a
low heat. Heat for 5 minutes, until steaming, but not boiling.

2 Place **100g (3½oz) caster sugar** in a heatproof bowl. Strain
the hot milk mixture into the bowl and whisk well until
the sugar dissolves. Then whisk in the gelatine mixture until
combined. Return the mixture to the pan and heat until the
gelatine has dissolved (see Green tea panna cotta, step 3).

3 Remove from the heat. Use **1 tbsp sunflower oil** to lightly
grease **four 150ml (5fl oz) ramekins**, and pour in the hot
mixture evenly. Cool to room temperature, then chill for 4–6
hours, until set.

4 Carefully turn out the panna cottas onto individual serving
plates (see Green tea panna cotta, step 4). Serve sprinkled
with the **seeds from 1 pomegranate**. You can store the panna
cottas, covered in the fridge, for up to 2 days.

🕐 **15 mins**
plus cooling and chilling 🍴 **MAKES 4**

PANNA COTTA yogurt
and pistachio

Rather like an upmarket version of Greek yogurt
and honey, this recipe is ideal to serve as a finale
to a Mediterranean-inspired meal.

1 Whisk **4 tbsp orange juice** and **7g (1 heaped tsp) powdered
gelatine** in a bowl and leave to rest for 5 minutes. Place **375ml
(13fl oz) whipping cream** and **finely grated zest of 1 orange**
in a heavy-based saucepan over a low heat. Heat for 5 minutes,
until steaming, but not boiling.

2 Place **100g (3½oz) caster sugar** in a heatproof bowl. Strain
the cream milk mixture into the bowl and whisk until the
sugar dissolves. Whisk in the gelatine mixture until combined.
Return the mixture to the pan and heat until the gelatine has
dissolved (see Green tea panna cotta, step 3).

3 Remove from the heat and stir in **250g (9oz) full-fat Greek
yogurt**. Use **1 tbsp sunflower oil** to lightly grease **four 150ml
(5fl oz) ramekins**, and pour in the hot mixture evenly. Cool
completely, then chill for 3–4 hours, until set.

4 Carefully turn out the panna cottas onto individual serving
plates (see Green tea panna cotta, step 4). Serve with a
drizzle of runny honey and **chopped unsalted and skinned
pistachios** sprinkled over the top. You can store the panna
cottas, covered in the fridge, for up to 2 days.

10 mins
plus cooling and chilling

MAKES 4

POSSET lemon

A posset is a classic English dessert that dates back hundreds of years. It is egg free – lemon juice is used effectively to curdle and set hot cream and sugar. Serve alongside delicate, freshly baked sablés (see pp260–61).

INGREDIENTS
100ml (3½fl oz) lemon juice
400ml (14fl oz) double cream
finely grated zest of 1 lemon, plus extra to decorate

125g (4½oz) caster sugar
sablés, to serve (optional)

SPECIAL EQUIPMENT
4 x 150ml (5fl oz) glasses

1 Strain the lemon juice into a heatproof bowl and set aside. Heat the cream, lemon zest, and sugar in a large heavy-based saucepan over a medium heat until just beginning to boil.

2 Reduce the heat to a low simmer and cook the mixture for 5 minutes, stirring occasionally, until slightly thickened.

3 Remove from the heat. Pour the mixture over the lemon juice, whisking constantly to combine. Leave to cool for 5 minutes.

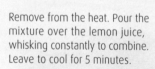

4 Transfer the mixture to the glasses and chill for 6 hours, or overnight. Decorate with lemon zest and serve with sablés, if desired. You can store the possets, covered in the fridge, for up to 3 days.

POSSET blood orange

Blood orange juice gives this posset a bright colour. Serve with candied citrus – for super-thin slices, freeze the fruit for 30 minutes and cut with a sharp knife.

INGREDIENTS

120ml (4fl oz) blood orange juice

3 tbsp lemon juice

400ml (14fl oz) double cream

finely grated zest of 1 orange

100g (3½oz) caster sugar

1 sprig of rosemary

For the candied citrus

250g (9oz) caster sugar

1 large, firm orange, thinly sliced

1 firm seedless lemon, thinly sliced

1 firm seedless lime, thinly sliced

SPECIAL EQUIPMENT

4 x 150ml (5fl oz) shallow bowls or glasses

PLAN AHEAD

You can prepare and store the candied fruit, in an open container to keep dry, up to 2 days ahead.

1 For the candied citrus, boil the sugar and 500ml (16fl oz) water in a large saucepan, stirring occasionally, until the sugar dissolves. Spread the citrus slices evenly in the pan and cover them with a sheet of greaseproof paper. Reduce the heat to a low simmer.

2 Cook for 1 hour, until the white parts of the slices are translucent. Carefully remove them from the pan and pat dry on a thick sheet of kitchen paper. Spread the slices on a wire rack and leave in a warm place for 1–2 days, turning them occasionally, until completely dry.

3 Strain both the juices into a heatproof bowl. Place the cream, orange zest, sugar, and rosemary in a heavy-based saucepan and heat until just beginning to boil. Reduce the heat to a low simmer.

4 Cook the cream mixture for 5 minutes, stirring occasionally, until it thickens slightly. Remove from the heat and whisk into the juices in the bowl, until well combined. Cool for 5 minutes, then discard the rosemary.

5 Transfer the mixture to the shallow bowls and chill for up to 6 hours, or overnight until set. Serve with the candied citrus slices. You can store the possets, covered in the fridge, for up to 3 days.

POSSET rhubarb and ginger

The sweet creaminess of this posset is offset by the pleasingly astringent rhubarb and a touch of warm spicy ginger.

INGREDIENTS

250g (9oz) rhubarb, washed, trimmed, and cut into 3cm (1in) pieces

3cm (1in) piece of fresh root ginger, finely sliced

150g (5½oz) caster sugar

30g (1oz) preserved ginger, finely chopped

juice of 2 lemons

juice of 1 large orange

400ml (14fl oz) double cream

finely grated zest of 1 orange

1 tsp ground ginger

SPECIAL EQUIPMENT

4 x 150ml (5fl oz) shallow bowls or glasses

PLAN AHEAD

You can store the cooked rhubarb, covered in the fridge, up to 3 days ahead. Strain before use.

1 Place the rhubarb, sliced ginger, and 50g (1¾oz) of the sugar in a lidded heavy-based saucepan. Add 4 tablespoons of water, cover, and bring to the boil. Then reduce the heat to a low simmer and cook for a further 5–7 minutes, until the rhubarb has softened and breaks down when stirred.

2 Remove the mixture from the heat, discard the ginger, and leave to cool completely. Then strain to remove any excess liquid and stir in the preserved ginger. Chill the mixture for 2 hours, or until needed.

3 Strain both the juices into a heatproof bowl. Heat the cream, orange zest, ground ginger, and remaining sugar in a heavy-based saucepan. Bring almost to the boil, then reduce the heat, and cook for 5 minutes, stirring occasionally, until it thickens slightly.

4 Remove from the heat and whisk it into the juices in the bowl, until well combined. Leave to cool. Drain any excess liquid from the rhubarb mixture and divide it evenly between the shallow bowls. Spread it out in a smooth layer and pour over the cream mixture evenly. Chill for up to 6 hours, or overnight, until set. Serve chilled. You can store the possets, covered in the fridge, for up to 3 days.

🕐 **15 mins**
plus cooling and chilling

🍴 **MAKES 4**

POSSET lime and coconut

You can use any acidic citrus juice to set possets. Here, lime juice and coconut combine to give this typically English dessert a tropical twist. Serve topped with toasted coconut, to add more texture.

INGREDIENTS

400ml (14fl oz) double
   cream

finely grated zest of 1 lime,
   plus extra for serving

125g (4½oz) caster sugar

30g (1oz) desiccated
   coconut

120ml (4fl oz) lime juice

toasted coconut shavings,
   to decorate

SPECIAL EQUIPMENT

4 x 150ml (5fl oz) shallow
   cups or bowls

1 Heat the cream, lime zest, sugar, and coconut in a heavy-based saucepan. Bring to the boil, then reduce the heat to a simmer. Cook for 5 minutes, stirring occasionally, until the cream thickens slightly.

2 Remove from the heat and leave to cool slightly. Use a hand-held blender to blend the mixture until smooth. Return to the heat and bring to a simmer. Remove from the heat.

3 Strain the lime juice into a large heatproof bowl. Gradually pour the cream mixture over the top, whisking constantly until it is well combined. Leave to cool for about 5 minutes.

4 Transfer the mixture to the cups and chill for at least 6 hours, or overnight. Sprinkle with coconut shavings and lime zest before serving. You can store the possets, covered in the fridge, for up to 3 days.

10 mins
plus chilling   **MAKES 4**

FOOL summer fruit

Traditionally, fruit fools contained only stewed fruit and custard. Modern fools feature fresh fruit purée and whipped cream to create a brighter flavour and fluffier texture – they have now become a classic in their own right.

INGREDIENTS
400g (14oz) mixed hulled strawberries, raspberries, and blueberries
30g (1oz) caster sugar, plus 1 tbsp extra
200ml (7fl oz) double cream
150g (5½oz) full-fat Greek yogurt
½ tsp vanilla extract

SPECIAL EQUIPMENT
4 x 100ml (3½fl oz) glass jars or glasses

1 Slice the strawberries so that they are a similar size as the other fruit. Combine all the fruit with 1 tablespoon of sugar in a large bowl. Then pulse two-thirds of the mixture in a food processor to form a purée.

2 Whisk the cream in a bowl until fluffy. Add the yogurt, vanilla extract, and remaining sugar. Fold the mixture gently, so that you lose as little air as possible.

3 Gently fold the fruit purée into the cream mixture until no streaks remain.

The mixture should be well combined.

4 Fold the reserved fruit into the mixture. Divide the mixture between the jars, cover, and chill for 2 hours, before serving. You can cover and store them in the fridge for up to 1 day.

30 mins
plus cooling and chilling

MAKES 4

FOOL gooseberry and elderflower

This fool is perfect for a warm day. Enhance tart gooseberries with the floral flavours of elderflower cordial – both flavours of British summertime.

1 Place **350g (12oz) topped and tailed gooseberries**, **100g (3½oz) caster sugar**, and **1 tbsp elderflower cordial** in a lidded saucepan and stir to dissolve the sugar. Cover and cook over a low heat for 5 minutes, until the gooseberries have given out some water and have started to swell.

2 Uncover and cook for a further 5 minutes. Then remove from the heat and mash the gooseberries with a potato masher to break them up. Leave to cool completely, before chilling until cold. In a large bowl, whisk **200ml (7fl oz) double cream** to form stiff peaks.

3 Fold the fruit mixture into the cream. Then fold in **240g (8¾oz) good-quality, ready-made custard** into the fruit and cream mixture. Mix well until light and fluffy and spoon the fool into **four 100ml (3½fl oz) glass jars**. Chill for at least 2 hours before serving. You can store them, covered in the fridge, for up to 1 day.

PLAN AHEAD
You can prepare and store the gooseberry purée, covered in the fridge, up to 3 days ahead.

Mango and passionfruit

Gooseberry and elderflower

10 mins
plus chilling   **MAKES 4**

FOOL mango and passionfruit

Ripe mangoes purée easily, making them perfect for a smooth fool. Contrast their sweetness with tangy Greek yogurt and sharp, acidic passionfruit.

1. Finely chop **2 ripe mangoes** to form a pulp and chill until needed. Whisk **150ml (5fl oz) double cream** in a bowl to form peaks. Whisk in **30g (1oz) icing sugar** to form soft peaks.

2. Gently fold **250g (9oz) full-fat Greek yogurt** and **½ tsp vanilla extract** into the cream mixture, so that you lose as little air as possible, until combined. Then scoop out the pulp from **2 ripe passionfruit** and fold into the cream mixture.

3. Place a spoonful of the cream mixture in **four 100ml (3½fl oz) jars**. Top with a layer of the mango pulp. Repeat the process, finishing with a third layer of the cream mixture. Cover the fruit fool and chill for 2 hours.

4. Scoop out the pulp from **1 passionfruit** and use to top the fruit fools evenly. Sprinkle over some **finely chopped unsalted and skinned pistachios** and serve immediately. You can store them, covered in the fridge, for up to 1 day.

Rhubarb and custard

25 mins
plus cooling and chilling   **MAKES 4**

FOOL rhubarb and custard

You can mellow sharp, spring rhubarb with a sweet home-made custard and whipped cream. Its pretty pink colour is always a delight.

1. Place **400g (14oz) washed and trimmed rhubarb, cut into 3cm (1in) pieces** in a lidded heavy-based saucepan. Add **60g (2oz) caster sugar** and **4 tbsp water**, cover, and bring to the boil. Reduce the heat to a low simmer and cook for 3–5 minutes, until the rhubarb has softened. Increase the heat slightly and uncover.

2. Cook the rhubarb for a further 2 minutes, stirring frequently, until it has broken down completely and the juices have reduced. Remove from the heat. Cool completely, drain any excess liquid, and chill the rhubarb for 2 hours.

3. Whisk **2 egg yolks**, **1 tsp vanilla extract**, **1 tbsp cornflour**, and **2 tbsp caster sugar** in a heatproof bowl until smooth. Heat **120ml (4fl oz) whole milk** and **120ml (4fl oz) single cream** in a heavy-based saucepan until hot, but not boiling. Pour it into the egg yolk mixture, whisking until the sugar dissolves.

4. Pour the mixture into a clean pan and bring to the boil over a medium heat, stirring constantly. Reduce the heat to low. Cook for 3–4 minutes, stirring, until the custard is thick enough to coat the back of a spoon. Pour it into a shallow dish, cover the surface with cling film, and leave to cool for at least 1 hour.

5. Whisk the **120ml (4fl oz) double cream** in a bowl to form stiff peaks. Gently fold it into the custard. Then fold in the rhubarb until combined, yet a little streaky. Divide the fruit fool into **four 100ml (3½fl oz) jars**. Cover and chill for at least 2 hours before serving. You can store them, covered in the fridge, for up to 1 day.

PLAN AHEAD
You can prepare and store the custard, covered in the fridge, up to 1 day ahead.

🕐 **30 mins**
plus chilling and setting

🍴 **SERVES 4**

JELLY strawberry

Shop-bought jelly is rubbery and full of artificial colours and flavours. It is so easy to make your own – gently poach ripe, bright fruit to give you the flavour and colour you need. Add fresh fruit to the mixture ahead of setting for an elegant touch.

INGREDIENTS

900g (2lb) strawberries, hulled and quartered

100g (3½oz) caster sugar, plus extra if needed

½ tsp vanilla extract

⅛ tsp salt

24g (scant 1oz) powdered gelatine

SPECIAL EQUIPMENT

4 x 200ml (7fl oz) serving bowls

1 Place the strawberry quarters in a saucepan, reserving 20. Add the sugar and 240ml (8fl oz) cold water. Simmer with a lid on over a medium–low heat for 15 minutes.

2 Strain the liquid into a bowl. Do not press down on the fruit, as it will turn the jelly cloudy. Discard the fruit and return the liquid to the pan. Stir in the vanilla extract and salt. Taste and add more sugar, if needed.

3

Place 110ml (3¾fl oz) of cold water in a bowl. Stir in the gelatine and leave for 3–4 minutes, until it blooms and firms. Then add it to the pan and cook the mixture over a low heat, until dissolved.

4

Divide the mixture between the serving bowls and top with the reserved fruit. Cover and place in the fridge to chill and set for 2–3 hours, or overnight, before serving. You can store the jellies, covered in the fridge, for up to 8 days.

15 mins
plus resting, chilling, and setting

SERVES 4

JELLY mango and milk

When milk is used to make jelly the results are creamy and pudding-like – a rich and smooth dessert.

1 Place **120ml (4fl oz) milk** and **24g (scant 1oz) powdered gelatine** in a saucepan. Stir to combine and leave to rest for 5–10 minutes, until the gelatine blooms and thickens.

2 Add **500ml (16fl oz) mango juice or nectar, 80ml (2¾fl oz) whole milk, 50g (1¾oz) caster sugar**, and **a pinch of salt** to the pan. Cook over a low heat, stirring frequently, until the sugar dissolves and the mixture is smooth. Do not boil the mixture. Remove from the heat.

3 Divide the mixture between **four 200ml (7fl oz) jars**. Cover with cling film. Leave to chill and set in the fridge for 2–3 hours, or overnight, before serving. You can store the jellies in the fridge for up to 5 days.

15 mins
plus resting, chilling, and setting

SERVES 4

JELLY Prosecco and raspberry

Serve these stylish jellies as a stunning climax to a celebratory meal.

1 Place **60ml (2fl oz) water, 60ml (2fl oz) white grape juice,** and **24g (scant 1oz) powdered gelatine** in a saucepan. Stir to combine and leave to rest for 2–4 minutes, until the gelatine blooms and thickens.

2 Add **50g (1¾oz) caster sugar** and **180ml (6fl oz) white grape juice** to the pan. Cook over a low heat, stirring frequently, until the sugar dissolves and the mixture is smooth. Do not boil the mixture. Remove from the heat and leave to cool for 3–4 minutes.

3 Gradually add **300ml (10fl oz) Prosecco** to the mixture, stirring gently to combine. Then divide the mixture between **four 200ml (7fl oz) jars**. Cover with cling film and leave to chill and set in the fridge for 20–25 minutes.

4 Push **3–4 raspberries** into each jelly jar, and chill them for a further 2–3 hours, or overnight, until set and firm. Serve chilled. You can store the jellies in the fridge for up to 7 days.

Prosecco and raspberry

Mango and milk

🕐 **20 mins**
plus steeping, chilling, and setting

🍴 **SERVES 4**

JELLY mulled red wine

These striking dark jellies make great additions to a festive dessert table. The recipe is also a great way to use up leftover mulled wine.

1 Place **350ml (12fl oz) red wine**, **1 cinnamon stick**, **5 cloves**, and **grated zest of 1 orange** in a saucepan. Heat over a medium-low heat until the mixture begins to simmer gently. Remove from the heat and leave to steep for 15–20 minutes.

2 Place **200ml (7fl oz) apple juice** and **24g (scant 1oz) powdered gelatine** in a bowl. Stir to combine and leave for 3–4 minutes, until the gelatine blooms and thickens. Strain the wine mixture, discarding the spices, and place in a large pan.

3 Add **50g (1¾oz) caster sugar** and the gelatine mixture to the pan. Warm over a low heat, stirring until the sugar dissolves. Do not boil the mixture. Remove from the heat.

4 Divide the mixture between **four 200ml (7fl oz) jars** and cover with cling film. Leave to chill and set in the fridge for 2–3 hours, or preferably overnight. Serve with a little **sweetened whipped cream**, if desired. You can store the jellies in the fridge for up to 5 days.

Mulled red wine

Simple alternatives

Fruits with good colour and high water content make the best choice for jellies. These recipes adapt the classic Strawberry jelly (see pp198–99).

Blackberry Ripe blackberries, known for their deeply coloured juices, look and taste delicious when used in jelly. Use the same quantity of blackberries as the strawberries (see pp198–99).

Rhubarb Bright rhubarb gives jellies a beautifully pale pink colour. Instead of the strawberries, stew 900g (2lb) rhubarb and the caster sugar in 240ml (8fl oz) water for 15 minutes, Make sure you have about 650ml (22fl oz) liquid – discard any excess and continue with the recipe (see p198–99).

Gooseberry and elderflower Instead of stewing the strawberries, place 900g (2lb) gooseberries, the caster sugar, and 240ml (8fl oz) water in a lidded saucepan and cook over a low heat for 15 minutes. Make sure you have about 650ml (22fl oz) liquid – discard any excess and continue with the recipe (see pp198–99).

Blood orange Instead of the strawberries and water, pour 650ml (22fl oz) freshly squeezed blood orange juice into a lidded saucepan with the caster sugar (see pp198–99). Cover and stew for 15 minutes. Drain 175g (6oz) canned mandarin segments, and use to top the jellies in the serving bowls before chilling.

Strawberry and mango For a twist on the flavour and added colour, instead of the reserved strawberries, add 1 diced ripe mango to the jelly mixture and leave it to chill and set as normal (see p199, step 4).

Raspberry Fresh raspberries make a delicious change from strawberries, especially when they are in season. Use the same quantity of raspberries as the strawberries (see pp198–99).

🕐 **20 mins**
plus cooling and chilling

🍴 **SERVES 4**

FRUIT SALAD with minted sugar syrup

A fruit salad is a refreshing and light dessert option. Cut the fruit into small pieces, so that it is easy to mix a few flavours in a single spoonful. This minted sugar syrup helps to bring out the flavour of the ingredients.

INGREDIENTS

1 ripe mango, peeled and cut into 1cm (½in) cubes

2 ripe kiwis, peeled and cut into 1cm (½in) cubes

100g (3½oz) ripe papaya, peeled and cut into 1cm (½in) cubes

100g (3½oz) pineapple, cut into 1cm (½in) cubes

seeds from 1 ripe pomegranate

For the syrup

50g (1¾oz) caster sugar

1 tbsp lemon juice

10 large mint leaves

PLAN AHEAD

You can prepare and store the syrup in the fridge up to 1 week ahead.

1 For the syrup, place the ingredients in a small heavy-based saucepan. Pour over 50ml (1¾fl oz) cold water.

2 Bring to the boil, stirring frequently until the sugar dissolves. Remove from the heat, pour into a heatproof bowl, and leave to cool. Then chill until needed.

3 Combine all the fruit, in a large serving bowl, reserving one-quarter of the pomegranate seeds. Strain the syrup into a jug. Discard the mint leaves.

4 Pour the syrup over the fruit and toss well to coat. Scatter over the reserved pomegranate seeds and serve. It is best served within 4 hours of preparation.

FRUIT SALAD
ice pops

Serve these healthy ice pops after a summer's meal. They are incredibly simple to prepare.

INGREDIENTS
250g (9oz) just-ripe mixed fruit, such as pineapple, kiwi, strawberries, blueberries, and mangoes

300ml (10fl oz) white grape juice

SPECIAL EQUIPMENT
6 x 100ml (3½fl oz) ice-lolly moulds

6 lolly sticks

1 Cut the fruit into small pieces, roughly the size of the blueberries. Place them in a large bowl and toss well to combine. Divide the fruit between the ice-lolly moulds, packing them in loosely.

2 Pour the grape juice over the mixed fruit evenly, making sure you fill the moulds just below the brim. Insert the sticks into the moulds and transfer them to the freezer.

3 Freeze the moulds for 4–6 hours, or until frozen solid. Place them briefly under hot running water to loosen and turn out the ice pops. Serve immediately. You can store them in the freezer for up to 1 month.

⏱ **20 mins**
plus chilling   🍴 **SERVES 4**

FRUIT SALAD summer fruit with balsamic glaze

Pairing strawberries with balsamic vinegar originated in Italy, and it is now popular internationally. Here, sweetened balsamic is used to glaze an array of summer fruits.

INGREDIENTS
2 tbsp good-quality balsamic vinegar

3 tbsp caster sugar

300g (10oz) strawberries, hulled and quartered

100g (3½oz) blueberries

100g (3½oz) raspberries

2 ripe peaches, peeled, stoned, and diced to the size of the raspberries

1 Combine the vinegar, sugar, and 1 tablespoon water in a small heavy-based saucepan. Bring to the boil, then reduce the heat to a low simmer. Cook, stirring, until the sugar melts.

2 Remove from the heat and cool to room temperature. Place the strawberries and blueberries in a large bowl. Pour in the balsamic glaze and toss gently to coat.

3 Chill the mixture for 30 minutes. Then add the raspberries and peaches, toss gently to coat, and chill for a further 30 minutes. Toss gently and serve immediately.

🕐 **25 mins** plus cooling   🍴 **SERVES 4**   🌡️ Also great **HOT**

FRUIT SALAD roasted winter fruit

Whatever the weather outside, bring some heat to your dinner table with these roasted fruits and warming spices. Pecans add a welcome crunch that contrasts with the soft fruit.

INGREDIENTS

2 large apples, peeled, cored, and quartered

2 large just-ripe pears, peeled, cored, and quartered

150g (5½oz) blackberries

juice of 2 large oranges

½ tsp ground cinnamon

30g (1oz) soft light brown sugar

30g (1oz) pecans, roughly chopped

For the yogurt

200g (7oz) full-fat Greek yogurt

1 tsp vanilla extract

1 tbsp icing sugar

grated zest of 1 orange

1. Preheat the oven to 180°C (350°F/Gas 4). Slice the apple and pear pieces in half, lengthways. Place them in a large bowl and add the blackberries, orange juice, cinnamon, and brown sugar. Toss the fruit well to coat.

2. Transfer the mixture to a baking tray and spread it out in an even layer. Scatter over the pecans and bake for 20 minutes, until the apples and pears are just soft when pierced with a knife. Remove from the heat and leave to cool for 5 minutes.

3. Place the yogurt, vanilla extract, icing sugar, and orange zest in a large bowl and fold them well to combine. Serve the fruit salad warm with the yogurt, or leave to cool to room temperature. You can store the salad, covered in the fridge, for up to 2 days.

Sticks and skewers

You can skewer a variety of fruits. Dip, freeze, or barbecue them to create fun, healthy, and easy desserts – perfect for a summer's day.

Chocolate fondue Dice 500g (1lb 2oz) fresh fruit, such as mango, kiwi, and banana, into bite-sized pieces. Melt 100g (3½oz) good-quality dark chocolate and 100ml (3½fl oz) double cream in a small bowl over just simmering water. Remove from the heat, and serve alongside the fruit for dipping.

Frozen bananas Trim the ends off 2 firm bananas and cut them in half. Insert a wooden ice lolly stick into each banana half, and freeze them for 4 hours. Melt 200g (7oz) white chocolate (as above). Submerge each frozen banana in the chocolate, and leave to set. Melt 50g (1¾oz) dark chocolate, and drizzle it over the top. Serve immediately.

Pineapple kebabs Chop ½ large, ripe pineapple into chunks and marinate them in 4 tbsp dark rum and 4 tbsp brown sugar for 1–2 hours. Skewer the pineapple chunks and grill on the barbecue for 2–3 minutes each side, until caramelized and warm. Serve immediately.

Dipped strawberries Hull 20 firm, bite-sized strawberries. Gently push a round lolly stick into each one. Melt 100g (3½oz) white chocolate (see Chocolate fondue, above), and submerge each strawberry in the melted chocolate. Allow to set, then serve.

🕐 **1 hr 25 min–1 hr 35 mins**
plus cooling and setting

🍴 **SERVES 8**

SACHERTORTE
chocolate

This rich dark chocolate torte was invented in 19th century Vienna. The simple apricot jam filling and rich ganache topping make it a truly special dessert. Try serving it with a little whipped cream.

INGREDIENTS

250g (9oz) butter, softened

250g (9oz) caster sugar

250g (9oz) good-quality dark chocolate, melted

½ tsp pure vanilla extract

5 eggs, separated

250g (9oz) plain flour

6–8 tbsp apricot glaze, or sieved apricot jam

whipped cream, to serve

For the ganache

200ml (7fl oz) double cream

150g (5½ oz) good-quality dark chocolate, finely chopped

SPECIAL EQUIPMENT

23cm (9in) round cake tin

piping bag fitted with a fine plain round nozzle

PLAN AHEAD

You can store the unglazed cake in an airtight container in the freezer up to 3 months ahead.

Beat the batter well after each
ingredient is added to ensure
that it is evenly incorporated.

 Preheat the oven to 180ºC (350ºF/Gas 4). Line the tin with greaseproof paper. Beat the butter and sugar in a large bowl until light and fluffy. Then beat in the chocolate and vanilla extract. Add the egg yolks, one at a time, and beat well to combine. Fold in the flour until incorporated.

2 In a separate bowl, whisk the egg whites to form stiff peaks. Spoon a little of the egg white into the chocolate mixture and combine well. Then gently fold in the remaining egg whites, until evenly incorporated. Pour the batter into the tin and spread it out evenly.

3 Bake the cake in the oven for 45–50 minutes, until it feels just firm to the touch and an inserted skewer comes out clean. Remove from the heat and place the tin on a wire rack. Leave the cake to cool completely. Then turn it out of the tin and slice in half horizontally.

4 Heat the apricot glaze in a small saucepan until runny. Place one of the cakes on a wire rack, over a baking tray. Brush over the glaze and top with the other cake, making sure the flat side of the cake is facing the top. Brush the remaining glaze over the top and sides of the cake and leave to set.

 For the ganache, gently melt the cream and chocolate in a heatproof bowl over a saucepan of simmering water, making sure it does not touch the water. Stir the ganache occasionally, until thick and glossy. Remove from the heat.

6 Leave the ganche to cool slightly, stirring occasionally, until it reaches a smooth, coating consistency. If it becomes cold and thick, re-warm it over a pan of gently simmering water. Set aside 3 tablespoons of the ganache in a separate bowl.

7 Pour the ganache over the cake, a little at a time, and use a palette knife to spread it evenly over the top and sides of the cake. Leave the cake to set in a cool place. Then use the palette knife to transfer it carefully to a large serving dish.

8 Gently heat the reserved ganache, if it has become too thick. Then spoon it into the piping bag and carefully pipe the word "Sacher" across the top of the cake. Leave to set briefly before serving with whipped cream. You can store the cake in an airtight container for up to 3 days.

🕐 **1 hr 10 mins**
plus cooling and chilling

🍴 **SERVES 8**

TORTE chocolate and salted caramel

This luxurious dessert is as eye-catching as it is delicious. For a mouth-watering contrast in flavour, dark chocolate ganache is studded with sea salt flakes. Apply the ganache when it is cool but still spreadable to achieve a smooth finish.

INGREDIENTS

3 eggs
125g (4½oz) caster sugar
60g (2oz) plain flour
30g (1oz) cocoa powder

For the mousse

200g (7oz) caster sugar
85g (3oz) unsalted butter, diced
220ml (7½fl oz) double cream
12g (¼oz) powdered gelatine

For the ganache

90ml (3fl oz) double cream
115g (4oz) good-quality dark
 chocolate, finely chopped
sea salt flakes, to decorate

SPECIAL EQUIPMENT

20cm (8in) springform
 cake tin

1 Preheat the oven to 190°C (375°F/Gas 5). Line the tin with baking parchment. Whisk the eggs and sugar in a large bowl for 5 minutes, until the mixture is pale, thick, and has tripled in volume.

2 Sift the flour and cocoa powder into the egg mixture and gently fold them in. Pour the batter evenly into the tin. Bake for 20–25 minutes, until the cake is well risen and an inserted toothpick comes out clean. Cool in the tin for 10 minutes, then turn the cake out and place on a wire rack to cool completely.

3 For the mousse, melt the sugar in a large, heavy-based saucepan over a medium heat, until the edges start to melt. Gently swirl the pan to distribute the heat, until it forms a thick, dark caramel. Then reduce the heat and gradually stir in the butter.

4 Increase the heat to medium. Add 120ml (4fl oz) of the cream in a thin stream, stirring constantly until combined. Then increase the heat and bring to the boil for 1 minute, whisking constantly. Transfer the mousse to a heatproof bowl. Leave to cool, then whisk in the remaining cream until combined.

5 Mix the gelatine with 2 tablespoons of cold water in a cup and leave to rest for 1 minute. Then whisk in 1 tablespoon of boiling water, until the gelatine dissolves. Whisk the mixture into the mousse, until well combined.

6 Slice the cake in half, lengthways. Place the bottom half in the tin, and spread the mousse evenly. Top with the remaining half of the cake, cut-side up, pressing down slightly. Chill until needed.

7 For the ganache, heat the cream in a small, heavy-based saucepan until hot, but not boiling. Remove from the heat, add the chocolate, and leave to melt. Then stir the ganache well to combine and chill until cool and thick enough to pour.

8 Pour the ganache over the cake and spread it out evenly. Sprinkle with sea salt and chill for at least 4 hours before serving. You can store it in an airtight container in the fridge for up to 2 days.

🕐 **1 hr–1 hr 10 mins** plus cooling and chilling   🍴 **SERVES 8**

TORTE lemon and raspberry

This pretty torte is a perfect dish to serve at a summer celebration. The whisked sponge is as light as a feather, and the filling is creamy and tangy at the same time.

INGREDIENTS
3 eggs

125g (4½oz) caster sugar

85g (3oz) plain flour

grated zest of ½ small lemon

For the filling
12g (¼oz) powdered gelatine

5 tbsp lemon juice

200ml (7fl oz) good-quality lemon curd

225g (8oz) mascarpone cheese

125g (4½oz) raspberries, plus extra to decorate

30g (1oz) caster sugar

icing sugar, to decorate

SPECIAL EQUIPMENT
20cm (8in) springform cake tin

PLAN AHEAD
You can store the unfilled sponge cake in an airtight container in the freezer up to 3 months ahead.

1 Preheat the oven to 190°C (375°F/Gas 5). Line the tin with baking parchment. Whisk the eggs and caster sugar in a bowl for at least 5 minutes (see Chocolate and salted caramel torte, step 1). Sift the flour into the egg mixture and fold it in gently. Then fold in the lemon zest.

2 Pour the mixture evenly into the tin and bake for 20–25 minutes, until done (see Chocolate and salted caramel torte, step 2). Cool in the tin for 10 minutes, then turn out and place on a wire rack to cool completely.

3 For the filling, whisk the gelatine with 3 tablespoons of lemon juice in a bowl and leave to stand for 1 minute. Add 2 tablespoons of hot water to the gelatine, whisking until the gelatine dissolves. Whisk the lemon curd and mascarpone in a bowl with a hand-held whisk.

4 Add the gelatine to the mascarpone mixture and continue to whisk until it is thick. Slice the sponge cake in half, lengthways. Place the bottom half in the tin, and spread the filling evenly. Place the raspberries evenly over the filling. Top with the remaining half of the cake, and press down firmly.

5 Melt the caster sugar and remaining lemon juice in a saucepan over a low heat, until just dissolved. Spoon the drizzle evenly over the cake. Cover the cake with cling film and chill for 4 hours, or overnight. Dust with icing sugar, top with raspberries, and serve. You can store it in an airtight container in the fridge for up to 2 days.

Dusts and powders

With a smooth surface and even colour, a torte is the perfect canvas for dusting. Make sure you dust no more than an hour before serving.

Citrus powder This powder has a sharp flavour, rather like sherbet. To make it, bake candied citrus slices (see Blood orange posset, p192). Grind 2–3 slices to a fine powder in a clean spice or coffee grinder. Use it to dust citrus-flavoured tortes, such as the Lemon and raspberry torte (see left).

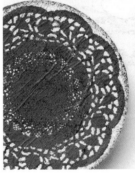

Doily design Place a paper doily or homemade stencil on top of your torte. Sift icing sugar over the surface, then remove the doily carefully – it will leave a delicate and pretty finish. This works well on any unglazed torte.

Matcha powder With a beautiful pale-green colour, matcha powder has a very strong green tea flavour, so use a ratio of 1 tsp icing sugar for every ¼ tsp matcha. Lay strips of ribbon, spaced apart, on the surface of your unglazed torte. Dust over the powder, remove the ribbons carefully, and serve.

Sugar sprinkles To make sprinkles, preheat the oven to 180°C (350°F/Gas 4). Mix 60g (2oz) granulated sugar with your choice of food colouring, a drop at a time, until you get the right colour. Spread it out on a foil-lined baking sheet and bake for 10 minutes. Allow to cool, then sprinkle it over your torte.

30 mins plus chilling   🍴 **SERVES 8**

CHILLED CHEESECAKE
lime and blueberry

This fruity cheesecake is chilled rather than baked. The filling has a lighter consistency than a baked one, and it is less susceptible to cracking. Make sure you measure the gelatine carefully, as it can affect how the filling sets.

INGREDIENTS
250g (9oz) digestive biscuits, finely crushed
100g (3½oz) unsalted butter, melted

For the topping
100g (3½oz) blueberries
1 tbsp caster sugar
grated zest of ½ lime

For the filling
juice of 2 limes
12g (¼oz) powdered gelatine

300g (10oz) soured cream
100g (3½oz) caster sugar
500g (1lb 2oz) full-fat cream cheese
grated zest of 1 lime, plus extra to serve
1 tsp vanilla extract

SPECIAL EQUIPMENT
23cm (9in) springform cake tin

1 Line the tin with greaseproof paper. Mix the biscuit crumbs and butter in a bowl, until well combined. Spread the mixture in the tin, pressing it down firmly to form a smooth and even base. Chill until needed.

2 For the topping, gently heat the blueberries, sugar, lime zest, and 1 tablespoon water in a heavy-based saucepan. Stir until the blueberries start to release their juices. Remove from the heat and leave to cool.

3 For the filling, whisk the lime juice and gelatine in a heavy-based saucepan and leave for 5 minutes. Then heat gently, whisking, until the gelatine dissolves and leave to cool. Whisk the remaining ingredients in a bowl, until combined. Then whisk in the gelatine mixture, and spread the filling evenly over the biscuit base.

4 Spoon over the topping and decorate with the strained juices. Chill for 4–6 hours, or overnight. Remove from the tin and sprinkle with lemon zest to serve. You can store it, covered in the fridge, for up to 2 days.

30 mins plus chilling   **SERVES 8–10**

CHILLED CHEESECAKE
triple chocolate

A chocoholic's dream, this cheesecake features a rich white chocolate filling. Top it with milk and dark chocolate swirls that provide added crunch.

INGREDIENTS

250g (9oz) Oreo or bourbon biscuits, filling removed and finely crushed

100g (3½oz) unsalted butter, melted

300g (10oz) good-quality white chocolate, broken into pieces

30g (1oz) each good-quality dark chocolate and milk chocolate, broken into pieces

225g (8oz) full-fat cream cheese

200g (7oz) mascarpone

60g (2oz) caster sugar

1 tsp vanilla extract

100ml (3½fl oz) double cream, whipped

SPECIAL EQUIPMENT

22cm (8½in) springform cake tin

1 Line the tin with baking parchment. Combine the biscuits and butter in a large bowl. Tip the crumbs out into the prepared tin and press them down firmly, using the back of a spoon, to form a thin, even layer. Chill until needed.

2 Melt the white chocolate in a heatproof bowl over a saucepan of simmering water, making sure it does not touch the water. Stir until smooth, remove from the heat, and leave to cool. Repeat the process for the dark and milk chocolate, using two separate heatproof bowls.

3 Whisk the cream cheese, mascarpone, sugar, and vanilla extract in a large bowl, until well combined and smooth. Whisk in the cooled white chocolate, then fold in the whipped cream. Tip the filling over the biscuit base, and spread it out into a smooth layer.

4 Drizzle the melted dark and milk chocolate over the cheesecake and use a skewer to swirl it. Chill the cheesecake for at least 6 hours, or overnight, before serving. You can store the cheesecake, covered, in the fridge for up to 2 days.

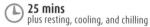 **25 mins** plus resting, cooling, and chilling   **MAKES 4**

MINI CHILLED CHEESECAKES lemon

With a lemon curd topping that produces a dark golden-yellow layer, these mini cheesecakes look very professional.

INGREDIENTS

45g (1½oz) unsalted butter, melted, plus extra for greasing

125g (4½oz) digestive biscuits, finely crushed

For the filling

7g (1 heaped tsp) powdered gelatine

4 tbsp lemon juice

100g (3½oz) full-fat cream cheese

150g (5½oz) ricotta cheese

60g (2oz) caster sugar

grated zest of 1 lemon

For the topping

150g (5½oz) thick-set lemon curd

7g (1 heaped tsp) powdered gelatine

SPECIAL EQUIPMENT

4 x 7.5cm (3in) baking rings

1 Grease the baking rings and set aside. Combine the biscuits and butter in a large bowl. Tip the crumbs out into the prepared rings and press them down firmly, using the back of a spoon, to form a thin, even layer. Chill until needed.

2 For the filling, sprinkle the gelatine over the lemon juice in a small, heavy-based saucepan. Whisk well and leave to rest for 5 minutes. Then gently heat the mixture, whisking constantly, until the gelatine has just dissolved. Remove from the heat and leave to cool.

3 Whisk the remaining filling ingredients in a large bowl, until well combined and smooth. Whisk in the cooled gelatine mixture until combined. Divide the filling between the biscuit bases and smooth out to an even layer. Chill the cakes for 30 minutes.

4 For the topping, whisk 1 tablespoon of water with the lemon curd in a small, heavy-based saucepan. Sprinkle over the gelatine and leave to rest for 5 minutes. Then gently heat the mixture, whisking constantly, until smooth. Remove from the heat and leave to cool.

5 Pour the topping over the cheesecakes, spreading it out into an even layer. Chill the cheesecakes for at least 4–6 hours, or overnight. To serve, run a knife round the edges of the rings and turn out the cheesecakes. You can store them, covered, in the fridge for up to 2 days.

CHILLED CHEESECAKES
Alternative curds and coulis

To adapt the classic Lime and blueberry chilled cheesecake (see pp212–13) or the variation recipes (opposite), pair them with these vibrant and full-flavoured curds and coulis.

◀ Tangerine curd
Transform the Mini lemon cheesecakes (see opposite) into Mini tangerine cheesecakes. For the topping, use the same quantity of thick-set orange curd instead of the lemon curd, and prepare it as described. You can also replace the lemon juice in the filling with the same quantity of tangerine juice.

▲ Blueberry and vanilla coulis
Simplify the Lime and blueberry version (see pp212–13). Blend 100g (3½oz) fresh blueberries, 1 tbsp icing sugar, and a little water. Strain the coulis, then top the cake and chill as directed. You can also omit the lime juice and zest from the filling – simply add 2 tsp vanilla extract and 2 tbsp water.

◀ Strawberry coulis
Serve the Triple chocolate cheesecake (see opposite) with a strawberry coulis instead of the melted chocolate. Purée 150g (5½oz) strawberries with 1 tbsp each lemon juice and icing sugar. Strain to remove the pips and serve with the chilled cheesecake.

◀ Kiwi and lime coulis
Replace the blueberries in the coulis for the Lime and blueberry cheesecake (see pp212–13) with 1 kiwi, diced into 5mm (¼in) cubes. Briefly simmer the juice of 1 lime, 1 tbsp caster sugar, and 1 tbsp water in a pan until the sugar dissolves. Then add the kiwi, use to top the cheesecake, and chill as directed.

Peach coulis ▶
Replace the blueberries in the coulis for the Lime and blueberry cheesecake (see pp212–13) with 100g (3½oz) stoned and diced ripe peaches. You can also omit the lime zest from the coulis, and add 1 tsp almond extract to the filling instead of the lime zest and juice.

Mango coulis ▲
Use a mango coulis instead of the Lime and blueberry version (see pp212–13). Purée the flesh of 2 ripe mangoes with juice of 1 lemon and 1 tbsp icing sugar until it is completely smooth. Use to top the cheesecake and chill as directed.

 **1 hr 30 mins** plus cooling and chilling   **SERVES 8**

BAKED CHEESECAKE with strawberry sauce

Less delicate than chilled varieties, baked cheesecakes keep for longer in the fridge. The lemon juice and zest gives this velvet-like filling a brightness of flavour. Once you master this classic, you could change the flavourings or sauce, if you prefer.

INGREDIENTS

75g (2½oz) unsalted butter, at room temperature, plus extra for greasing

150g (5½oz) digestive biscuits, crushed into fine crumbs

For the filling

675g (1½lb) cream cheese, at room temperature

150ml (5fl oz) soured cream, at room temperature

150g (5½oz) caster sugar

1 tsp vanilla extract

pinch of fine sea salt

grated zest of ½ lemon

1 tbsp lemon juice

2 eggs

For the sauce

400g (14oz) strawberries, hulled and thinly sliced lengthways

1 tbsp lemon juice

1 tbsp caster sugar

4 tbsp strawberry jam, sieved to remove seeds

SPECIAL EQUIPMENT

20cm (8in) springform cake tin

Preheat the oven to 180°C (350°F/Gas 4). Grease and line the cake tin with greaseproof paper. Melt the butter in a small saucepan over a low heat, then combine it with the biscuit crumbs in a large bowl.

1

Transfer the mixture to the prepared tin. Using the back of a spoon, gently press it into the bottom of the tin to form a thin, even layer. Bake for about 10 minutes, then remove and set aside to cool.

2

3

For the filling, whisk the cream cheese, soured cream, sugar, vanilla extract, salt, and lemon zest and juice until combined. Add the eggs, one at a time, and whisk well to combine.

4

Cover the sides and base of the cake tin with thick foil and place it in a large roasting tin. Pour the filling evenly over the biscuit base. Pour enough boiling water into the roasting tin to come halfway up the sides of the cake tin.

Bake for 1 hour, until the cheesecake is set and shrinking away from the sides. Turn off the heat and leave the cheesecake to cool in the oven for 30 minutes, so that it is less likely to crack as it cools. Leave it to cool completely on a wire rack, before chilling for at least 4 hours.

5

6

For the sauce, combine the strawberries, lemon juice, and sugar in a bowl and leave to macerate for about 30 minutes. Gently heat the jam in a small heavy-based saucepan. Combine it with the strawberry mixture and leave to cool. Remove the cheesecake from the tin and serve with the sauce. You can keep the cheesecake, well wrapped, in the fridge for up to 3 days.

🕐 **1 hr 50 mins**
plus cooling and chilling

🍴 **SERVES 8**

BAKED CHEESECAKE chocolate orange

Dark chocolate biscuits, such as bourbons or Oreos, can replace digestive biscuits to create a rich cheesecake base. The cream cheese and mascarpone filling is perfectly smooth with a distinct orange flavour.

INGREDIENTS

100g (3½oz) unsalted butter, melted and cooled, plus extra for greasing

200g (7oz) Oreo or bourbon biscuits, filling removed and crushed

For the filling

450g (1lb) cream cheese, at room temperature

225g (8oz) mascarpone cheese, at room temperature

100g (3½oz) caster sugar

½ tsp orange extract

4 tbsp freshly squeezed orange juice

grated zest of ½ large orange

2 eggs

For the orange curd

115g (4oz) caster sugar

1 tbsp cornflour

3 egg yolks

75ml (2½fl oz) freshly squeezed orange juice

grated zest of ½ large orange, plus extra for decorating

25g (scant 1oz) unsalted butter, at room temperature, diced

SPECIAL EQUIPMENT

20cm (8in) spring-form cake tin

1 Preheat the oven to 180°C (350°F/Gas 4). Grease and line the cake tin with greaseproof paper. Combine the biscuit crumbs and butter in a bowl. Spread the mixture in the tin in an even layer. Place on a baking sheet and bake for 10 minutes. Remove and set aside to cool.

2 For the filling, pulse all the ingredients, except the eggs, in a food processor until smooth. Transfer to a bowl and add the eggs, one at a time, whisking well after each addition. Cover the sides and base of the cake tin with foil.

3 Place the cake tin in a large roasting tin. Pour the filling over the biscuit crust, in an even layer. Pour just enough boiling water into the roasting tin, so it comes halfway up the sides of the cake tin.

4 Bake the cheesecake for 1 hour, until the filling is just set and shrinking away from the sides. Turn off the heat and leave it to cool in the oven for 30 minutes. Then remove the cheesecake from the oven and leave to cool completely.

5 For the orange curd, combine the sugar and cornflour in a heavy-based saucepan. Whisk in the egg yolks until combined. Then add the orange juice and zest and mix well.

6 Heat the mixture for 8–10 minutes, stirring until thickened. Do not allow it to boil. Remove from the heat and gradually beat in the butter, until the orange curd is thick and glossy. Leave to cool completely.

7 Spread the orange curd over the top of the cheesecake, avoiding the sides. Cover the cake with cling film and chill for 4 hours, before removing from the tin to serve. You can keep it, wrapped, in the fridge for up to 3 days.

CROSTATA di ricotta

🕐 **1 hr**
plus chilling and cooling

🍴 **SERVES 8**

This well-loved Italian dessert combines ricotta and candied peel with a sweet and lemony pastry crust.

INGREDIENTS

175g (6oz) unsalted butter, softened, plus extra for greasing

250g (9oz) plain flour, sifted, plus extra for dusting

grated zest of 1 lemon

50g (1¾oz) caster sugar

4 egg yolks

pinch of salt

1 egg, beaten, to glaze

For the filling

1.25kg (2¾lb) ricotta cheese

100g (3½oz) caster sugar

1 tbsp plain flour

pinch of salt

grated zest of 1 orange

2 tbsp chopped candied orange peel

1 tsp vanilla extract

45g (½oz) sultanas

30g (1oz) flaked almonds

4 egg yolks

SPECIAL EQUIPMENT

23–25cm (9–10in) round springform cake tin

1. Grease the tin and set aside. Place the flour in a bowl. Make a well in the centre and add the butter, lemon zest, sugar, egg yolks, and salt. Mix well. Gradually work in the flour to form a dough. Knead it on a floured surface for 2 minutes until smooth. Shape it into a ball, wrap in cling film, and chill for 30 minutes.

2. On a floured surface, roll out three-quarters of the pastry to a 35–37cm (14–15in) round. Use it to line the tin, pressing it down well. Trim the excess. Chill the pastry case and remaining pastry for 15 minutes.

3. For the filling, beat the ricotta, sugar, flour, and salt in a bowl. Then beat in the remaining ingredients, until combined. Spoon the filling into the pastry case, evenly, and tap the tin lightly to remove air pockets. Brush the edges of the pie with the egg.

4. Preheat the oven to 180°C (350°F/Gas 4). On a floured surface, roll out the remaining pastry to a 25cm (10in) round. Cut it into 1cm (½in) wide strips and use to create a lattice top for the pie. Brush with the remaining egg and chill for 15–30 minutes until firm.

5. Bake the cheesecake on a baking sheet, on the bottom shelf of the oven for 1 hour, until golden. Leave to cool slightly, then remove from the tin. Serve cooled to room temperature. Serve on the same day.

🕐 **50–55 mins**
plus cooling

🍴 **MAKES 4**

BAKED CHEESECAKES tiramisu

Tiramisu flavours work perfectly with a creamy cheesecake filling. Serve these little treats alongside a glass of Amaretto or strong coffee.

INGREDIENTS

50g (1¾oz) digestive biscuits, finely crushed

50g (1¾oz) Amaretti biscuits, finely crushed

50g (1¾oz) unsalted butter, melted and cooled

300g (10oz) ricotta cheese

200g (7oz) full-fat cream cheese

100g (3½oz) caster sugar

2 eggs

1 tsp vanilla extract

1 tbsp Amaretto liqueur

1 tsp instant espresso powder

1 tbsp coffee liqueur

cocoa powder, for dusting

SPECIAL EQUIPMENT

4 x 10cm (4in) round loose-bottomed cake tins

1. Preheat the oven to 180°C (350°F/Gas 4). Line the cake tins with greaseproof paper. Combine both lots of biscuit crumbs and the butter in a bowl. Distribute the mixture equally between the tins, pressing it into thin layers. Bake in the oven for 5 minutes. Remove and set aside to cool.

2. Pulse the ricotta, cream cheese, sugar, eggs, vanilla extract, and Amaretto in a food processor until smooth. Dissolve the espresso powder in 1 tablespoon of boiling water. Stir in the coffee liqueur and cool slightly. Then combine with 3 tablespoons of the cheese mixture.

3. Place the tins on a baking sheet. Divide the filling between them and drizzle over the coffee mixture. Bake in the oven for 25–30 minutes, until the filling is just set and shrinking away from the sides.

4. Turn off the heat and leave them in the oven to cool for 30 minutes. Then remove and cool completely, before chilling for 4 hours or overnight. Remove the cakes from the tins and serve dusted with cocoa powder. You can keep them, wrapped, in the fridge for up to 3 days.

1 hr 10 mins
plus cooling

SERVES 8–10

SPONGE vanilla and strawberry

In this recipe, the egg yolks and whites are whisked separately to give you the perfect sponge cake: light, airy, and well-risen. The combination of whipped cream and strawberries makes this a classic summer dessert.

INGREDIENTS

45g (1½oz) unsalted butter, melted, plus extra for greasing

125g (4½oz) plain flour

¾ tsp baking powder

¼ tsp salt

2 tbsp cornflour

6 large eggs, separated

1 tsp cream of tartar

200g (7oz) caster sugar

1½ tsp vanilla extract

3 tbsp whole milk, at room temperature

For the filling

150ml (5fl oz) double cream

1 tsp icing sugar

200g (7oz) strawberries, hulled and halved

For the frosting

350ml (12fl oz) whipping cream

3 tbsp icing sugar

½ tsp vanilla extract

SPECIAL EQUIPMENT

2 x 20cm (8in) cake tins

PLAN AHEAD

You can store the unfilled sponge cakes in an airtight container 2-3 days ahead.

1

Preheat the oven to 180°C (350°F/Gas 4). Lightly grease and line the cake tins with baking parchment. Sift the flour, baking powder, salt, and cornflour into a small bowl and set aside.

2

Whisk the egg whites in a large bowl, until light and foamy. Whisk in the cream of tartar until soft peaks form, then add half of the sugar. Beat the mixture well to form stiff peaks.

3

Gradually fold in the flour mixture until incorporated.

In a separate bowl, beat the egg yolks and remaining sugar for 4–5 minutes until thick and pale yellow. Add the vanilla extract, butter, and milk, and mix well. Then fold in the flour mixture, until combined.

4

Add the egg white mixture a little at a time.

Fold in the egg white mixture, until combined. Divide the batter evenly between the tins. Bake for 20–25 minutes, until the cakes are golden and an inserted toothpick comes out clean. Cool in the tin for 10 minutes, then leave on a wire rack to cool completely.

5

For the filling, beat the double cream and icing sugar in a bowl to form stiff peaks. Roughly chop half the strawberries and fold into the cream and sugar mixture.

6

Spread the filling on one of the cakes and top with the other. For the frosting, whisk the whipping cream, icing sugar, and vanilla extract to form stiff peaks and spread over the cake. Top with the remaining strawberries and serve. You can store the cake in the fridge for 1–2 days.

🕐 **1 hr 30 mins**
plus chilling

🍴 **SERVES 12**

TRES LECHES with cherries

The name for this cake translates from Spanish into "three-milk cake". It is popular throughout South America. To achieve the delicately moist texture and sweet flavour, soak the sponge in a sauce made from cream, condensed milk, and evaporated milk.

INGREDIENTS

unsalted butter, for greasing

150g (5½oz) plain flour, plus extra for dusting

6 large eggs, separated

¼ tsp cream of tartar

250g (9oz) caster sugar

75ml (2½fl oz) whole milk

1½ tsp vanilla extract

1¾ tsp baking powder

¼ tsp salt

12 Maraschino cherries

For the tres leches

240ml (8fl oz) double cream

200ml (7fl oz) condensed milk

120ml (4fl oz) evaporated milk

1 tsp vanilla extract

For the frosting

350ml (12fl oz) double cream

3 tbsp icing sugar

½ tsp pure vanilla extract

SPECIAL EQUIPMENT

23 x 33cm (9 x 13in) cake tin

1 Preheat the oven to 180°C (350°F/Gas 4). Grease and flour the cake tin. Whisk the egg whites in a large bowl until fluffy. Add the cream of tartar and whisk to form soft peaks. Gradually add 50g (1¾oz) of the caster sugar and whisk to form stiff peaks. Set aside.

2 Whisk the egg yolks and remaining sugar in a large bowl until thick and pale yellow in colour. Add the milk and vanilla extract and whisk until smooth. Place the flour, baking powder, and salt in a separate bowl and mix well to combine.

3 Add the dry ingredients to the egg yolk mixture, gradually, and whisk until smooth. Then fold in the egg white mixture, a little at a time, until combined. Pour the batter into the tin and smooth over the top.

4 Bake for 30–35 minutes. Remove and cool the cake in the tin for 5 minutes, before leaving to cool completely on a wire rack. For the tres leches, combine all the ingredients in a bowl.

5 Place the cooled cake on a serving dish and pierce it in several places with a skewer, making sure it goes all the way through. Pour the tres leches over the top and sides of the cake. Cover with cling film and chill for 3 hours, until the liquid has been absorbed.

6 For the frosting, whisk all the ingredients to form stiff peaks and spread over the cake. Slice the cake into 12 even-sized pieces, top each with a Maraschino cherry, and serve chilled. You can store the cake in an airtight container in the fridge for 4 days.

55 mins
plus cooling

SERVES 8-10

SPONGE Victoria

Give the traditional British cake a fresh spin with this cream–raspberry filling – lovely to serve in the summer months.

INGREDIENTS

225g (8oz) unsalted butter, plus extra for greasing

250g (9oz) caster sugar

4 large eggs, at room temperature

1½ tsp pure vanilla extract

4 tbsp whole milk

225g (8oz) self-raising flour

½ tsp salt

175g (6oz) raspberries, halved

For the filling

225g (8oz) mascarpone cheese, at room temperature

200ml (7fl oz) double cream

30g (1oz) icing sugar, plus extra for dusting

½ tsp vanilla extract

SPECIAL EQUIPMENT

2 x 23cm (9in) round cake tins

PLAN AHEAD

You can store the unfilled sponge cakes in an airtight container 2-3 days ahead.

1 Preheat the oven to 180°C (350°F/Gas 4). Grease and line the tins with baking parchment. Place the butter and caster sugar in a large bowl and whisk well with a hand-held whisk until light and fluffy. Add the eggs, one at a time, whisking well after each addition.

2 Add the vanilla extract and milk, and whisk until evenly combined. Sift the flour and salt into a bowl and add to the wet mixture, a little at a time, whisking until just combined. Do not overmix.

3 Divide the batter evenly between the cake tins and smooth over the tops with a spatula. Bake for 20–25 minutes, until a skewer inserted into the centre of the cakes comes out clean. Leave the cakes to cool in the tins for 10 minutes, then remove and place on a wire rack to cool completely.

4 For the filling, place all the ingredients in a large bowl and beat well to form stiff peaks. Spread the filling on one of the cakes and top with a layer of the raspberries. Cover it with the second cake, dust with icing sugar, and serve. You can store the cake in the fridge for 1-2 days.

1 hr
plus cooling

SERVES 8

SPONGE angel food

The name "angel food cake" comes from the airy texture of the bake – so light, it is suitable for angels. There is no fat in the recipe, so it does not keep. Serve on the same day.

INGREDIENTS

125g (4½oz) plain flour

2 tbsp cornflour

¼ tsp salt

300g (10oz) caster sugar

11 egg whites, at room temperature

1½ tsp cream of tartar

1½ tsp vanilla extract

1 tsp lemon juice

175g (6oz) blueberries, to serve

icing sugar, for dusting

SPECIAL EQUIPMENT

25cm (10in) tube cake tin

1 Preheat the oven to 180°C (350°F/Gas 4). Sift the flour, cornflour, salt, and half the caster sugar into a bowl. Set aside. Place the egg whites in a separate bowl and whisk with a hand-held whisk until foamy. Add the cream of tartar, and whisk again to form soft peaks.

2 Gradually add the remaining caster sugar and whisk until the mixture is combined and forms soft peaks. Fold in the vanilla extract and lemon juice with a spatula until just combined. Gradually sift the flour mixture over and fold it in gently until just combined. Do not overmix.

3 Pour the batter into the tin and smooth over the top. Tap the tin on a work surface a few times, to release any air bubbles. Bake the cake for 30–35 minutes, until golden and firm to the touch. Invert the tin over a serving plate, and leave to cool for 2–3 hours.

4 Run a knife around the cake edge to help to remove it from the tin. Place the cake, bottom-side up, on a large plate. Scatter over the blueberries, and dust with icing sugar. Serve on the same day.

 **45 mins**
plus cooling and macerating

MAKES 4

SHORTCAKES strawberry

This recipe is a classic American one, beloved throughout the country. The texture resembles an English scone. These shortcakes are large – in true American style – but they are so delicious that they will quickly disappear.

INGREDIENTS
75g (2½oz) unsalted butter, chilled and diced, plus extra for greasing

250g (9oz) plain flour, plus extra for dusting

2 tsp baking powder

60g (2oz) caster sugar

pinch of salt

1 egg, beaten

150ml (5fl oz) buttermilk

icing sugar, for dusting

For the filling
150g (5½oz) strawberries, hulled and thinly sliced

1 tbsp caster sugar

150ml (5fl oz) double cream

1 tsp vanilla extract

SPECIAL EQUIPMENT
7.5cm (3in) round pastry cutter

1. Preheat the oven to 200°C (400°F/Gas 6). Grease and line a baking sheet with baking parchment. Combine the flour, baking powder, caster sugar, and salt in a large bowl. Rub in the butter until the mixture resembles coarse breadcrumbs.

2. Whisk the beaten egg and buttermilk in a separate bowl and pour into the dry mixture. Using your fingertips, bring the mixture together to form a soft, loose dough.

3. On a floured surface, roll out the dough to a large circle, 2cm (¾in) thick. Cut out 4 rounds with the pastry cutter and place on the baking sheet. Bake on the top shelf of the oven for 15 minutes, until risen. Remove and place on a wire rack to cool completely.

For the filling, combine the strawberries and caster sugar in a bowl and leave to macerate for 1 hour. Whisk the cream and vanilla extract in a bowl to form stiff peaks. Split the shortcakes and sandwich with the cream and the strawberries. Dust with icing sugar, and serve immediately.

1 hr plus cooling   **SERVES 4–6**

SHORTCAKE roasted peach

Play around with proportions and serve an over-sized peach shortcake. Shortcakes – like scones – are incredibly easy to make, but should be served straight away, or within a few hours of cooling.

INGREDIENTS

2 peaches, stoned and cut into thin wedges

30g (1oz) unsalted butter, chilled and diced

30g (1oz) soft light brown sugar

For the shortcake

250g (9oz) plain flour, plus extra for dusting

2 tsp baking powder

60g (2oz) caster sugar

pinch of salt

75g (2½oz) unsalted butter, chilled and diced

1 egg, beaten

150ml (5fl oz) buttermilk

For the filling

150ml (5fl oz) double cream

1 tsp vanilla extract

icing sugar, to serve

PLAN AHEAD

You can store the roasted peaches in an airtight container in the fridge up to 3 days ahead. Bring to room temperature before serving with the shortcake.

1 Preheat the oven to 200°C (400°F/Gas 6). Arrange the peaches in an ovenproof dish large enough to hold them in a single layer. Dot with the butter and sprinkle over the brown sugar.

2 Bake the peaches on the top shelf of the oven for 10–15 minutes, until just soft when pierced with a knife. Remove from the oven and leave to cool.

3 For the shortcake, combine the flour, baking powder, caster sugar, and salt in a large bowl. Rub in the butter until the mixture resembles breadcrumbs.

4 Whisk the egg and buttermilk in a separate bowl, and add to the dry mixture. Use your fingertips to bring them together to form a soft, loose dough.

5 Gently roll out the dough on a lightly floured work surface to a 15cm (6in) circle, about 2cm (¾in) thick. Place on a baking sheet.

6 Bake on the top shelf of the oven for 20–25 minutes, until well risen and lightly coloured. Remove from the heat. Cool completely on a wire rack, then use a knife to split the shortcake in half.

7 For the filling, whisk the cream and vanilla extract in a bowl to form soft peaks. Sandwich the shortcake with the filling and peaches, and pour over a little cooking liquid. Serve dusted with icing sugar.

⏱ **45 mins**
plus cooling and chilling

🍴 **MAKES 6**

SHORTCAKE SANDWICHES
ice cream

For a playful take on the classic, speckle your shortcakes with fresh strawberries and sandwich them with ice cream.

INGREDIENTS

115g (4oz) unsalted butter, softened

175g (6oz) caster sugar, plus extra for dusting

½ tsp vanilla extract

1 egg yolk

200g (7oz) plain flour

½ tsp baking powder

100g (3½oz) strawberries, hulled and diced

175g (6oz) good-quality vanilla ice cream

PLAN AHEAD

You can store the unfilled shortcake cookies in an airtight container up to 1 day ahead.

1 Preheat oven to 180°C (350°F/Gas 4). Line two baking sheets with greaseproof paper and set aside. Use a hand-held whisk to whisk the butter and sugar in a large bowl, until light and fluffy.

2 Whisk in the vanilla extract and egg yolk. Sift the flour and baking powder into the mixture, and whisk to combine. Add the strawberries, and mix well. Shape the dough into 12 equal-sized balls, rolling them briefly between your hands.

3 Flatten the balls slightly, and place on the baking sheets. Sprinkle with the sugar. Bake for 15–18 minutes, until the shortcakes are risen and lightly golden at the edges. Remove and leave to cool on the sheet for 10 minutes, then place on a wire rack to cool completely.

4 To assemble the sandwiches, leave the ice cream to soften at room temperature for a few minutes. Then sandwich two of the shortcake cookies with a spoonful of the softened ice cream. Place in the freezer for 5–10 minutes before serving.

⏱ **20 mins**
plus chilling and cooling

🍴 **MAKES 4**

SHORTCAKES stacked strawberry

This elegant dessert looks wonderful served with a little fruit coulis (see p215). Chilling the stacks in the fridge helps to soften the layers of buttery biscuits.

INGREDIENTS

85g (3oz) unsalted butter, softened

140g (5oz) caster sugar

1 egg yolk

½ tsp vanilla extract

175g (6oz) plain flour, plus extra for dusting

For the filling

250ml (9fl oz) double cream

1 tbsp icing sugar, plus extra for dusting

250g (9oz) strawberries, hulled and thinly sliced

SPECIAL EQUIPMENT

8cm (3¼in) cookie cutter

4 x 8cm (3¼in) pastry rings

PLAN AHEAD

You can store the unfilled shortcake biscuits in an airtight container up to 3 days ahead.

1 Whisk the butter and caster sugar in a bowl until light and fluffy. Whisk in the egg yolk and vanilla extract. Add the flour, and add 2 tablespoons cold water, and bring together to form a soft, loose dough. Cover in cling film and chill for 30 minutes.

2 Preheat the oven to 180°C (350°F/Gas 4) and line three baking sheets with baking parchment. On a floured surface, roll out the dough thinly. Use the cookie cutter to cut out 16 circles and place them on a baking sheet. Bake for 10 minutes, until the edges begin to colour.

3 Remove from the heat and cool completely on a wire rack. Then place one shortcake biscuit in each pastry ring on a lined baking sheet. For the filling, whisk the cream and icing sugar in a bowl to form stiff peaks.

4 Spread a spoonful of the cream over each shortcake biscuit to make a 5mm (¼in) thick layer. Cover with a layer of the strawberries. Repeat to add two more layers each of the shortcake biscuits, cream, and strawberries. Add another layer of cream and top with a shortcake.

5 Cover with cling film and chill for at least 6 hours, or overnight. Then carefully remove the pastry rings and dust the shortcake stacks with icing sugar to serve. You can store the stacked dessert, covered in cling film, in the fridge for up to 1 day.

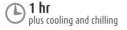

🕐 **1 hr**
plus cooling and chilling

🍴 **SERVES 8–10**

CAKE devil's food

This rich cake is dark and moist, with the espresso powder adding an extra layer of flavour to the chocolate sponge. You could serve devil's food cake with a bowl of whipped cream, sweetened with a little icing sugar and a drop of vanilla extract.

INGREDIENTS

240ml (8fl oz) vegetable or grapeseed oil, plus extra for greasing

1 tsp instant espresso powder

75g (2½oz) natural cocoa powder

2 large eggs, plus 1 yolk, lightly beaten

100g (3½oz) caster sugar

200g (7oz) dark brown sugar

1 tsp vanilla extract

250g (9oz) plain flour

1 tsp salt

1½ tsp bicarbonate of soda

½ tsp baking powder

230ml (8fl oz) soured cream, at room temperature

For the icing

400ml (14fl oz) double cream

¼ tsp salt

350g (12oz) good-quality dark chocolate, finely chopped

3 tbsp unsalted butter, softened

1 tsp vanilla extract

SPECIAL EQUIPMENT

2 x 20cm (8in) round cake tins

PLAN AHEAD

You can store the unglazed cake, wrapped in cling film, up to 2 days ahead.

1

Preheat the oven to 180°C (350°F/Gas 4). Lightly grease and line the cake tins with baking parchment. Place the espresso powder and cocoa powder in a small bowl. Pour over 240ml (8fl oz) hot water, mix well, and leave to cool.

2

In a large bowl, whisk the oil, eggs, egg yolk, and both lots of sugar until smooth. Add the vanilla extract and whisk well to combine. In a separate bowl, sift together the flour, salt, bicarbonate of soda, and baking powder. Mix well.

3

Gradually add the dry ingredients and soured cream to the wet mixture, alternately, and combine well. Add the espresso mixture, and stir lightly until incorporated.

Keep stirring until the mixture is smooth and without streaks.

4

Divide the batter evenly between the cake tins. Bake the cakes for 35–40 minutes, until an inserted skewer comes out clean. Remove and cool the cakes in the tins for 15 minutes. Then transfer to a wire rack to cool completely.

5

Whisk the frosting until smooth, before chilling.

For the icing, bring the double cream to a simmer over a medium-low heat. Place it in a large bowl. Whisk in the salt and chocolate, then stir in the butter and vanilla extract. Cover and chill for 2 hours, stirring occasionally, until thick.

6

Beat the chilled icing for 1 minute, until light and fluffy. Sandwich the cakes with a generous amount of the frosting. Then cover the top and sides with the remaining icing, and serve. You can keep the cake in an airtight container in the fridge for 2–3 days.

🕐 **55 mins**
plus cooling

🍴 **SERVES 8–10**

CAKE German chocolate

Everything about this American classic is rich and decadent. With its triple-layered sponge and fantastic frosting, the cake makes a perfect centrepiece to a dessert table.

INGREDIENTS

175g (6oz) unsalted butter, softened and diced, plus extra for greasing

115g (4oz) good-quality very dark chocolate

200g (7oz) caster sugar

200g (7oz) dark brown sugar

4 large eggs, lightly beaten

1½ tsp vanilla extract

300ml (10fl oz) buttermilk

250g (9oz) plain flour

1¼ tsp baking powder

¾ tsp bicarbonate of soda

1 tsp salt

For the icing

180ml (6fl oz) whole milk

140g (5oz) light brown sugar

⅛ tsp salt

2 large egg yolks, lightly beaten

1 tsp vanilla extract

85g (3oz) unsalted butter, diced

175g (6oz) desiccated coconut

85g (3oz) walnuts, chopped

SPECIAL EQUIPMENT

3 x 20cm (8in) cake tins

PLAN AHEAD

You can store the unglazed cakes, wrapped in cling film, 1–2 days ahead.

1 Preheat the oven to 180°C (350°F/Gas 4). Grease and line the tins with baking parchment. Melt the chocolate in a heatproof bowl over a saucepan of simmering water, making sure it does not touch the water. Remove and cool to room temperature.

2 Beat the butter and both lots of sugar in a large bowl, until light and fluffy. Gradually beat in the eggs until combined. Then beat in the vanilla extract until smooth. Add the chocolate and combine well, scraping down the sides of the bowl.

3 Mix the buttermilk with 60ml (2fl oz) lukewarm water. Sift the flour, baking powder, bicarbonate of soda, and salt into a bowl. Gradually add the dry mixture and buttermilk mixture alternately to the chocolate batter. Mix until combined and smooth.

4 Divide the batter evenly between the cake tins and bake for 30–35 minutes, until an inserted toothpick comes out clean. Cool the cakes in the tins for 10–15 minutes. Then transfer to a wire rack to cool completely.

5 For the icing, place the milk, brown sugar, salt, egg yolks, vanilla extract, and butter in a large saucepan over a medium heat. Whisk until smooth and bring to the boil. Reduce the heat to a simmer, cooking for a further 5–6 minutes, until thickened.

6 Remove from the heat, add the coconut and walnuts, and mix well. Cool to room temperature, and sandwich the cakes with two-thirds of the icing. Top the cake with the remaining icing, and serve. You can store the cake in an airtight container for 3–4 days.

🕐 **1 hr 15 mins** plus cooling 🍴 **SERVES 6–8**

GÂTEAU black forest

The name "black forest" comes from the use of Kirsch, a liqueur that originated in the Black Forest region, Germany.

INGREDIENTS

3 tbsp unsalted butter, melted, plus extra for greasing

6 large eggs, separated

225g (8oz) caster sugar

1½ tsp vanilla extract

3 tbsp whole milk, at room temperature

85g (3oz) plain flour

¾ tsp baking powder

2 tbsp cornflour

¼ tsp salt

6 tbsp natural cocoa powder

1 tsp cream of tartar

For the filling

5 tbsp cherry juice

2½ tbsp Kirsch

pinch of salt

3½ tbsp caster sugar

400g (14½oz) tart cherries, pitted

225g (8oz) mascarpone cheese, at room temperature

350ml (12fl oz) double cream

¼ tsp vanilla extract

45g (1½oz) grated chocolate, to decorate

SPECIAL EQUIPMENT

23cm (9in) springform cake tin

PLAN AHEAD

You can store the unglazed cake, wrapped in cling film, up to 1 day ahead.

1 Preheat the oven to 180°C (350°F/Gas 4). Grease and line the tin with baking parchment. Set aside. Beat the egg yolks and half the sugar in a bowl, until thick and pale. Then beat in the vanilla extract, butter, and milk until combined.

2 Sift the flour, baking powder, cornflour, salt, and cocoa powder into a bowl. Gradually fold in the egg yolk mixture and set aside. In a separate bowl, beat the egg whites until foamy. Beat in the cream of tartar to form soft peaks, then gradually beat in the remaining sugar to form stiff peaks.

3 Gradually fold the egg white mixture into the batter, until just combined. Then pour it into the tin, bake for 40–45 minutes, and leave to cool (see German chocolate cake, step 4). Use a long, serrated knife to slice the cake into two.

4 For the filling, heat the cherry juice, Kirsch, salt, and 1½ tablespoons of the sugar in a saucepan over a medium-low heat. Stir until the sugar has dissolved. Add the cherries and stir to coat. Remove the cherries from the pan, reserving the syrup, and place them in a bowl. Leave to cool.

5 Beat the mascarpone in a bowl until smooth. Gradually add the cream and beat well to combine. Then gradually add the vanilla extract and remaining sugar and beat to form soft peaks.

6 Place one of the cakes on a serving dish and brush generously with the cherry syrup. Spread over half of the cream mixture and top with two-thirds of the cherries. Sprinkle with half of the chocolate shavings.

7 Top with the second cake and brush with the syrup. Top with the remaining cream, grated chocolate, and cherries, and serve. You can store the cake, covered in the fridge, for 2–3 days.

🕐 **50 mins** plus cooling 🍴 **SERVES 8–10**

CAKE red velvet

This vividly coloured cake is light and fluffy, thanks to the buttermilk in the sponge layers.

INGREDIENTS

240ml (8fl oz) vegetable oil, plus extra for greasing

250g (9oz) plain flour

2 tbsp natural cocoa powder

1 tsp salt

1 tsp bicarbonate of soda

2 large eggs, plus one yolk, lightly beaten

300g (10oz) caster sugar

300ml (10fl oz) buttermilk

1½ tsp vanilla extract

1 tsp apple cider vinegar

2–3 tsp red food colouring paste

For the icing

350g (12oz) cream cheese

85g (3oz) unsalted butter, room temperature

¾ tsp vanilla extract

pinch of salt

350g (12oz) icing sugar

SPECIAL EQUIPMENT

2 x 20cm (8in) cake tins

PLAN AHEAD

You can store the unglazed cake, wrapped in cling film, for 1–2 days ahead.

1 Preheat the oven to 180°C (350°F/Gas 4). Grease and line the cake tins with baking parchment. Combine the flour, cocoa powder, salt, and bicarbonate of soda in a bowl. In a separate bowl, whisk the oil, eggs and yolk, sugar, buttermilk, vanilla extract, cider vinegar, and food colouring paste until well combined.

2 Gradually fold the dry mixture into the wet mixture, until smooth and combined. Divide the batter between the tins. Bake the cake and leave to cool (see German chocolate cake, step 4). For the icing, beat together all the ingredients in a bowl until well combined.

3 Spread the icing generously over one cake, then cover with the second cake, rounded side up. Use the remaining icing to cover the top and sides, and serve. You can store the cake in an airtight container for 3–4 days.

 **1 hr 30 mins** plus cooling **SERVES 8-10**

CARROT CAKE with cream cheese icing

Adding grated carrots to a cake batter makes it moist and sweet. Their flavour is not discernible once the cake is cooked, but they impart a moist texture. Walnuts add extra crunch, while the icing gives it a rich, creamy finish.

INGREDIENTS

300ml (10fl oz) sunflower oil, plus extra for greasing
300g (10oz) self-raising flour, sifted
1 tsp ground cinnamon
½ tsp ground ginger
¼ tsp grated nutmeg
300g (10oz) caster sugar
4 eggs
250g (9oz) grated carrots, squeezed to remove excess moisture
75g (2½oz) walnuts, roughly chopped

For the icing
100g (3½oz) unsalted butter, softened
100g (3½oz) cream cheese, at room temperature
400g (14oz) icing sugar
grated zest of 1 large orange, plus extra to decorate

SPECIAL EQUIPMENT
2 x 23cm (9in) cake tins

PLAN AHEAD
You can store the unglazed cakes in an airtight container up to 5 days ahead.

Preheat the oven to 180°C (350°F/Gas 4). Grease and line the tins with baking parchment. Combine the flour, spices, and caster sugar in a bowl. Beat the eggs and oil in a jug and add to the dry ingredients. Then add the carrots and walnuts and stir well to form a stiff batter.

1

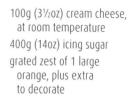

Divide the batter equally between the tins. Bake for 45–50 minutes, until the cakes are golden brown and an inserted toothpick comes out clean. Cool in the tins on a wire rack for 10 minutes. Then turn them out and place on a wire rack to cool completely.

The icing should be smooth and fluffy.

For the icing, whisk the butter and cream cheese in a bowl until smooth. Gradually whisk in the icing sugar, until combined. Then add the orange zest and whisk well.

3

Sandwich the cakes with one-third of the icing. Use the remaining icing to cover the top and sides of the cake. Sprinkle over a little orange zest and serve. You can store the cake in an airtight container for up to 5 days.

4

🕐 **1 hr 5 mins** plus cooling 🍴 **SERVES 8** 🌡 Also great **HOT**

CAKE courgette and hazelnut

Healthier than carrot cake, this recipe is perfect for when courgettes are in season. The cake is also delicious warm.

INGREDIENTS
225ml (7¾fl oz) sunflower oil, plus extra for greasing
100g (3½oz) hazelnuts
3 large eggs
1 tsp vanilla extract
225g (8oz) caster sugar
200g (7oz) grated courgettes, squeezed to remove excess moisture
200g (7oz) self-raising flour
75g (2½oz) wholemeal self-raising flour
pinch of salt
1 tsp ground cinnamon
finely grated zest of 1 lemon
icing sugar, for dusting

SPECIAL EQUIPMENT
23cm (9in) springform cake tin

1 Preheat the oven to 180°C (350°F/Gas 4). Grease the tin, line with baking parchment, and set aside. Spread the hazelnuts on a baking sheet and bake for 5 minutes, until lightly browned. Remove from the heat, and rub them with a clean kitchen towel to remove any excess skin. Roughly chop them and set aside.

2 Whisk the oil, eggs, vanilla extract, and caster sugar in a large bowl until light and smooth. Fold in the courgettes and hazelnuts until combined. Then sift over the flour, tipping any bran left in the sieve. Add the remaining ingredients and fold well to combine.

3 Pour the batter into the tin and bake for 45 minutes, until well risen and springy to the touch. Remove from the heat and cool in the tin for 10 minutes, then turn it out and place on a wire rack to cool completely. Serve dusted with icing sugar. You can keep the cake in an airtight container for up to 3 days.

🕐 **45 mins** plus cooling and setting 🍴 **SERVES 8**

CAKE beetroot and chocolate

Adding puréed beetroot to chocolate cake gives it a deep and earthy flavour and an extra moist crumb.

INGREDIENTS
180ml (6fl oz) sunflower oil, plus extra for greasing
200g (7oz) cooked and peeled beetroot
2 eggs
200g (7oz) caster sugar
175g (6oz) plain flour
1 tsp baking powder
15g (½oz) cocoa powder
1 tbsp freeze-dried raspberry pieces

For the ganache
90ml (3fl oz) double cream
115g (4oz) dark chocolate, finely chopped

SPECIAL EQUIPMENT
23cm (9in) springform cake tin

PLAN AHEAD
You can store the unglazed cake in an airtight container up to 3 days ahead.

1 Preheat the oven to 180°C (350°F/Gas 4). Grease the tin, line with baking parchment, and set aside. Pulse the beetroot in a food processor to form a smooth purée, scraping down the sides if needed. In a large bowl, whisk the eggs, oil, and sugar until combined.

2 Sift the flour, baking powder, and cocoa powder into the egg mixture until combined. Then fold in the beetroot purée and combine well. Pour the batter into the tin and bake for 30–35 minutes, until it is well risen and an inserted toothpick comes out clean.

3 Remove from the heat and leave to cool in the tin for 10 minutes. Then turn it out and place on a wire rack to cool completely. For the ganache, heat the cream in a small, heavy-based saucepan until steaming.

4 Remove from the heat, add the chocolate, and stir well to melt and combine. Leave to cool and thicken. Then pour it over the cake and smooth it out with a palette knife. Sprinkle over the raspberries and leave to set at room temperature before serving.

CAKES honey spice

⏱ **55 mins** plus cooling   🍴 **MAKES 6**   🌡 Also great **HOT**

These spiced cakes are served with a delicately flavoured orange and cardamom cream. They are wonderful served fresh from the oven.

INGREDIENTS

75g (2½oz) unsalted butter, plus extra for greasing

75g (2½oz) runny honey

30g (1oz) soft dark brown sugar

100g (3½oz) plain flour

1 tsp baking powder

½ tsp ground cinnamon

½ tsp ground ginger

⅛ tsp grated nutmeg

⅛ tsp ground cloves

grated zest of 1 orange

1 egg

For the cream

100ml (3½fl oz) whipping cream or double cream

1 tbsp icing sugar, plus extra for dusting

grated zest of 1 orange

pinch of ground cardamom

SPECIAL EQUIPMENT

6 x 120ml (4fl oz) muffin tins

PLAN AHEAD

You can prepare and store the orange cream, covered in the fridge, up to 1 day ahead.

1 Preheat the oven to 180°C (350°F/Gas 4). Grease the muffin tins and set aside. Melt the honey, butter, and brown sugar in a large saucepan over a medium heat, stirring frequently, until the sugar dissolves. Transfer to a heatproof jug and leave to cool.

2 Sift the flour, baking powder, and spices into a large bowl. Stir in the orange zest and make a well in the centre. Beat the egg into the cooled honey mixture. Add the liquid mixture to the dry mixture, gently folding them together to make a smooth batter.

3 Pour the batter into the prepared muffin tins, making sure they are only three-quarters full. Bake the cakes for 30 minutes, until well risen and golden brown. Remove from the heat and leave to cool slightly before turning them out.

4 For the cream, whisk the cream, icing sugar, and zest in a bowl to form soft peaks. Then add the cardamom, a little at a time, to taste. Dust the cakes with icing sugar and serve immediately with the cream. Best served on the same day.

50 mins–1 hr
plus cooling

SERVES 10

BUNDT CAKE vanilla

This ring-shaped cake originated in northern Germany and is now popular all over the world. It is traditionally a simply flavoured cake that is dusted with icing sugar or drizzled with icing before serving.

INGREDIENTS

225g (8oz) butter, plus extra for greasing

350g (12oz) plain flour, plus extra for dusting

2 tsp baking powder

1 tsp salt

200g (7oz) caster sugar

150g (5½oz) light brown sugar

3 large eggs, plus one yolk, lightly beaten

1 tbsp vanilla extract

200ml (7fl oz) whole milk

raspberries, to serve (optional)

For the icing

3–4 tbsp double cream

225g (8oz) icing sugar

¼ tsp vanilla extract

SPECIAL EQUIPMENT

25cm (10in) bundt tin

PLAN AHEAD

You can store the cooled unglazed cake, wrapped in cling film, up to 1 day ahead.

1

Preheat the oven to 180°C (350°F/Gas 4). Lightly grease and flour the bundt tin, tapping out any excess flour. Set aside. Sift the flour and baking powder into a bowl. Add the salt, mix well, and set aside.

2

Whisk the butter and both lots of sugar in a large bowl with a hand-held whisk for 3–4 minutes, until light and fluffy. Add half of the beaten eggs, and whisk until well combined.

3

Whisk in the remaining beaten eggs, until well combined. Beat in the vanilla extract until smooth. Scrape down the sides of the bowl as needed.

4

Add the flour and milk, a little at a time, and whisk the mixture until well combined and smooth. Scrape down the sides of the bowl and pour the batter into the tin.

5

Bake for 40–50 minutes, rotating the tin at the halfway mark, until golden. Transfer to a wire rack and cool for 1 hour, before removing the cake from the tin.

Insert a skewer into the baked cake – it should come out clean.

6

For the icing, place the double cream in a bowl. Whisk in the icing sugar and vanilla extract, gradually, until thick. Pour it over the cake. Serve with raspberries, if desired.

Drizzle spoonfuls of the icing over the cake, allowing it to run down the sides.

🕐 **1 hr 30 mins**
plus cooling

🍴 **SERVES 10**

BUNDT CAKE lemon and blueberry

Lemon and blueberry are a classic flavour pairing – sweet and sharp at the same time. Toss the berries in plain flour before you fold them into the batter – this stops them from sinking to the bottom of the cake.

INGREDIENTS

225g (8oz) unsalted butter, plus extra for greasing

375g (13oz) plain flour, plus 2-3 tbsp extra, for dusting

350g (12oz) caster sugar

3 large eggs, lightly beaten

1½ tsp vanilla extract

1 tbsp grated lemon zest, plus extra to serve

2¾ tsp baking powder

1 tsp salt

200ml (7fl oz) buttermilk, at room temperature

250g (9oz) blueberries, plus extra to serve

For the glaze

225g (8oz) icing sugar

1 tbsp lemon juice

pinch of salt

2 tbsp milk

SPECIAL EQUIPMENT

25cm (10in) bundt tin

PLAN AHEAD

You can store the cooled unglazed cake, wrapped in cling film, up to 1 day ahead.

1 Preheat the oven to 180°C (350°F/Gas 4). Lightly grease and flour the bundt tin, tapping out excess flour. Whisk the butter and caster sugar in a bowl until light and fluffy. Gradually whisk in the eggs until combined.

2 Whisk the vanilla extract and lemon zest into the butter mixture until smooth. Combine the flour, baking powder, and salt in a separate bowl. Gradually add the flour mixture and buttermilk to the butter mixture alternately, whisking to combine.

3 Toss the blueberries in 2-3 tablespoons of flour and gently fold into the batter. Scrape down the sides of the bowl, and mix well.

4 Pour the batter into the prepared tin and bake for 50-60 minutes, rotating the tin at the halfway mark, until golden. Insert a skewer into the baked cake - it should come out clean. Cool on a wire rack for 1 hour, before removing the cake from the tin.

5 For the glaze, whisk the icing sugar, lemon juice, and salt in a bowl until combined. Gradually add the milk, whisking until smooth, and pour over the cake. Sprinkle the cake with lemon zest and serve immediately, with a handful of blueberries. You can store the cake in an airtight container for up to 3 days.

BUNDT CAKE lemon and poppyseed

Poppy seeds add a lovely crunch to this tangy cake. Grease and flour the tin well, as it helps you to turn the cake out.

INGREDIENTS
225g (8oz) unsalted butter, plus extra for greasing

375g (13oz) plain flour, plus extra for dusting

450g (1lb) caster sugar

5 large eggs, lightly beaten

1 tsp vanilla extract

1 heaped tbsp grated lemon zest

1¾ tsp baking powder

½ tsp bicarbonate of soda

1 tsp salt

60ml (2fl oz) lemon juice

240ml (8fl oz) yogurt

1 tablespoon poppy seeds

For the glaze
225g (8oz) icing sugar

pinch of salt

60g (2oz) softened cream cheese

1 tbsp butter

3 tbsp milk

SPECIAL EQUIPMENT
25cm (10in) bundt tin

PLAN AHEAD
You can store the cooled unglazed cake, wrapped in cling film, up to 1 day ahead.

1 Preheat the oven and prepare the bundt tin (see Lemon and blueberry bundt cake, step 1). Whisk the butter and caster sugar in a bowl until light and fluffy. Gradually whisk in the eggs until combined. Add the vanilla extract and lemon zest, whisking until smooth.

2 Place the flour, baking powder, bicarbonate of soda, and salt in a bowl. In a separate bowl, combine the lemon juice and yogurt. Gradually whisk both mixtures into the butter mixture, alternately, until well combined.

3 Fold in the poppy seeds, mix well, then pour into the prepared tin. Bake for 50–55 minutes, rotating the tin at the halfway mark, until golden. Test for doneness (see Lemon and blueberry bundt cake, step 4). Transfer to a wire rack to cool for 1 hour, then remove the cake from the tin.

4 For the glaze, place the icing sugar, salt, cream cheese, and butter in a large bowl and whisk to combine. Gradually add the milk, whisking until smooth and glossy. Pour it over the cake. Serve the cake immediately after glazing. You can store the cheesecake in an airtight container for up to 3 days.

MINI BUNDTS marbled

Mini bundt tins are available in specialist baking shops and produce appealing individual cakes. These delights are great when paired with coffee at the end of a meal.

INGREDIENTS
115g (4oz) unsalted butter, plus extra for greasing

190g (6¾ oz) plain flour, plus extra for dusting

2 tbsp cornflour

½ tsp salt

½ tsp baking powder

½ tsp instant espresso powder

3 tsp natural cocoa powder, plus extra to decorate

200g (7oz) caster sugar

2 large eggs, lightly beaten

1 tsp pure vanilla extract

90g (3¼oz) soured cream

icing sugar, to decorate

SPECIAL EQUIPMENT
Bundt-lette muffin tin, each mould measuring 100ml (3½fl oz)

1 Preheat the oven and prepare the bundt-lette tin (see Lemon and blueberry bundt cake, step 1). Boil a kettle half-full of water and leave to cool for 5 minutes. Sift the flour, cornflour, salt, and baking powder into a bowl. In a separate bowl, place the espresso and cocoa powders, pour over 1 tablespoon of the water, and set aside.

2 Whisk the butter and caster sugar in a bowl until fluffy. Gradually add the eggs, and whisk to combine. Add the vanilla extract and whisk until smooth.

3 Gradually fold in the flour mixture and cream into the butter mixture alternately, until well incorporated and smooth. Place half the batter in a separate bowl, add the espresso mixture, and whisk well to combine.

4 Fill each bundt mould with equal quantities of both batters. Swirl the batters with a toothpick to create a marbled effect. Bake for 15–20 minutes, rotating the tin at the halfway mark, until golden. Insert a toothpick into the baked cakes – it should come out clean.

5 Transfer the tin to a wire rack to cool for 45 minutes, then remove the cakes from the tin. Dust with icing sugar and cocoa powder to serve. You can store them in an airtight container for up to 3 days.

🕐 **30 mins**
plus chilling and cooling

🍴 **SERVES 10–12**

ROULADE chocolate and summer fruit

A roulade is a fabulous dessert choice for entertaining as it is one of the best recipes to feed a crowd. Rolling up a roulade is not as difficult as it seems – as shown here, wrap it in baking parchment and then a kitchen towel for guaranteed success.

INGREDIENTS

1 tbsp unsalted butter, melted, for brushing

35g (1¼oz) cocoa powder, plus extra for dusting

5 eggs, separated

150g (5½oz) caster sugar

1 tbsp plain flour

For the filling

250ml (9fl oz) double cream

1 tsp vanilla extract

1 tbsp icing sugar

125g (4½oz) strawberries, hulled and quartered

125g (4½oz) raspberries

SPECIAL EQUIPMENT

30 x 37cm (12 x 15in) Swiss roll tin

PLAN AHEAD

You can make the sponge cake 1 day ahead. Roll it in the kitchen towel, then cover with a layer of foil.

1

Preheat the oven to 220°C (425°F/Gas 7). Line the tin with baking parchment, brush it lightly with butter, and chill for 5 minutes. Then dust the parchment evenly with cocoa powder, tipping off any excess.

Dust very lightly using a small sieve.

2

In a large bowl, whisk the egg yolks and 100g (3½oz) caster sugar with a hand-held whisk until light and fluffy. In a separate bowl, whisk the egg whites to form stiff peaks. Then whisk in the remaining caster sugar until glossy. Sift the cocoa powder and flour into a small bowl.

3

In three batches, gradually fold the cocoa and the egg white mixtures into the egg yolk mixture. Fold carefully so that you lose as little air as possible, until combined. Pour the batter into the tin. Tip the tin lightly to ensure the batter spreads evenly.

4

Bake for 7–10 minutes, until an inserted toothpick comes out clean. Remove from the oven and cool the sponge in the tin for 2 minutes, then turn out onto a sheet of baking parchment dusted with cocoa powder. Roll up the sponge in the parchment, wrap in a clean kitchen towel, and leave to cool completely.

Carefully roll up the sponge in the kitchen towel.

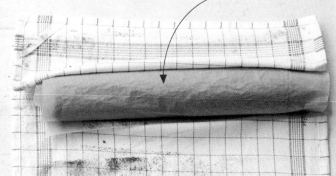

5

For the filling, whisk the cream, vanilla extract, and icing sugar in a bowl to form stiff peaks. Unroll the sponge and spread over the cream, leaving a 1cm (½in) border. Scatter over the berries and gently press them into the cream.

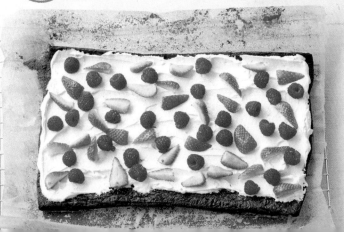

6

Re-roll the cake as before, using the parchment to support it, and trim the edges. Carefully transfer the roulade to a serving plate, dust with cocoa powder, and serve immediately.

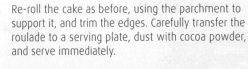

🕐 **35 mins**
plus cooling

🍴 **SERVES 10–12**

ROULADE peach melba

With a meringue base, this roulade is incredibly light. Softening the base with vinegar and cornflour helps it to remain flexible and easy to roll around the filling. A bonus of this recipe is that you can make it entirely from freezer or store-cupboard ingredients.

INGREDIENTS

5 egg whites, at room temperature

225g (8oz) caster sugar

½ tsp white wine vinegar, or rice wine vinegar

1 tsp cornflour

½ tsp vanilla extract

icing sugar, for dusting

For the coulis

125g (4½oz) frozen raspberries

30g (1oz) caster sugar

For the filling

250ml (9fl oz) double cream

400g can peaches, drained and diced

SPECIAL EQUIPMENT

30 x 37cm (12 x 15in) Swiss roll tin

1 Preheat the oven to 180°C (350°F/Gas 4). Line the tin with baking parchment and set aside. Whisk the egg whites in a bowl to form stiff peaks. Gradually add the caster sugar, whisking constantly until the mixture is well combined, thick, and glossy.

2 Fold the vinegar, cornflour, and vanilla extract into the meringue mixture. Mix gently, trying to lose as little air as possible, and pour into the prepared tin. Bake the meringue for 15 minutes. Remove from the heat and leave to cool in the tin.

3 For the coulis, place the raspberries and caster sugar in a small, heavy-based saucepan over a gentle heat. Cook for 5–7 minutes, stirring occasionally, until the raspberries soften and the sugar dissolves. Strain the mixture into a bowl and chill until needed.

4 For the filling, whisk the cream in a bowl to form stiff peaks. Spread a sheet of baking parchment over a clean work surface and sprinkle it with a little icing sugar. Place a large serving platter next to the parchment so that the roulade can be easily moved onto it after it is rolled.

5 Turn the meringue out over the parchment. Spread the cream over the meringue evenly, leaving a 1cm (½in) border. Spread the raspberry coulis over the cream. Gently pat the peaches dry with kitchen paper to remove any excess liquid.

6 Scatter the peaches over the coulis and gently press them into place. Carefully roll the meringue using the parchment to support it. Then roll it onto the serving platter, dust with icing sugar, and serve immediately.

ROULADE
black forest

Tinned cherries and fruity Kirsch pair well with thick cream in this decadent version of the classic roulade.

INGREDIENTS
30 x 37cm (12 x 15in) chocolate sponge cake (see Chocolate and summer fruit roulade pp240–41)

cocoa powder, for dusting

For the filling
250ml (9fl oz) double cream

1 tsp vanilla extract

1 tbsp icing sugar

3 tbsp Kirsch

400g can pitted black cherries, drained and halved

PLAN AHEAD
You can make the sponge cake 1 day ahead. Roll it in the kitchen towel, then cover with a layer of foil.

1 For the filling, place the cream, vanilla extract, and sugar in a large bowl and whisk well to form stiff peaks. Roll out the prepared sponge cake over a clean work surface covered with a clean kitchen towel.

2 Sprinkle the Kirsch evenly over the cake. Then spread the cream over the sponge cake evenly, leaving a 1cm (½in) border. Scatter over the cherries and gently press them into place.

3 Using the kitchen towel for support, gently roll up the sponge and trim the edges. Carefully transfer the roulade to a large serving plate and dust with cocoa powder. Serve immediately.

SWISS ROLL raspberry

Home-made Swiss rolls are a world away from crusty shop-bought varieties. Traditional raspberry jam is used here, but you could replace it with peach, apricot, or even fig jam.

INGREDIENTS
3 large eggs

100g (3½oz) caster sugar, plus extra for sprinkling

pinch of salt

75g (2½oz) self-raising flour, sifted

1 tsp vanilla extract

6 tbsp raspberry jam

SPECIAL EQUIPMENT
23 x 33cm (9 x 13in) Swiss roll tin

PLAN AHEAD
You can make the sponge cake 1 day ahead. Roll it in the kitchen towel, then cover with a layer of foil.

1 Preheat the oven to 200°C (400°F/Gas 6). Line the tin with baking parchment and set aside. Whisk the eggs, sugar, and salt in a heatproof bowl set over a saucepan of simmering water, making sure it does not touch the water, until thick. The mixture should leave trails on the surface when the whisk is lifted.

2 Remove from the heat and whisk the mixture for 1–2 minutes, until cool. Gently fold in the flour and vanilla extract, so that you lose as little air as possible. Pour the mixture evenly into the tin. Bake for 12–15 minutes, until the sponge is springy and shrinking away from the sides.

3 Place a sheet of baking parchment on a clean work surface. Sprinkle evenly with a little sugar and turn out the sponge over it. Cool for 5 minutes, then gently peel off the baking parchment.

4 Warm the jam in a saucepan over a gentle heat and spread over the sponge. Make a 2cm (¾in) indent along one short side, 2cm (¾in) from the edge. Roll the sponge from this edge, using the parchment to support it.

5 Leave the cake to cool completely. Then remove the parchment and place the roulade, join downwards, on a serving plate. Sprinkle with sugar and serve. You can keep it in an airtight container for 2 days, or freeze it for up to 8 weeks.

25 mins
plus cooling

MAKES 24

MACAROONS almond

These macaroons are the perfect after-dinner treat, especially for those with a gluten intolerance. They are made with a mixture of ground almonds and rice flour, which gives them a light, delicate texture.

INGREDIENTS

2 egg whites

225g (8oz) caster sugar

125g (4½oz) ground almonds

30g (1oz) rice flour

2–3 drops of almond extract

24 blanched almonds

SPECIAL EQUIPMENT

2 sheets of edible wafer paper

1 Preheat the oven to 180°C (350°F/ Gas 4). Line two baking sheets with edible wafer paper and set aside. Whisk the egg whites in a large bowl with a hand-held whisk until they are stiff and form soft peaks.

2 Add the sugar, a tablespoon at a time, and whisk until the mixture is thick and glossy. Then gently fold in the ground almonds, rice flour, and almond extract. Mix until combined.

3 Use two warmed tablespoons to scoop up and shape the dough into 24 rounds, placing them spaced well apart on the baking sheets. Clean the spoon between scoops. Place a blanched almond in the centre of each round.

4

Bake the macaroons in the oven for 12–15 minutes, until lightly coloured. Place on a wire rack to cool completely. Then tear the macaroons off the sheets and serve. You can store them in an airtight container for 2–3 days.

🕐 **30 mins** plus chilling 　🍴 **MAKES 24**

MACAROONS coffee and hazelnut

Ground hazelnuts provide a darker, nuttier flavour than ground almonds – perfect when matched with strong coffee. You could also crumble them over a coffee granita (see p281).

INGREDIENTS

2 egg whites

225g (8oz) caster sugar

150g (5½oz) ground hazelnuts

30g (1oz) rice flour

1 tsp strong instant coffee powder, dissolved in 1 tsp boiling water and cooled

24 blanched hazelnuts

SPECIAL EQUIPMENT

2 sheets of edible wafer paper

1 Preheat the oven to 180°C (350°F/Gas 4). Line two baking sheets with edible wafer paper. Whisk the egg whites in a bowl to form stiff peaks. Add the sugar, a tablespoon at a time, and whisk until thick and combined.

2 Gently fold the ground hazelnuts and rice flour into the mixture. Then fold in the coffee mixture, and mix until evenly incorporated. Cover and chill for about 30 minutes.

3 Use two warmed tablespoons to shape the dough into 24 rounds, placing them spaced apart on the baking sheets. Clean the spoons between scoops. Place a blanched hazelnut in the centre of each round.

4 Bake the macaroons on the top shelf of the oven for 12–15 minutes, until lightly coloured. Leave to cool on the sheets for 5 minutes. Then place on a wire rack to cool completely, before tearing them from the sheets and serving. You can store them in an airtight container for 2–3 days.

🕐 **45 mins** plus cooling 　🍴 **MAKES 15**

MACAROONS pineapple and coconut

Pineapple provides a good contrast to sweet coconut in these little delicacies, inspired by tropical flavours.

INGREDIENTS

200g (7oz) sweetened shredded coconut

200ml (7fl oz) condensed milk

85g (3oz) diced pineapple

2 large egg whites

pinch of cream of tartar

1 Preheat the oven to 190°C (375°F/Gas 5). Line a baking sheet with baking parchment. In a large bowl, place the coconut, milk, and pineapple, and mix well. In a separate bowl, beat the egg whites and cream of tartar to form stiff peaks.

2 Gently fold the egg white mixture into the coconut mixture, a little at a time, until it is well combined. Use two tablespoons to scoop and shape the dough into 15 rounds, placing them spaced well apart on the lined baking sheet. Clean the spoons between scoops.

3 Bake the macaroons for 20–25 minutes, rotating the sheets after 15 minutes, until golden. Leave to cool completely on the baking sheets, then serve. You can store the macaroons in an airtight container in the fridge for up to 4 days, or freeze them for up to 1 month. Thaw before serving.

🕐 **45 mins**
plus cooling and chilling

🍴 **MAKES 24**

MACAROONS chocolate and raspberry

Mixing fresh raspberries into this macaroon mixture gives it a wonderfully vibrant colour, and distributes nuggets of tangy fruit throughout the bake.

INGREDIENTS

175g (6oz) raspberries
350g (12oz) shredded
    coconut
180ml (6fl oz) condensed
    milk

2 large egg whites
⅛ tsp cream of tartar
350g (12oz) good-quality
    dark chocolate

1 Preheat the oven to 190°C (375°F/Gas 5). Line two baking sheets with baking parchment. In a small bowl, crush the raspberries with the back of a spoon. In a separate bowl, combine the raspberries, coconut, and milk, and set aside.

2 Beat the egg whites and cream of tartar to form stiff peaks. Gently fold the egg whites into the coconut mixture, a little at a time, until well combined. Use two tablespoons to scoop and shape 24 rounds of dough (see Coffee and hazelnut macaroons, step 3).

3 Bake the macaroons for 20–25 minutes, rotating the sheets after 15 minutes, until lightly golden. Leave to cool completely on the baking sheets. Melt the chocolate in a heatproof bowl over a saucepan of gently simmering water, making sure it does not touch the water.

4 Remove from the heat and cool for 3–4 minutes. Then dip the base of the macaroons in the chocolate and place them on a baking sheet, lined with greaseproof paper. Drizzle chocolate over the macaroons, if desired.

5 Chill the macaroons for 15–20 minutes, until the chocolate has hardened. Serve at room temperature. You can store the macaroons in an airtight container in the fridge for up to 4 days, or freeze them for up to 1 month. Thaw before serving.

INGREDIENTS

175g (6oz) unsalted butter, softened, plus extra for greasing

200g (7oz) plain flour

100g (3½oz) caster sugar

For the caramel filling

50g (1¾oz) unsalted butter

50g (1¾oz) light brown sugar

400g can condensed milk

For the topping

200g (7oz) good-quality milk chocolate

25g (scant 1oz) unsalted butter

50g (1¾oz) good-quality dark chocolate

SPECIAL EQUIPMENT

20cm (8in) square cake tin

🕐 **1 hr 25 mins**
plus cooling and setting

🍴 **MAKES 16**

TRAYBAKE millionaire's shortbread

There is a variety of very rich ingredients in this recipe, and this is said to be the reason for its indulgent name. You can cut the traybake into bite-sized pieces and serve it with coffee. It also works well as a sweet canapé.

Preheat the oven to 160°C (325°F/Gas 3). Grease and line the tin with baking parchment. Combine the flour and sugar in a bowl. Rub in the butter until the mixture resembles breadcrumbs. Spread it in the tin and bake for 35–40 minutes. Remove and leave to cool in the tin.

1

Press the mixture down for a smooth, even layer.

2

For the filling, melt the butter and sugar in a heavy-based saucepan over a medium heat. Add the milk and bring to the boil, stirring. Then reduce the heat to a simmer and cook for 5 minutes, stirring, until it is thick and lightly coloured. Pour it over the base and leave to cool.

For the topping, melt the milk chocolate and butter in a heatproof bowl over a pan of simmering water, making sure it does not touch the water. Stir until smooth. Then melt the dark chocolate in a separate bowl, until smooth.

3

Pour the milk chocolate mixture over the caramel and smooth over the top. Top with the dark chocolate, in a zigzag pattern, and drag a skewer through both layers of chocolate. Leave to cool and harden. Cut it into 16 even-sized squares to serve. You can store the shortbread in an airtight container for up to 5 days.

4

Use the skewer to create a marbled effect.

⏱ **30 mins** plus chilling 🍴 **MAKES 16**

TRAYBAKE Nanaimo

These rich and moist no-bake bars are said to originate from Nanaimo, which is a town in British Columbia, Canada.

1 Grease and line a **20cm (8in) square baking tin**. Melt **115g (4oz) unsalted butter** in a heavy-based saucepan over a low heat. Add **30g (1oz) cocoa powder** and **60g (2oz) caster sugar**, and cook for 2 minutes, whisking, until the sugar has dissolved.

2 Remove the cocoa mixture from the heat. Whisk in **1 large beaten egg**, until well combined. Return the mixture to a low heat and cook it for 1–2 minutes, whisking frequently, until it has thickened. Remove from the heat.

3 Place **200g (7oz) crushed biscuits**, **75g (2½oz) sliced almonds**, and **50g (1¾oz) unsweetened desiccated coconut** in a large bowl. Pour over the cocoa and egg mixture and combine well. Transfer the mixture to the tin, pressing down to form an even, firm layer. Chill for 30 minutes.

4 Whisk **50g (1¾oz) softened unsalted butter** in a large bowl until light and fluffy. Add **300g (10oz) icing sugar**, **2 tbsp custard powder**, **½ tsp vanilla extract**, and **2–3 tbsp milk**, and whisk until it is a smooth, spreadable frosting. Smooth it over the base and chill for 30 minutes.

5 Melt **150g (5½oz) good-quality dark chocolate** and **25g (scant 1oz) unsalted butter** in a heatproof bowl over a pan of simmering water. Cool it to room temperature and pour over the vanilla layer in the tin. Spread it out evenly and chill for 1 hour. Then remove from the tin and slice into 16 even-sized pieces. You can store the bars in an airtight container for up to 5 days.

Tiffin

Nanaimo

⏱ **20 mins** plus chilling 🍴 **MAKES 25**

TRAYBAKE tiffin

Crunchy and chewy at the same time, these delicious bars were invented in Scotland at the beginning of the 20th century.

1 Grease and line a **20cm (8in) square baking tin**. Melt **150g (5½oz) unsalted butter**, **125g (4½oz) golden syrup**, and **45g (1½oz) cocoa powder** in a saucepan over a low heat, whisking constantly until smooth.

2 Combine **300g (10oz) crushed digestive biscuits** and **150g (5½oz) dried fruit** in a large bowl. Pour over the butter mixture and mix until combined. Transfer the mixture to the prepared tin and spread it out to a firm, even layer. Chill for at least 30 minutes.

3 Meanwhile, melt **250g (9oz) milk chocolate** in a heatproof bowl over a saucepan of simmering water. Do not allow the bowl to touch the water. Cool to room temperature, before spreading it over the biscuit and fruit base. Chill for 30 minutes. Then remove from the tin and slice into 25 even-sized pieces. You can store the bars in an airtight container for up to 5 days.

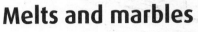

🕐 **20 mins** plus chilling   🍴 **MAKES 16**

TRAYBAKE rocky road

This American classic derives its name from its craggy texture and is stuffed with dried fruits, nuts, and sweet treats.

1 Grease and line a **20cm (8in) square baking tin**. Melt **250g (9oz) good-quality dark chocolate**, **100g (3½oz) unsalted butter**, and **2 tbsp golden syrup** in a large heatproof bowl over a pan of simmering water. Cool to room temperature.

2 Add **150g (5½oz) roughly chopped pretzel sticks**, **100g (3½oz) mini marshmallows**, **50g (1¾oz) roughly chopped almonds**, and **50g (1¾oz) roughly chopped dried cherries** to the chocolate mixture. Stir well until combined.

3 Transfer the mixture to the prepared tin. Spread it out to a firm and even layer and chill for at least 2 hours. Remove from the tin and slice into 16 even-sized pieces. You can store the bars in an airtight container for up to 5 days.

Rocky road

Melts and marbles

It is so easy to mix molten chocolate or sugar to create stunning decorations for traybakes. Use good-quality chocolate for best results.

Marbling Marble Millionaire's shortbread (see pp248–49) with 60g (2oz) melted white chocolate. Spread the melted milk chocolate over the base, as described in the recipe, then pour the white chocolate over the top, dragging a wooden chopstick through both layers. Allow to set, and chill.

Feathering This gives a professional look to Millionaire's shortbread (see pp248–49). Top the filling with the milk chocolate and smooth it out. Working quickly, use a piping bag to pipe thin lines of the melted dark chocolate across the surface. Drag a toothpick through the lines to feather them, then leave to set.

Spun sugar Melt 250g (9oz) caster sugar over a low heat until it turns to a dark, liquid caramel. Use a fork to drizzle the caramel quickly in thin zigzag lines over baking parchment. When each little knot of spun sugar sets, use to top small pieces of Millionaire's shortbread (see pp248–49).

Zigzag shapes Divide the base for the Nanaimos (see opposite) between 12 mini muffin tins. Pack them down, and chill for 30 minutes. Turn them out and pipe mini rosettes of the filling on each one. Chill for 30 minutes. On a lined baking sheet, drizzle melted chocolate into zigzags, and allow to set. Use them to top the Nanaimos, and serve.

INGREDIENTS

100g (3½oz) dark brown sugar

50g (1¾oz) caster sugar

115g (4oz) unsalted butter, softened

1 egg, at room temperature

¾ tsp vanilla extract

150g (5½oz) plain flour

½ tsp salt

½ tsp baking powder

150g (5½oz) dark chocolate chips

PLAN AHEAD

You can prepare and store the dough, wrapped in cling film, in the fridge up to 3 days ahead, or freeze it 4–5 months ahead. Bring to room temperature before baking.

20 mins
plus chilling and cooling

MAKES 12

COOKIES chocolate chip

Not only a tea-time snack, these cookies are also the perfect after-dinner choice, especially when served with coffee or ice cream. You could also crumble them and serve them on top of sundaes or parfaits.

1 Whisk both lots of sugar and the butter in a large bowl for 3–4 minutes, until light and fluffy. Whisk in the egg, scraping down the sides of the bowl. Beat in the vanilla extract. Combine the flour, salt, and baking powder in a separate bowl.

2 Gradually fold the dry ingredients into the wet mixture until just combined. Then fold in the chocolate chips until they are evenly incorporated. Wrap the dough in cling film. Chill for 2–3 hours, or overnight, until firm.

3

Preheat the oven to 180°C (350°F/Gas 4). Line two baking sheets with baking parchment. Shape the dough into 12 equal-sized balls, each weighing 45g (1½oz). Place them on the baking sheets, spaced at least 5cm (2in) apart.

4

Bake for 13–14 minutes, rotating the baking sheets halfway through. Remove and cool the cookies on the baking sheets for 5 minutes. Transfer to a wire rack to cool completely, and serve. You can store the cookies in an airtight container in the fridge for 4–5 days, or freeze them for up to 8 months.

🕐 **20 mins**
plus chilling and cooling   🍴 **MAKES 10**

COOKIES snickerdoodles

These soft cookies are really a cross between a cake and a biscuit. Their light and buttery texture is best enjoyed fresh from the oven.

1 Whisk **85g (3oz) unsalted butter**, **100g (3½oz) dark brown sugar**, and **50g (1¾oz) caster sugar** in a large bowl until light and fluffy. Add **1 egg** and whisk to combine. Then whisk in **½ tsp vanilla extract** until well combined, scraping down the sides of the bowl if needed.

2 Place **150g (5½oz) plain flour**, **½ tsp salt**, **⅛ tsp cinnamon**, **½ tsp baking power**, **½ tsp cream of tartar**, and **1 tbsp cornflour** in a separate bowl, and mix well. Gradually add to the sugar and butter mixture, whisking until just incorporated. Cover the dough with cling film and chill for 2–3 hours, or until firm.

3 Preheat the oven to 180°C (350°F/Gas 4). Line two large baking sheets with baking parchment and set aside. Place **50g (1¾oz) caster sugar** and **1½ tbsp ground cinnamon** in a small bowl. Mix well to combine.

4 Divide and shape the dough into 10 equal-sized balls, weighing about 45g (1½oz) each. Lightly coat each dough ball with the cinnamon mixture. Transfer them to the lined baking sheets, spacing them at least 5cm (2in) apart.

5 Bake the cookies for 14–16 minutes, rotating the baking sheets halfway through, until golden at the edges and shiny. Remove and cool them on the baking sheets for 5 minutes, before placing on a wire rack to cool completely. You can store them in an airtight container for up to 4–5 days, or freeze them for up to 8 months.

PLAN AHEAD
You can prepare and store the dough, wrapped in cling film, in the fridge up to 3 days ahead, or freeze it 4–5 months ahead. Bring to room temperature before baking.

Snickerdoodles

Snickerdoodles

🕐 **30 mins**
plus cooling   🍴 **MAKES 16**

COOKIES cranberry and oatmeal

Vitamin-rich cranberries and heart-healthy oats make these cookies a healthy dessert option. Serve them with Greek yogurt and honey.

1 Preheat the oven to 180°C (350°F/Gas 4). Whisk **100g (3½oz) softened unsalted butter**, **50g (1¾oz) dark soft brown sugar**, and **150g (5½oz) caster sugar** in a large bowl, until light and fluffy. Add **1 egg** and whisk well to combine.

2 Sift **125g (4½oz) plain flour**, **¼ tsp baking powder**, **¼ tsp ground cinnamon**, and **a pinch of salt** into a bowl. Combine the dry ingredients with the wet mixture. Then gently fold in **100g (3½oz) rolled oats** and **60g (2oz) dried cranberries**.

3 Line two baking sheets and place 8 heaped tablespoons of the mixture on each, spaced well apart. Bake the cookies in the oven for 15 minutes, or until they begin to brown at the edges, but are still chewy in the centre.

4 Remove and cool them on the baking sheets for 5 minutes, before placing on a wire rack to cool completely. You can store the cookies in an airtight container for up to 3 days.

PLAN AHEAD
You can prepare and store the dough, wrapped in cling film, in the fridge up to 3 days ahead, or freeze it 4–5 months ahead. Bring to room temperature before baking.

Cranberry and oatmeal

⏱ **30 mins**
plus chilling and cooling

🍴 **MAKES 16**

COOKIES s'mores

Reminiscent of childhood campfires, the flavours of s'mores are comforting, indulgent, and oh so moreish.

1 Whisk **150g (5½oz) dark brown sugar**, **100g (3½oz) caster sugar**, and **115g (4oz) unsalted butter** in a large bowl, until light and fluffy. Add **1 egg** and whisk well to combine. Then whisk in **1 tsp vanilla extract** until combined, scraping down the sides of the bowl if needed.

2 Place **185g (6½oz) plain flour**, **¾ tsp bicarbonate of soda**, and **½ tsp salt** in a small bowl and mix until well combined. Add the dry ingredients to the wet mixture, a little at a time, until just combined.

3 Use a spatula to fold **30g (1oz) mini marshmallows**, **50g (1¾oz) crushed digestive biscuits**, and **85g (3oz) each of dark and milk chocolate chips** into the mixture until incorporated. Cover the dough with cling film and chill for 2–3 hours, or until firm.

4 Preheat the oven to 180°C (350°F/Gas 4), and line two large baking sheets with baking parchment. Divide and shape the dough into 16 equal-sized balls, each weighing about 45g (1½oz). Place eight balls on each baking sheet, at least 5cm (2in) apart.

5 Bake the cookies for 13–14 minutes, rotating the baking sheets halfway through, until browning at the edges. Remove and cool them on the baking sheets for 5 minutes, before placing on a wire rack to cool completely. You can store them in an airtight container in the fridge for up to 4–5 days, or freeze them for up to 8 months.

PLAN AHEAD
You can wrap the dough in cling film and store it in the fridge up to 3 days ahead, or freeze it 4–5 weeks ahead. Bring to room temperature before baking.

S'mores

🕐 **1 hr**
plus cooling

🍴 **MAKES 12–15**

BISCOTTI almond

These crisp Italian biscuits are often served with dessert wine at the end of a meal. Twice baked, they are usually dry and hard, but soften well when dipped into sweet, heady wine. Their lack of moisture means that they store well.

INGREDIENTS

100g (3½oz) whole almonds, shelled and skinned

50g (1¾oz) unsalted butter

225g (8oz) self-raising flour, plus extra for dusting

100g (3½oz) caster sugar

2 eggs

1 tsp vanilla extract

1 Preheat the oven to 180°C (350°F/Gas 4). Spread the almonds on a non-stick baking sheet. Bake in the for 5–10 minutes, tossing them at the halfway mark, until slightly coloured. Remove and leave to cool.

2 Melt the butter in small saucepan over a low heat. Remove and leave to cool slightly. Sift the flour into a large bowl. Roughly chop the almonds and add them to the flour along with the sugar, and mix well.

3 Whisk together the butter, eggs, and vanilla extract in a bowl, until combined. Gradually stir the wet mixture into the dry ingredients. Bring them together to form a dough, adding more flour if it is too wet and difficult to shape.

4 On a lightly floured surface, shape the dough into two logs, each about 20cm (8in) long. Place the logs on a lined baking sheet and bake in the oven for 20 minutes.

Make sure the logs are spaced apart on the baking sheet, as they will increase in size.

5 Remove and leave the logs to cool slightly on a chopping board. Then use a serrated knife to chop them, on a slant, into 3–5cm (1–2in) thick slices. Place the slices on a baking sheet and bake for 10 minutes.

6 Remove the biscotti from the oven, turn them over, and bake for a further 5 minutes. Remove and place on a wire rack to cool and harden, before serving. You can store the biscotti in an airtight container for up to 1 week, or freeze them, spaced out on a sheet, for up to 8 weeks.

Chocolate

🕐 **1 hr 15 mins**
plus cooling 🍴 **MAKES 20**

BISCOTTI chocolate

Simple biscotti dough is easy to embellish. Here, cocoa powder is added to the mixture, along with some roughly chopped pecans.

1 Preheat the oven to 180°C (350°F/Gas 4). Spread **50g (1¾oz) pecans** on a baking sheet and bake for 5 minutes, until slightly coloured. Leave them to cool slightly, and then chop into small pieces.

2 Sift **175g (6oz) plain flour**, **1 tsp baking powder**, and **25g (scant 1oz) cocoa powder** into a large bowl. Add **115g (4oz) caster sugar**, **30g (1oz) dark chocolate chips**, and the pecans, and mix well. Whisk together **2 eggs** in a separate bowl and combine with the dry ingredients.

3 Bring the mixture together to form a dough. On a lightly floured surface, shape the dough into two logs, each about 20cm (8in) long and 5cm (2in) wide. Place the logs on a lined baking sheet and bake for about 25 minutes.

4 Remove and leave to cool for 20 minutes on a chopping board. Using a serrated knife, cut the logs diagonally into 2cm (¾in) thick slices. Place the slices on baking sheets, making sure they are spaced well apart.

5 Bake the biscotti for 10 minutes. Then turn them over and bake for a further 10 minutes. Remove and transfer to a wire rack to harden and cool completely, before serving. You can store the biscotti in an airtight container for up to 1 week.

Pistachio and cranberry

1 hr plus cooling   **MAKES 12–15**

BISCOTTI pistachio and cranberry

Flecked with green and red, these pretty biscotti make a fantastic addition to the table during the festive season.

1. Preheat the oven to 180°C (350°F/Gas 4). Spread **100g (3½oz) unsalted and shelled whole pistachios** on a baking sheet, and bake for 5–10 minutes. Remove, cool to room temperature, and rub between kitchen towels to remove the skins. Roughly chop the pistachios and place them in a large bowl.

2. Add **50g (1¾oz) dried cranberries, 225g (8oz) self-raising flour, 100g (3½oz) caster sugar**, and **finely grated zest of 1 orange**, and mix well. In a separate bowl, whisk **2 eggs, 1 tsp vanilla extract**, and **50g (1¾oz) melted and cooled unsalted butter**. Combine the wet mixture with the dry ingredients to form a dough.

3. On a lightly floured surface, shape the dough into two logs, each about 20cm (8in) long and 7.5cm (3in) thick. Place them on a baking sheet lined with silicone paper, and bake in the oven for 20 minutes.

4. Remove and leave to cool slightly on a chopping board. Use a serrated knife to chop the logs on a slant into 3–5cm (1–2in) thick slices. Place on a baking sheet, making sure the slices are spaced well apart.

5. Bake the biscotti for 10 minutes. Then turn them over and bake for a further 5 minutes. Remove and transfer to a wire rack to harden and cool completely, before serving. You can store the biscotti in an airtight container for up to 1 week.

1 hr 5 mins plus cooling   **MAKES 20**

BISCOTTI ginger

Using both powdered and crystallized ginger gives these gently spiced biscotti a complex flavour and texture.

1. Preheat the oven to 180°C (350°F/Gas 4). Sift **250g (9oz) self-raising flour** into a large bowl. Add **125g (4½oz) caster sugar** and **60g (2oz) finely chopped crystallized ginger**, and mix well. Then add **1½ tsp ground ginger, 1½ tsp cinnamon**, and **¼ tsp grated nutmeg**. Mix well to combine.

2. In a separate bowl, whisk together **2 eggs, 1 tsp vanilla extract**, and **60g (2oz) melted and cooled unsalted butter** until well mixed. Combine the wet mixture with the dry ingredients to form a loose dough. On a lightly floured surface, shape the dough into two logs, each about 20cm (8in) long and 5cm (2in) wide. Place the logs on a lined baking sheet.

3. Bake for 25 minutes. Remove and leave the logs to cool for 20 minutes on a chopping board. Then use a serrated knife to cut the logs diagonally into 2cm (¾in) thick slices. Place the slices on baking sheets, making sure they are spaced well apart.

4. Bake the biscotti for 10 minutes. Then turn them over and bake for a further 10 minutes, until golden and hard. Remove and leave to harden and cool completely on a wire rack, before serving. You can store the biscotti in an airtight container for up to 1 week.

Ginger

30 mins plus cooling   **MAKES 30**

SABLÉS classic

These all-butter shortbread cookies are a French classic. They are a versatile dessert choice – you could use them to sandwich ice cream, as shown here, or roll them as thinly as you dare and use them to decorate a mousse or parfait.

INGREDIENTS
225g (8oz) plain flour, plus extra for dusting

100g (3½oz) caster sugar

150g (5½oz) unsalted butter, softened and diced

1 egg yolk

1 tsp vanilla extract

vanilla ice cream, to serve (optional)

blueberries, to serve (optional)

SPECIAL EQUIPMENT
7cm (2¾in) round pastry cutter

PLAN AHEAD
You can prepare and store the dough, wrapped in the fridge, up to 3 days ahead. Or freeze it up to 3 months ahead – thaw it in the fridge overnight before baking.

1 Preheat the oven to 180°C (350°F/Gas 4). Sift the flour and sugar into a large bowl and mix well. Rub in the butter until the mixture resembles coarse breadcrumbs. Add the egg yolk and vanilla extract, then bring together to form a soft dough.

2 On a lightly floured surface, briefly knead the dough until smooth and roll it out to a thickness of 5mm (¼in). Use a palette knife to move the dough around to prevent it from sticking, if needed.

If the dough is too sticky to roll, chill it for 15 minutes and try again.

3 Use the pastry cutter to cut out 30 rounds and transfer them to non-stick baking sheets.

Re-roll the offcuts to the same thickness and cut out more rounds.

4 Bake in batches, for 10–15 minutes, until the biscuits are golden brown at the edges. Cool them on the baking sheets until firm enough to handle. Then transfer to a wire rack to cool completely. Sandwich the sablés with vanilla ice cream and serve with blueberries, if desired. You can store them in an airtight container for up to 5 days.

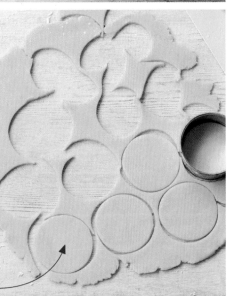

🕐 **30 mins**
plus cooling 🍴 **MAKES 30**

SABLÉS ginger

Crystallized ginger gives these elegant sablés extra crunch, sweetness, and a lovely warmth of flavour.

1 Preheat the oven to 180°C (350°F/Gas 4). Place **100g (3½oz) caster sugar** and **225g (8oz) sifted plain flour** in a large bowl and mix well. Rub in **150g (5½oz) softened unsalted butter** until the mixture resembles breadcrumbs.

2 Stir in **1 tsp ground ginger** and **50g (1¾oz) finely chopped crystallized ginger**. Then add **1 egg yolk** and **1 tsp vanilla extract**, and bring together to form a dough. On a floured surface, briefly knead the dough until smooth.

3 On a well-floured surface, roll the dough out to a 5mm (¼in) thickness. Use a **7.5cm (3in) pastry cutter** to cut out 30 rounds, re-rolling the offcuts to the same thickness until you have used all of the dough. Place the biscuits, spaced apart, on two non-stick baking sheets.

4 Bake the biscuits in batches, for 12–15 minutes each, or until golden brown at the edges. Cool them on the baking sheets until firm enough to handle, then transfer to a wire rack to cool completely. You can store the biscuits in an airtight container for up to 5 days, or freeze them for up to 8 weeks.

PLAN AHEAD
You can prepare and store the dough, well wrapped in the fridge up to 3 days ahead, or freeze it up to 3 months ahead. Thaw overnight in the fridge before baking.

Maple pecan

🕐 **30 mins**
plus chilling and cooling 🍴 **MAKES 25**

SABLÉS maple pecan

Pecans are full of flavour and bring crunch to these sablés. Be sure to chop the nuts finely, so that it is easy to slice the log of dough.

1 Place **115g (4oz) softened unsalted butter** in a large bowl. Add **50g (1¾oz) caster sugar** and **50g (1¾oz) soft light brown sugar**, and beat with a hand-held whisk until light and fluffy.

2 Add **60ml (2fl oz) maple syrup**, **1 egg yolk**, and **½ tsp vanilla extract** and beat well to combine. Sift in **225g (8oz) plain flour** and **¼ tsp fine sea salt**. Add **100g (3½oz) finely chopped pecans** and bring the mixture together to form a dough. Shape it into a 25 x 5cm (10 x 2in) log, wrap tightly in greaseproof paper, and chill for 1 hour.

3 Preheat the oven to 180°C (350°F/Gas 4). Remove the paper and place the dough on a chopping board. Use a sharp knife to cut it into 1cm (½in) thick rounds. Place the rounds, spaced apart, on two non-stick baking sheets and transfer to the oven.

4 Bake the biscuits in batches, for 15 minutes each, until they are golden brown at the edges. Cool them on the baking sheets for about 15 minutes, before placing on a wire rack to cool completely. You can store the biscuits in an airtight container for up to 5 days, or freeze them for up to 8 weeks.

PLAN AHEAD
You can store the dough, well wrapped in the fridge up to 3 days ahead, or freeze it for up to 3 months. Thaw overnight in the fridge, then bake.

Ginger

⏱ **30 mins**
plus chilling and cooling

🍴 **MAKES 25**

SABLÉS chocolate

Green pistachios add flecks of colour to these dark chocolate sablés. For the fullest pistachio flavour, use raw, unsalted nuts.

1 Place **250g (9oz) softened unsalted butter** and **200g (7oz) caster sugar** in a large bowl and beat with a hand-held whisk until light and fluffy. Add **2 egg yolks** and **2 tsp vanilla extract**, and beat well to combine.

2 Sift **250g (9oz) plain flour**, **60g (2oz) cocoa powder**, and **½ tsp fine sea salt** into the bowl. Add **50g (1¾oz) finely chopped pistachios** and bring the mixture together to form a dough. Shape the dough into a 30 x 5cm (12 x 2in) log, wrap it tightly in greaseproof paper, and chill for 1 hour.

3 Preheat the oven to 180°C (350°F/Gas 4). Remove the paper and place the dough on a chopping board. Use a sharp knife to cut it into 1cm (½in) thick rounds. Place the rounds, spaced apart, on two non-stick baking sheets and transfer to the oven.

4 Bake the biscuits, in batches, for 12–15 minutes. Cool them on the baking sheets for 15 minutes, before placing on a wire rack to cool completely. You can store the biscuits in an airtight container for up to 5 days, or freeze them for up to 8 weeks.

PLAN AHEAD
You can prepare and store the dough, well wrapped in the fridge up to 3 days ahead, or freeze it up to 3 months ahead. Thaw overnight in the fridge before baking.

Chocolate

Dips and double dips

Plunge sablés into rich chocolate, melted over a bain-marie. As always, make sure the base of your bowl does not touch the water in the pan.

Half dips Melt 175g (6oz) dark chocolate in a heatproof bowl over a pan of simmering water. Remove from the heat. Dip a Classic sablé (see pp260–61) halfway into the chocolate. Allow excess to drip off into the bowl, then place on a lined baking sheet to set. Repeat with the remaining sablés.

Double dips Half-dip Classic sablés (see p260–61) in dark chocolate, as above, and allow to dry on a lined baking sheet. Melt 175g (6oz) white chocolate in a separate bowl, then remove from the heat. Dip in the other half of each sablé and leave to set.

Dipped edges Prepare the Chocolate sablés (see left), reserving the crushed pistachios from the batter. Bake them and leave to cool. Roll the edges in a shallow plate of melted dark chocolate (see above) and then in the reserved bowl of crushed pistachios. Leave to set.

Total immersion Melt 175g (6oz) dark chocolate (see above). Remove the bowl from the heat and immerse each of the Ginger sablés (see opposite) into the chocolate. Place on a lined baking sheet, sprinkle with 50g (1¾oz) chopped crystallized ginger, and leave to set.

🕐 **20 mins**
plus cooling

🍴 **MAKES 16**

TUILES simple

Classic tuiles are easy to make, but the art lies in timing the bake and shaping them properly. Serve them with cream and fruit, or use them to decorate desserts such as possets, mousses, and sorbets.

INGREDIENTS

50g (1¾oz) unsalted butter, softened

50g (1¾oz) icing sugar, sifted

1 egg, beaten

50g (1¾oz) plain flour, sifted

vegetable oil, for greasing

whipped cream, to serve (optional)

raspberries, to serve (optional)

Preheat the oven to 200°C (400°F/Gas 6). Place the butter and sugar in a large bowl and whisk together until light and fluffy. Add the egg and whisk well to combine. Then fold in the flour.

1

Gently fold in the flour with a metal spoon, taking care not to overmix.

Draw four 8cm (3¼in) wide circles on four sheets of baking parchment, turn them over, and place on baking sheets. Spoon the batter into the traced circles, using the back of a wet spoon to smooth it out to a thin layer. Bake on the top shelf of the oven for 5–7 minutes, until the edges are golden brown.

2

Remove from the oven, and use a palette knife to lift and drape the tuiles over a greased rolling pin. You have only seconds to shape them before they harden. Bake for a further minute to soften them, if needed.

Leave the tuiles to cool on the rolling pin for 2–3 minutes.

Once cooled, gently transfer the tuiles to a wire rack to cool and dry completely. Serve them with whipped cream and raspberries, if desired. You can store the tuiles in an airtight container for up to 5 days.

4

BRANDY SNAPS

A classic British treat, these crisp biscuits are best served filled with whipped cream and dusted with icing sugar.

INGREDIENTS
100g (3½oz) unsalted
  butter, diced
100g (3½oz) caster sugar
60g (2oz) golden syrup
100g (3½oz) plain flour,
  sifted
1 tsp ground ginger
finely grated zest of
  ½ lemon
1 tbsp brandy
vegetable oil, for greasing

For the filling
250ml (9fl oz) double
  cream, whipped
1 tbsp icing sugar
1 tsp brandy

SPECIAL EQUIPMENT
piping bag fitted with a
  large nozzle

PLAN AHEAD
You can store the
unfilled brandy snaps
in an airtight container
up to 2 days ahead.

1 Preheat the oven to 180°C (350°F/Gas 4). Melt the butter and caster sugar in a saucepan over a medium heat. Add the syrup and mix well. Remove from the heat and beat in the flour, ginger, and lemon zest until well combined. Add the brandy and mix well to combine.

2 Draw four or five 8cm (3¼in) wide circles each on four sheets of baking parchment, turn them over, and place on baking sheets. Spoon the batter into the traced circles (see Lime and coconut tuiles, step 2).

3 Bake on the top shelf of the oven for 6–8 minutes, until they are golden brown and the edges have darkened slightly. Leave them to cool on the baking sheets for 3 minutes, until soft enough to shape and move with a spatula. Return to the oven for 1-2 minutes to soften, if needed.

4 Shape the biscuits over the greased handle of a wooden spoon. Leave to cool and harden on the spoon, before transferring to a wire rack to cool completely. Place the filling ingredients in a bowl and mix well to combine. Pipe the filling into the cooled, rolled brandy snaps. Once filled, the biscuits will soften, so serve them immediately.

TUILES lime and coconut

These biscuits are so thin that any additions to the mixture must be very finely chopped or sliced. Simple fruit zest and coconut flakes add flavour and texture.

INGREDIENTS
50g (1¾oz) unsalted
  butter, softened
50g (1¾oz) icing sugar
1 egg
grated zest of 1 lime
50g (1¾oz) plain flour
3-4 tbsp unsweetened,
  desiccated coconut
vegetable oil, for greasing

1 Preheat the oven to 200°C (400°F/Gas 6). Place the butter and sugar in a bowl and whisk until light and fluffy. Add the egg and whisk to combine. Then whisk in the lime zest, gently fold in the flour, and mix well.

2 Draw four 8cm (3¼in) wide circles on four sheets of baking parchment, turn them over, and place on baking sheets. Spoon the batter into the traced circles and use the back of a wet spoon to smooth it out to a thin layer.

3 Sprinkle the coconut over the circles. Bake for 6–8 minutes, until golden brown at the edges. Remove, cool, and shape the tuiles over a greased rolling pin for 2–3 minutes. Place on a wire rack to cool completely before serving. You can store the tuiles in an airtight container for up to 2 days.

🕐 **30 mins** plus cooling   🍴 **MAKES 12**

CANNOLI TUILES Amaretto

Traditional Italian cannoli are deep fried. For a lighter variety that is easy to make, try these baked tuiles that are stuffed with an Amaretto and ricotta filling.

INGREDIENTS

125g (4½oz) caster sugar
2 tbsp runny honey
60g (2oz) unsalted butter, softened
2 tbsp double cream
1 tbsp Amaretto
60g (2oz) plain flour
vegetable oil, for greasing

For the filling

150g (5½oz) ricotta cheese
300g (10oz) mascarpone
50g (1¾oz) icing sugar
zest of 1 large lemon
1–2 tbsp Amaretto
1 tsp vanilla extract
½ tsp cinnamon
30g (1oz) grated dark chocolate, to decorate

SPECIAL EQUIPMENT

piping bag fitted with a large star nozzle

PLAN AHEAD

You can store the unfilled cannoli in an airtight container up to 2 days ahead.

1 Preheat the oven to 200°C (400°F/Gas 6). Melt the caster sugar, honey, butter, cream, and Amaretto in a saucepan over a low heat for 5 minutes, stirring, until the mixture is smooth and the sugar has melted.

2 Remove from the heat, add the flour, and beat well to combine. Use a greased tablespoon to place spoonfuls of the mixture on lined baking sheets in neat circles, spaced well apart. Place only 2–3 tablespoons on each sheet to avoid overcrowding.

3 Bake on the top shelf of the oven for 5–7 minutes, until golden brown all over. Leave the tuiles to cool on the baking sheets for 2–3 minutes until set, but still soft enough to shape.

4 Wrap the tuiles loosely around the greased handle of a large wooden spoon. Bake them for a further 1–2 minutes to soften, if they cool too quickly. Leave to set and harden on the spoon, then transfer to a wire rack to cool completely.

5 For the filling, whisk the ricotta in a bowl until smooth. Whisk in the remaining ingredients until thick and smooth, and pipe the mixture into the cannoli. Sprinkle each end of the cannoli with chocolate. Once filled, the tuiles will soften, so serve them immediately.

Cups and cones

Warm tuile biscuits (see pp264–65) are flexible and perfect for shaping. Cool them for a few seconds, then shape while they are still pliable.

Cones Mould tightly crumpled tin foil into a cone shape, and wrap a still warm of tuile biscuit around it to form the cone. It cools and sets in a few seconds. Serve with a small ice cream boule, if desired.

Spirals Shape your tuile batter into 3 x 10cm (1¼ x 4in) strips on a lined baking sheet. Bake in the oven, and when warm, wrap around the handle of a greased wooden spoon. Slip them off once hardened.

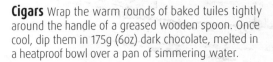

Cigars Wrap the warm rounds of baked tuiles tightly around the handle of a greased wooden spoon. Once cool, dip them in 175g (6oz) dark chocolate, melted in a heatproof bowl over a pan of simmering water.

Brandy snap baskets
Use an upturned, lightly buttered ramekin to mould still warm and flexible Brandy snaps (see opposite) into a basket shape. Allow to cool and set, fill with fresh fruit or sorbet, and serve immediately.

FROZEN

Ice creams and sorbets ▪ Iced desserts

INGREDIENTS

500ml (16fl oz) double
  cream
300ml (10fl oz) whole milk
1–2 tsp pure vanilla extract
pinch of salt
100g (3½oz) caster sugar
50g (1¾oz) light brown
  sugar
4 large egg yolks

SPECIAL EQUIPMENT

ice-cream maker
1.5 litre (2¾ pint) shallow
  freezer-proof airtight
  container

PLAN AHEAD

You can prepare, cover,
and store the custard in
the fridge up to 1 day
ahead of freezing.

🕐 **25 mins**
plus chilling and freezing

🍴 **SERVES 4**

ICE CREAM vanilla

Nothing beats the smooth, creamy flavour of good vanilla ice
cream. Home-made ice cream is surprisingly simple. Store the
bowl of the ice-cream maker in the freezer, if possible, so
that you can whip up a treat whenever you feel like it.

Prepare the ice-cream maker
as per the instructions. Heat
the cream, milk, vanilla extract,
salt, and both lots of sugar in
a saucepan over a low heat,
stirring until the sugar dissolves.
Whisk the egg yolks in a large
heatproof bowl.

1

2

When it is steaming, whisk
a little of the milk mixture
into the egg yolks. Then
whisk in the remaining
milk until combined.
Transfer back to the pan and
cook over a medium–low
heat until thick enough to
coat the back of a spoon.

3

Remove from the heat and pour the custard back into a large bowl set over an ice bath. Leave to cool for about 20 minutes, then remove the bowl from the ice bath, cover with cling film, and chill for 6–7 hours, or overnight, until completely chilled.

Remove the mixture from the fridge and pour into the ice-cream maker. Churn for 10–15 minutes, until thick. Pour the ice cream into the airtight container and freeze for 4–5 hours, until firm. Remove from the freezer 20 minutes before serving. You can store the ice cream in a freezer-proof container in the freezer for up to 2 months.

4

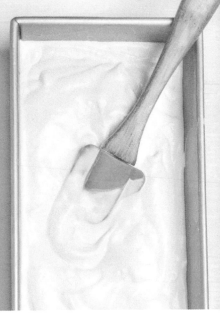

50 mins plus chilling and freezing   **SERVES 4**

ICE CREAM pecan and salted caramel

The addictive marriage of salt and caramel works perfectly for ice cream. Use good-quality sea salt flakes that dissolve easily.

INGREDIENTS
500ml (16fl oz) double cream
300ml (10fl oz) whole milk
⅛ tsp sea salt flakes
100g (3½oz) caster sugar
50g (1¾oz) light brown sugar
7 large egg yolks, beaten
1 tsp pure vanilla extract
85g (3oz) chopped pecans

For the caramel
100g (3½oz) caster sugar
120ml (4fl oz) double cream
15g (½oz) unsalted butter
½ tsp salt
¾ tsp vanilla extract

SPECIAL EQUIPMENT
ice-cream maker
2.5 litre (4⅓ pint) shallow, freezer-proof lidded airtight container

PLAN AHEAD
You can prepare, cover, and store the custard in the fridge, up to 1 day ahead of freezing.

1. Prepare the ice-cream maker as per the instructions. For the caramel, boil the caster sugar and 2 tablespoons of water in a saucepan over a medium–high heat, brushing down the sides of the pan with a damp pastry brush. Cook the sugar for 5 minutes, swirling the pan to ensure that it cooks evenly. Remove from the heat.

2. Gradually add the remaining caramel ingredients, stirring with a wooden spoon. Melt again over a medium–low heat. Transfer to a bowl and leave to cool. Heat the cream, milk, salt, and both lots of sugar in a saucepan over a low heat, stirring until the sugar dissolves.

3. In a bowl, whisk a little cream mixture into the beaten yolks, until combined. Whisk in the rest of the cream mixture. Transfer the custard to a clean pan. Cook over a medium–low heat until it is thick enough to coat the back of a spoon. Remove and stir in the vanilla extract.

4. Strain the custard into a bowl set over an ice bath. Leave to cool completely. Cover with cling film and chill for 1–2 hours. Pour into the ice-cream maker and churn, adding the pecans at the halfway mark, until thick.

5. Pour half of the ice cream into the airtight container followed by half the caramel. Then repeat with the remaining ice cream and caramel, creating a swirl effect with a knife. Cover and freeze for 4–5 hours, until firm. Remove from the freezer 20 minutes before serving. You can store the ice cream for 1–2 months in the freezer.

55 mins–1 hr plus chilling and freezing   **SERVES 4**

ICE CREAM peach

This simple fruity ice cream gives you delicious good-quality ice cream without an ice-cream maker.

INGREDIENTS
4 peaches, halved and stoned
2½ tbsp light brown sugar
500ml (16fl oz) double cream
300ml (10fl oz) whole milk
150g (5½oz) caster sugar
¾ tsp pure vanilla extract
pinch of salt
2½ tsp lemon juice

SPECIAL EQUIPMENT
2.5 litre (4⅓ pint) shallow, freezer-proof lidded airtight container

PLAN AHEAD
You can prepare and store the peach purée in an airtight container up to 1 day ahead.

1. Place the airtight container in the freezer. Preheat the oven to 200°C (400°F/Gas 6). Place the peaches in a shallow ovenproof dish and sprinkle the brown sugar over the top.

2. Bake the peaches for 25–30 minutes, until they are tender and lightly caramelized on top. Then transfer them to a food processor and pulse until smooth. Strain the peach purée into a bowl, cover, and place in the freezer until cold, but not frozen.

3. Combine the cream, milk, caster sugar, vanilla extract, salt, and lemon juice in a bowl, stirring until the sugar dissolves. Then add the peach purée, mix until smooth, and pour the mixture into the airtight container. Cover and freeze for 50–60 minutes.

4. Mix the ice cream to break up any crystals that may have formed, repeating every 45–55 minutes until fully frozen. Remove from the freezer 20 minutes before serving. You can store the ice cream for 1–2 months in the freezer.

Simple alternatives

An ice-cream base is so easy to adapt. Some ideas require an ice-cream maker (see pp270–71), whereas some transform the handmade varieties (see opposite).

Cookies and cream Prepare the Vanilla ice cream (see pp270–71, steps 1–4) and stir in 60g (2oz) roughly crumbled Oreos before freezing.

Coffee Combine 1 tbsp medium-strength coffee powder and 1 tbsp hot water in a small bowl and leave to cool. Prepare the Vanilla ice cream (see pp270–71, steps 1–4) and stir in the coffee mixture before freezing.

Rum and raisin Place 75g (2½oz) plump raisins and 3 tbsp dark rum in a small bowl. Leave to steep overnight. Prepare the Vanilla ice cream (see pp270–71, steps 1–4) and stir in the steeped raisin mixture before freezing.

Chocolate bar Roughly chop about 65g (2¼oz) of your favourite chocolate bars into small pieces. Prepare the Vanilla ice cream (see pp270–71, steps 1–4) and stir in the chocolate before freezing.

Apple and cinnamon Replace the peaches (see Peach ice cream, steps 1–4), with 4 apples, cored and quartered, add 1 tsp ground cinnamon, and continue with the recipe.

Mint choc chip Replace the lavender (see Lavender ice cream, steps 1–4) with 1 tsp finely chopped mint and 1 tsp green food colouring paste. Add 60g (2oz) finely chopped good-quality dark chocolate just before the initial freeze (step 2).

Cherry and walnut Replace the peaches (see Peach ice cream, steps 1–4) with 400g (14oz) ripe pitted cherries. Add 40g (1½oz) chopped walnuts to the ice-cream mixture before freezing.

🕐 **20 mins**
plus chilling and freezing

🍴 **SERVES 4**

ICE CREAM lavender

Culinary lavender gives a gentle floral fragrance to this ice cream, which does not require an ice-cream maker.

INGREDIENTS
500ml (16fl oz) double cream
300ml (10fl oz) whole milk
90ml (3fl oz) runny clover honey
75g (2½oz) caster sugar
3½ tbsp dried culinary lavender, plus extra to serve
pinch of salt
¼ tsp pure vanilla extract

SPECIAL EQUIPMENT
2.5 litre (4⅓ pint) shallow, freezer-proof lidded airtight container

1 Place the airtight container in the freezer. Heat all the ingredients in a large saucepan over a medium heat, stirring constantly until the sugar dissolves. Remove from the heat once the mixture begins to simmer and leave to infuse for 30 minutes.

2 Strain the mixture through a fine mesh sieve into a large bowl, discarding the lavender. Chill for 1–2 hours, then pour the mixture into the airtight container. Cover and freeze for 1 hour.

3 Remove the ice cream from the freezer and mix gently with a wooden spoon to break up any crystals that form. Return to the freezer and repeat every 45–55 minutes, until the ice cream is fully frozen.

4 Remove the ice cream from the freezer 20 minutes before serving, spoon into bowls, and sprinkle with the reserved lavender. You can store the ice cream for 1–2 months in the freezer.

 **35 mins**
plus cooling and freezing

SERVES 8

SEMI FREDDO coffee

An Italian dessert, semi freddo translates as "half frozen". To make a classic semi freddo, freeze a combination of mousse, custard, cream, and flavourings – the texture of the finished dessert will be somewhere between a mousse and an ice cream.

INGREDIENTS
4 eggs, separated

200g (7oz) caster sugar

2 tbsp instant coffee powder, plus extra for dusting

300ml (10fl oz) double cream, whipped to soft peaks

25g (scant 1oz) good-quality dark chocolate

SPECIAL EQUIPMENT
900g (2lb) loaf tin

1

Line the tin with cling film and set aside. Place the egg yolks and 50g (1¾oz) of the sugar in a heatproof bowl over a saucepan of simmering water, making sure it does not touch the water.

2

Whisk the mixture with a hand-held whisk for 5 minutes, until it is pale, light, and has tripled in volume.

3

Combine the coffee powder with 2 tablespoons of boiling water in a cup. Gradually whisk the coffee mixture into the egg yolk mixture. Then remove from the heat, and whisk for 3–5 minutes, until cool.

4

Whisk the egg whites and remaining caster sugar in a separate heatproof bowl over the pan of simmering water (see step 1) to form stiff peaks. Remove from the heat and whisk for a further 3–5 minutes, until it cools. Fold a little of the meringue into the coffee mixture.

5

Carefully fold the remaining meringue into the coffee mixture, so that you lose as little air as possible, until combined. Gently fold in the whipped cream and pour the mixture into the tin. Cover with cling film and freeze for 4–6 hours.

6

Melt the chocolate in a heatproof bowl over a pan of simmering water (see step 1). Invert the semi freddo onto a plate, discarding both sheets of cling film. Dust with coffee powder, decorate with the melted chocolate, and serve. You can store it, covered in the freezer, for up to 1 month.

SEMI FREDDO dark chocolate and brandied prune

You could serve this rich and boozy semi freddo as an alternative to a festive yule log – it is the perfect make-ahead dessert.

INGREDIENTS

100g (3½oz) soft prunes, diced

3 tbsp brandy

200g (7oz) good-quality dark chocolate, broken into pieces

4 eggs

100g (3½oz) caster sugar

300ml (10fl oz) double cream

dark chocolate curls, to decorate

SPECIAL EQUIPMENT

450g (1lb) loaf tin

1 Line the tin with cling film. Place the prunes and brandy in a small saucepan. Add just enough water to cover the prunes and bring to the boil. Then reduce the heat to a low simmer and cook for 5 minutes. Remove from the heat and leave to steep, until needed.

2 Melt the chocolate in a heatproof bowl over a pan of simmering water, making sure it does not touch the water. Remove from the heat. In a separate bowl, whisk the eggs and sugar over a pan of simmering water, until the mixture is pale, fluffy, and has tripled in volume.

3 Remove from the heat and whisk for a further 3–5 minutes, until cool. Whisk a spoonful of the egg mixture into the chocolate and combine, then add it all back into the egg mixture and fold it in gently. Whisk the cream in a bowl to form soft peaks.

4 Gradually fold the cream into the egg mixture, so that you lose as little air as possible. Then gently fold in the prunes until evenly combined. Pour the mixture into the prepared tin, cover with cling film, and freeze for at least 4–6 hours.

5 Remove the tin from the freezer and turn out the semi freddo, discarding both sheets of cling film (see Yogurt, honey, and pistachio semi freddo, steps 2–3). Serve decorated with dark chocolate curls. You can store the semi freddo, covered in the freezer, for up to 1 month.

SEMI FREDDO yogurt, honey, and pistachio

This modern take on semi freddo has a firm texture, as eggs are omitted from the recipe – this also means that it keeps for much longer in the freezer.

INGREDIENTS

400g (14oz) full-fat Greek yogurt

6 tbsp runny honey, plus extra to serve (optional)

grated zest of 1 large orange

200ml (7fl oz) double cream

60g (2oz) unsalted and skinned pistachios, finely chopped

SPECIAL EQUIPMENT

450g (1lb) loaf tin

1 Line the tin with cling film. Whisk the yogurt, honey, and orange zest in a large bowl until smooth and well combined. In a separate bowl, whisk the cream to form soft peaks and carefully fold into the yogurt mixture. Then fold in three-quarters of the pistachios.

2 Pour the mixture into the prepared tin, cover with cling film, and freeze for at least 6 hours. Then remove from the freezer, take off the cling film, and invert the tin over a large serving plate. Shake the tin lightly, if needed, to release the semi freddo.

3 Peel off the cling film. Sprinkle with the reserved pistachios and a drizzle of honey, if desired, and serve immediately. You can store the semi freddo, covered in the freezer, for up to 3 months.

🕐 **35 mins**
plus cooling and freezing

🍴 **SERVES 8**

SEMI FREDDO
raspberry meringue

This dessert takes inspiration from a classic raspberry pavlova. Freezing meringue, cream, and fruit creates a light and creamy semi freddo that is ideal for the summer months.

INGREDIENTS
4 eggs

100g (3½oz) caster sugar

200ml (7fl oz) double cream, whipped to soft peaks

45g (1½oz) ready-made meringues, broken into small pieces, plus extra to decorate

125g (4½oz) raspberries, lightly crushed, plus extra to serve

SPECIAL EQUIPMENT
450g (1lb) loaf tin

1 Line the tin with cling film. Place the eggs and sugar in a heatproof bowl over a saucepan of simmering water, making sure it does not touch the water. Whisk with a hand-held whisk, until the mixture is pale, fluffy, and has tripled in volume. Remove from the heat and whisk for a further 3–5 minutes, until cool.

2 Fold the whipped cream carefully into the egg mixture, so that you lose as little air as possible. Then fold in the meringues and raspberries. Pour the mixture into the prepared tin, cover with cling film, and freeze for at least 4–6 hours, until frozen.

3 Remove the tin from the freezer and turn out the semi freddo, discarding both sheets of cling film (see Yogurt, honey, and pistachio semi freddo, steps 2–3). Serve with crushed meringue pieces and raspberries. You can store the semi freddo, covered in the freezer, for up to 1 month.

🕐 **35 mins**
plus cooling, chilling, and freezing

🍴 **SERVES 8**

SEMI FREDDO
coconut, lime, and mango

This tropical iced indulgence has the perfect balance of flavours, thanks to sweet mango and sharp lime.

INGREDIENTS
3 egg yolks

60g (2oz) caster sugar

1 tbsp cornflour

400ml can coconut milk

200ml (7fl oz) double cream

30g (1oz) icing sugar

175g (6oz) ripe mango, diced and chilled

grated zest of 2 limes

toasted coconut shavings, to decorate

SPECIAL EQUIPMENT
450g (1lb) loaf tin

1 Line the tin with cling film. Whisk the egg yolks, caster sugar, and cornflour in a large heatproof bowl. Gently heat the milk in a small, heavy-based saucepan until hot, but not boiling. Carefully pour the milk over the egg yolk mixture, whisking constantly until combined.

2 Return the custard mixture to the pan and heat gently for 4–5 minutes, stirring constantly, until thick enough to coat the back of a spoon. Pour it into a shallow bowl and leave to cool completely. Cover the surface with cling film and chill until needed.

3 Whisk the cream and icing sugar in a bowl to form soft peaks. Chill until cold. Then fold the cream into the custard, followed by the mangoes and lime zest. Pour the mixture into the prepared tin, cover with cling film, and freeze for 6 hours, until frozen.

4 Remove the tin from the freezer and turn out the semi freddo, discarding both sheets of cling film (see Yogurt, honey, and pistachio semi freddo, steps 2–3). Decorate with the coconut shavings to serve. You can store the semi freddo, covered in the freezer, for up to 1 month.

🕐 **45–50 mins**
plus cooling, chilling, and freezing

🍴 **SERVES 4–6**

SORBET lemon

To make a refreshing sorbet, churn and freeze a mixture of sugar syrup and flavourings. There are thousands of flavour combinations to try, but lemon sorbet is the classic, and, some would argue, the best.

INGREDIENTS
300g (10oz) caster sugar
zest of 2 lemons, plus extra
   to serve
300ml (10fl oz) lemon juice

SPECIAL EQUIPMENT
ice-cream maker
800ml (1½ pint) airtight
   freezer-proof container

PLAN AHEAD
You can prepare and store the syrup in the fridge up to 3 days ahead.

Prepare the ice-cream maker as per the instructions. Heat the sugar and 300ml (10fl oz) cold water in a saucepan for 5 minutes, stirring occasionally, until the sugar dissolves.

1

Pour the syrup into a large heatproof bowl. Leave to cool completely, then chill until cold. Add the lemon zest to the syrup.

2

Strain the lemon juice and discard the pips. Add it to the syrup and whisk the mixture well to combine.

3

Pour the syrup into the ice-cream maker and churn for 30–40 minutes, or as per the instructions. Transfer it to the airtight container and freeze until needed. Serve topped with lemon zest. You can store the sorbet, in an airtight container in the freezer, for up to 1 month.

4

🕐 **30 mins**
plus cooling, chilling, and freezing   🍴 **SERVES 4–6**

SORBET raspberry and hibiscus

Dried hibiscus flowers impart a gorgeous dark red colour. You can find them in health food shops.

1 Prepare the **ice-cream maker** as per the instructions. Place **300g (10oz) caster sugar, 50g (1¾oz) dried hibiscus flowers**, and **500ml (16fl oz) cold water** in a large saucepan and bring to the boil. Then reduce to a simmer and cook for 5 minutes, stirring occasionally, until the sugar dissolves. Pour into a heatproof bowl.

2 Leave the juice to cool, then chill overnight. Then strain the juice into a blender, pressing the flowers with the back of a spoon. Discard the flowers. Add **500g (1lb 2oz) raspberries** and **juice of 1 lime** to the blender and pulse until smooth.

3 Strain the liquid into a large jug, pressing down with the back of a spoon. Pour it into the ice-cream maker and freeze as per the instructions. Then transfer it to a **1.5 litre (2¾ pint) shallow freezer-proof container** and freeze until needed. You can store the sorbet in the container in the freezer for up to 1 month.

Raspberry and hibiscus sorbet

🕐 **15 mins**
plus chilling and freezing   🍴 **SERVES 4–6**

SHERBET pink grapefruit and rose water

A sherbet is a cross between an ice cream and a sorbet. It is simple to prepare, and does not require a specialist ice-cream maker.

1 Place **250g (9oz) caster sugar**, grated zest of 1 large pink grapefruit, **450ml (15fl oz) pink grapefruit juice**, and **1 tbsp rose water** in a blender. Pulse for 2 minutes, until it is well combined and the sugar has dissolved.

2 Transfer the mixture to a bowl and chill for 1 hour. Then transfer to a blender, add **350ml (12fl oz) whole milk**, and pulse until well combined. Pour the liquid into a **1.5 litre (2¾ pint) shallow freezer-proof container.**

3 Transfer to the freezer, scraping the frozen edges into the centre of the container with a fork every 45 minutes, breaking up any larger ice crystals with the back of the fork. Repeat this process for 3 hours, or until the mixture is well frozen, but not solid, then freeze until needed.

4 Whisk **1 large egg white** in a bowl and use to brush **12–16 washed and dried large edible rose petals**. Sprinkle the petals evenly with **caster sugar**, shake off any excess, and leave to dry. Serve the sherbet decorated with the rose petals. You can store the sherbet in the container in the freezer for up to 1 month.

Pink grapefruit and rose water sherbet

Coffee granita

🕐 **15 mins**
plus cooling, chilling, and freezing

🍴 **SERVES 4**

GRANITA coffee

With its signature crystallized texture, this is a refreshing alternative to after-dinner coffee. It is easy to make, as there is no need for an ice-cream maker.

1 Place **2 tbsp espresso powder**, **2 tbsp caster sugar**, **2 tbsp coffee liqueur**, and **1 tsp vanilla extract** in a large heatproof jug. Pour over **500ml (16fl oz) boiling water**, whisking until the sugar dissolves.

2 Pour the liquid into the **1.2 litre (2 pint) shallow freezer-proof container**. Cool to room temperature, chill until cold, then transfer to the freezer.

3 Scrape the frozen edges of the granita into the centre of the container with a fork every 45 minutes, breaking up any larger ice crystals with the back of the fork.

4 Repeat this process for 3–4 hours, until the mixture is well frozen, but not solid. Serve. You can store the granita in the container in the freezer for up to 1 month.

25 mins
plus cooling **MAKES 4**

SUNDAE vanilla and chocolate with pecan brittle

Whether you make your own vanilla ice cream (see p270–71) or buy ready-made, there is no better way to serve it than as the basis of this sundae – drenched with warm chocolate sauce and sprinkled with crunchy brittle.

INGREDIENTS
50g (1¾oz) pecans, halved
150g (5½oz) caster sugar
500ml (16fl oz) good-quality vanilla ice cream

For the sauce
60g (2oz) unsalted butter
75g (2½oz) good-quality dark chocolate, chopped into small pieces
200g (7oz) condensed milk
½ tsp vanilla extract
¼ tsp sea salt flakes

SPECIAL EQUIPMENT
4 x 160ml (5½fl oz) sundae glasses

PLAN AHEAD
You can prepare and store the brittle in an airtight container up to 2 weeks ahead. You can prepare and store the sauce in an airtight container in the fridge up to 1 week ahead.

1

Preheat the oven to 180°C (350°F/Gas 4). Spread the pecans on a baking tray and bake on the top shelf of the oven for 5 minutes, until lightly toasted. Remove from the heat and leave to cool.

2

Roughly chop the pecans and place them in a tight, single layer on a baking tray lined with greaseproof paper. Heat the sugar in a heavy-based saucepan over a medium heat for 5 minutes, without stirring, until it begins to melt at the edges.

3

Cook the sugar, stirring gently, to form a light-coloured caramel. Pour it over the pecans and tip the tray gently to help spread it out evenly. Leave to cool completely. Then break the brittle into small pieces and set aside.

4

For the sauce, melt the butter and chocolate in a small heatproof bowl over a pan of simmering water, making sure it does not touch the water. Stir well until smooth and remove from the heat.

5

Remove the water from the heat. Whisk the remaining ingredients into the chocolate mixture until combined. Keep the sauce warm over the pan of water.

6

Divide the ice cream between the glasses and pour the sauce over the top. Sprinkle over the brittle and serve immediately.

35 mins
plus cooling and drying

MAKES 4

SUNDAE salted caramel and chocolate crunch

Salt has become a dessert staple, and it's easy to see why – good-quality salt contrasts with sweet flavours, while accenting them at the same time.

1 For the salted caramel, heat **200g (7oz) caster sugar** in a heavy-based saucepan over a medium heat until it has melted. Then whisk for 7–10 minutes, until the sugar is amber brown in colour. Add **115g (4oz) diced unsalted butter** and whisk well to combine.

2 Remove from the heat and add **120ml (4fl oz) double cream**, whisking constantly until smooth. Then whisk in **1 tsp vanilla extract** and **1 tsp sea salt flakes** until well combined. Set aside to cool.

3 Melt **75g (2½oz) good-quality dark chocolate chips** in a heatproof bowl over a pan of simmering water, making sure it does not touch the water. Dip **10 pretzels** two-thirds of the way into the chocolate, dripping off any excess. Place them to dry on a lined baking sheet.

4 Divide **500ml (16fl oz) good-quality vanilla ice cream** between **four 160ml (5½fl oz) sundae glasses**. Reserving four of the pretzels, roughly crush the rest and scatter over and around the ice cream. Drizzle over the salted caramel and top each sundae with one of the reserved pretzels. Serve immediately.

Salted caramel and chocolate crunch

🕐 20 mins   🍴 MAKES 4

SUNDAE summer fruit

This stunning and sophisticated sundae benefits from the hint of vanilla, which adds incredible depth to the sauce, and the crunch of meringue.

1 Combine **150g (5½oz) blackberries**, **100g (3½oz) halved and stoned cherries**, and **100g (3½oz) blueberries** in a small, lidded heavy-based saucepan. Add **60g (2oz) caster sugar**, **½ tsp vanilla extract**, and **2 tbsp of water** to the pan.

2 Cover and bring the mixture to the boil. Then reduce the heat to low, uncover, and cook for a further 5–7 minutes, until the berries start to break down and release their juices. Remove the compote from the heat and leave to cool slightly.

3 Whisk **120ml (4fl oz) double cream** in a bowl to form soft peaks. Break **60g (2oz) ready-made meringues** into small pieces. Place **1 scoop vanilla ice cream** into **four 160ml (5½fl oz) sundae glasses**.

4 Reserving a little for decoration, sprinkle over the meringue pieces. Top with **1 scoop of ice cream** and spoon over the warm berry compote. Top the sundae with a spoonful of the whipped cream and a sprinkling of the reserved meringue. Serve immediately.

PLAN AHEAD
You can prepare and store the compote in the fridge up to 3 days ahead. Reheat gently to serve.

Summer fruit

🕐 15 mins   🍴 MAKES 4

SPLIT banana

Give an old-fashioned sundae an update with a home-made warm chocolate sauce, pistachios, and good-quality vanilla ice cream.

1 For the sauce, heat **60g (2oz) chopped good-quality dark chocolate** and **90ml (3fl oz) double cream** in a small, heavy-based saucepan. Stir constantly until the chocolate has melted, then remove from the heat and keep warm.

2 Whisk **120ml (4fl oz) double cream** in a bowl to form soft peaks. Peel **4 ripe bananas** and split them down the middle, lengthways, to create two long slices. Place two slices each, cut-side up, in four **25cm (10in) glass sundae dishes**.

3 Top the banana slices with **2 small scoops good-quality vanilla ice cream** and **1 small scoop good-quality milk chocolate ice cream**. Make sure that the chocolate ice cream is in the centre.

4 Top the ice cream with small spoonfuls of the cream and drizzle over the chocolate sauce. Sprinkle the sundaes with **30g (1oz) chopped unsalted and skinned pistachios** and **60g (2oz) halved and stoned cherries**. Serve immediately.

Banana split

20 mins
plus freezing

SERVES 8

BOMBE chocolate and cherry

This show-stopping bombe is surprisingly easy to prepare. If cherry ice cream is difficult to find, a good-quality soft-serve raspberry ice cream works just as well. Take care not to over-whisk the ice cream, or it will no longer hold its shape.

INGREDIENTS
1.5 litres (2¾ pints) milk chocolate ice cream, or milk choc-chip ice cream

1.2 litres (2 pints) cherry ice cream

500ml (16fl oz) dark chocolate ice cream

For the glaze
175g (6oz) good-quality dark chocolate

3 tbsp coconut oil

SPECIAL EQUIPMENT
2.3 litre (4 pint) freezer-proof bowl, about 20cm (8in) wide

PLAN AHEAD
You can prepare and store the glaze in the fridge up to 2 days ahead. Reheat it gently before use.

1

Line the freezer-proof bowl with cling film, leaving some overhang. Place it in the freezer until needed. Place the milk chocolate ice cream in a large bowl and whisk with a hand-held whisk until slightly softened.

2

Cover the inside of the bowl with ice cream.

Spread the ice cream in an even layer in the prepared bowl, pressing it into shape. Place the bowl back in the freezer for 30–45 minutes, until the ice cream is solid.

3

Smooth out the chocolate layer before adding the second layer.

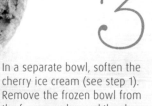

In a separate bowl, soften the cherry ice cream (see step 1). Remove the frozen bowl from the freezer and spread the cherry ice cream over the chocolate layer (see step 2). Freeze for a further 30 minutes, or until firm.

4

Soften the dark chocolate ice cream (see step 1) and pack it into the centre of the bombe. Freeze for 40 minutes.

5

Heat a large pan of water. Dip the base of the bombe bowl into the water for 15–20 seconds. Invert the bombe over a large serving dish and remove the bowl. Take off the cling film and place the bombe in the freezer.

6

For the glaze, melt both the ingredients in a heatproof bowl over a pan of simmering water, making sure it does not touch the water. Leave for 1–2 minutes, then drizzle it over the bombe and serve immediately. You can store the bombe, covered in the freezer, for up to 3 days.

🕐 **20 mins** plus freezing   🍴 **SERVES 8**

BOMBE mango and coconut

With a little patience and a simple technique, you can craft an ice-cream bombe that is sure to wow your guests. Coconut ice cream is readily available in most Asian supermarkets.

INGREDIENTS
2 litres (3½ pints) coconut ice cream

1 litre (1¾ pints) mango sorbet

For the glaze
175g (6oz) white chocolate
3 tbsp coconut oil

SPECIAL EQUIPMENT
2.3 litre (4 pint) freezer-proof bowl, about 20cm (8in) wide

PLAN AHEAD
You can prepare and store the glaze in the fridge up to 2 days ahead. Reheat gently before using.

1 Line the freezer-proof bowl with cling film, leaving some overhang, and place it in the freezer. Whisk half the ice cream in a bowl with a hand-held whisk until slightly softened. Spread it evenly in the prepared bowl, covering the inside of the bowl completely. Press it into shape and freeze for 40–45 minutes, until solid.

2 Soften the mango sorbet (see step 1). Spread it evenly over the ice cream layer and freeze for a further 30 minutes, or until firm. Whisk the remaining ice cream in a bowl until softened and use to fill the centre of the bombe. Freeze for 40 minutes.

3 Heat a large saucepan of water and dip the base of the bombe bowl in it for 15–20 seconds. Then invert the bombe over a large serving dish, remove the bowl, and discard the cling film. Freeze until needed.

4 For the glaze, melt both ingredients in a heatproof bowl over a pan of simmering water, making sure it does not touch the water. Leave to warm up briefly. Pour the glaze over the bombe and serve immediately. You can store it, covered in the freezer, for up to 3 days.

🕐 **20 mins** plus freezing   🍴 **SERVES 8**

BOMBE banana, toffee, and salted peanut

Mixing ice cream through the banana layer gives this bombe a light, soft texture. You could also top with peanuts.

INGREDIENTS
3 bananas, sliced
2 litres (3½ pints) toffee ice cream
30g (1oz) salted peanuts, chopped
1 litre (1¾ pints) vanilla ice cream

SPECIAL EQUIPMENT
2.3 litre (4 pint) freezer-proof bowl, about 20cm (8in) wide

1 Line a large baking sheet with baking parchment. Spread the banana slices on the parchment, spaced well apart. Freeze for 1 hour, or until they are solid.

2 Line the freezer-proof bowl with cling film, leaving some overhang, and place it in the freezer. Whisk the toffee ice cream in a large bowl with a hand-held whisk until slightly softened.

3 Spread the ice cream evenly in the prepared bowl, covering the inside of the bowl completely. Press it into shape and freeze for 40–45 minutes, until solid. Place the frozen banana slices in a bowl. Blend with a hand-held blender until smooth and fold in the peanuts.

4 Soften 600ml (1 pint) of the vanilla ice cream (see step 2) and fold into the banana and peanut mixture. Spread this mixture over the toffee ice cream evenly and freeze for 30 minutes, or until firm. Then soften the remaining vanilla ice cream and use to fill the centre of the bombe. Freeze for a further 40 minutes.

5 Using a large saucepan of hot water, turn out the bombe over a large serving dish (see Mango and coconut bombe, step 3). Remove the bowl, take off the cling film, and serve immediately. You can store the bombe, covered in the freezer, for up to 3 days.

ICE-CREAM BOMBES
Alternative sauces

A sauce can add fresh flavour to an ice-cream bombe. Some of these sauces are designed with bombe recipes in mind, but they also work well drizzled over a serving of ice cream.

◄ Dulce de leche sauce
Whisk a 397g can dulce de leche with 100ml (3½fl oz) single cream. Add a pinch of sea salt. This sauce makes a delicious accompaniment to the Banana, toffee, and salted peanut bombe (see opposite). Pour it over the bombe while still warm, as it thickens as it cools.

Pineapple and rum sauce ▲
Place 425g canned pineapple chunks in a blender, along with just 4 tbsp of the juices. Add 2 tbsp dark rum, blend to a smooth sauce, and chill until needed. You could serve it alongside the Mango and coconut bombe (see opposite).

◄ Strawberry sauce
Place 400g (14oz) roughly chopped strawberries, 1 heaped tbsp caster sugar, and juice of 1 lemon in a lidded saucepan. Cover and simmer for 10 minutes. Then purée and strain the sauce before chilling. Serve with any ice-cream bombe.

◄ Warm chocolate fudge sauce
Serve this with the Banana, toffee, and salted peanut bombe (see opposite). Melt 60g (2oz) unsalted butter and 50g (1¾oz) diced dark chocolate in a heatproof bowl over a pan of simmering water, making sure it does not touch the water. Remove from the heat and whisk in 200ml (7fl oz) condensed milk and ½ tsp vanilla extract. Serve warm, or at room temperature.

Choco mocha sauce ►
Heat 120ml (4fl oz) double cream and 60g (2oz) golden syrup until hot, but not boiling. Pour it over 115g (4oz) finely chopped dark chocolate and 1 tsp espresso powder, and whisk until melted. Serve warm as it thickens when it cools. Perfect with the Chocolate and cherry bombe (see pp286–87).

Dark cherry sauce ▲
Place 200g (7oz) pitted cherries, 2 tbsp caster sugar, and 1 tbsp water in a small lidded saucepan. Cover and heat gently for about 10 minutes, until the cherries start to release their juices and soften. Purée until completely smooth, chill, and serve drizzled over your choice of ice-cream bombe.

⏱ **40 mins**
plus chilling and freezing

🍴 **MAKES 6**

PARFAIT white chocolate and rose water

A parfait is a soft and light frozen dessert that combines eggs and cream, and sweetens them with sugar syrup. It doesn't require an ice-cream maker, but you do need a cooking thermometer to get the syrup to the correct temperature.

INGREDIENTS
240ml (8fl oz) double cream
125g (4½oz) white chocolate, finely chopped
100g (3½oz) caster sugar
⅛ tsp salt
4 large egg yolks
1 tsp rose water

30g (1oz) unsalted and skinned pistachios, roughly chopped

SPECIAL EQUIPMENT
sugar thermometer
6 x 150ml (5fl oz) glasses

1 Whisk the cream in a bowl to form soft peaks and chill until needed. Melt the chocolate in a heatproof bowl over a saucepan of simmering water, making sure it does not touch the water. Remove from the heat and set aside, stirring frequently to ensure it does not burn.

Stir the chocolate gently to ensure it is smooth.

2 Heat the sugar, salt, and 60ml (2fl oz) water in a pan over a low heat, stirring occasionally, until the sugar dissolves. Bring to the boil. Then reduce the heat to a simmer and cook until the temperature reaches 110°C (230°F). Remove from the heat.

Check the temperature at regular intervals.

3 Meanwhile, in the bowl of a standing mixer, whisk the egg yolks for 4–5 minutes, until pale and smooth. Then whisk in the hot sugar syrup in a steady stream, until combined. Add the rose water, beat well, then fold in the chocolate. Beat for a further 1 minute, or until well combined.

4 Gently fold in the whipped cream, until no streaks remain. Pour it into the glasses and freeze for 1 hour. Sprinkle the parfait with pistachios to serve. You can store the parfait, covered in the freezer, for 2–3 days.

45 mins
plus chilling and freezing

MAKES 6

PARFAIT vanilla and honey with strawberries

This is a summery twist on a classic parfait. Ripe strawberries and crisp flaked almonds provide a fantastic contrast in texture. Layer your dessert quickly, as parfaits tend to melt at room temperature.

INGREDIENTS

240ml (8fl oz) double cream

4 large egg yolks

70g (2¼oz) caster sugar

3 tbsp runny honey

⅛ tsp salt

1 tsp vanilla bean paste

450g (1lb) strawberries, hulled and diced

50g (1¾oz) flaked almonds

SPECIAL EQUIPMENT

sugar thermometer

6 x160ml (5½fl oz) glass jars

PLAN AHEAD

You can prepare and store the parfait in an airtight container in the freezer 2–3 days ahead.

1 Whisk the cream in a bowl to form soft peaks and chill until needed. In a separate bowl, whisk the egg yolks vigorously for 4–5 minutes, until they are pale yellow in colour. Set aside.

2 Heat the sugar, honey, salt, and 60ml (2fl oz) water in a small saucepan over a low heat, stirring frequently, until the sugar dissolves. Bring to the boil, then reduce the heat and simmer until the temperature reaches 110°C (230°F).

3 Remove the sugar syrup from the heat. Pour it into the egg yolk mixture, in a steady stream, whisking constantly until the mixture thickens and cools slightly. Gently fold in the vanilla bean paste, then the cream until no streaks remain. Transfer to an airtight container and freeze for at least 3 hours.

4 Remove from the freezer 10 minutes before serving. Place one scoop of the parfait mixture in each glass and top with a layer of the strawberries and almonds. Repeat the process to make another layer of each and serve immediately.

⏱ **25 mins**
plus chilling and freezing　🍴 **MAKES 4**

PARFAIT tropical fruit

Flavour a simple parfait with coconut, and then, just before serving, layer it with small diced tropical fruit to create a sundae-style dessert.

INGREDIENTS
240ml (8fl oz) double cream
4 large egg yolks
100g (3½oz) caster sugar
⅛ tsp salt
1¼ tsp coconut extract
2–3 kiwis, diced
175g (6oz) pineapple, diced
45g (1½oz) coconut shavings, plus extra to serve
1 mango, diced

SPECIAL EQUIPMENT
sugar thermometer
4 x160ml (5½fl oz) glass jars

PLAN AHEAD
You can prepare and store the parfait in an airtight container in the freezer 2–3 days ahead.

1 Whisk the cream in a bowl to form soft peaks and chill until needed. In a separate bowl, whisk the egg yolks and set aside (see Vanilla and honey parfait, step 1).

2 Heat the sugar, salt, and 60ml (2fl oz) water in a small saucepan over a low heat, stirring, until the sugar dissolves. Bring to the boil, then reduce the heat and simmer until the temperature reaches 110°C (230°F).

3 Pour the sugar syrup into the egg yolks and whisk well (see Vanilla and honey parfait, step 3). Then add the coconut extract and whisk until combined. Fold in whipped cream. Transfer the mixture to an airtight container, and freeze for 3 hours.

4 Remove from the freezer 10 minutes before serving. Make two layers each of the parfait mixture, fruit, and coconut in each glass jar (see Vanilla and honey parfait, step 4). Serve immediately.

Drips and drizzles

Parfait is often neutral in colour, so go wild with contrasting drizzled sauces – either on top of boules or over serving plates.

Zigzag Heat 60g (2oz) ready-made dulce de leche in a small bowl over gently simmering water until it is just warm. Transfer it to a disposable piping bag, snip off a corner, and zigzag the sauce over boules of Vanilla and honey parfait (see opposite).

Feather coulis Serve a mango coulis with the Tropical fruit parfait (see left). Purée the flesh of 2 mangoes with the juice of 1 lemon and 1 tbsp icing sugar until smooth. Pour into a piping bag and pipe lines over your plate, then drag a skewer through the lines at an angle for a feathered effect.

Chocolate crème anglaise Prepare crème anglaise (see Blueberry upside-down cakes with crème anglaise, p69), adding 50g (1¾oz) finely grated dark chocolate at step 5. Pool it on a serving plate and place a boule of Vanilla parfait (see opposite) on top. Serve.

Chocolate toppers For simple chocolate shapes, pipe 60g (2oz) melted and cooled chocolate onto parchment paper in decorative patterns. Allow to harden before peeling them off and using to decorate servings of parfait.

⏱ **30 mins**
plus cooling, chilling, and freezing

🍴 **SERVES 8**

ICE-CREAM PIE
rocky road

This ice-cream pie is the perfect dessert for the whole family –
it especially appeals to children and is quite easy to prepare.
As it keeps for a while in the freezer, you can prepare it days
in advance. Use good-quality ice cream for best results.

INGREDIENTS
250g (9oz) digestive
  biscuits, finely crushed
60g (2oz) caster sugar
125g (4½oz) unsalted
  butter, melted and cooled

For the filling
1 litre (1¾ pints) good-
  quality chocolate ice
  cream, softened
30g (1oz) mini marshmallows,
  plus extra to serve
50g (1¾oz) pecans,
  roughly chopped, plus
  extra to serve

50g (1¾oz) blanched
  almonds, roughly
  chopped, plus extra
  to serve

SPECIAL EQUIPMENT
23cm (9in) deep loose-
bottomed, fluted tart tin

PLAN AHEAD
You can store the blind-
baked biscuit base, wrapped
in cling film, in the fridge
up to 2 days ahead.

1
Preheat the oven to 180°C
(350°F/Gas 4). Combine
the biscuit crumbs, sugar,
and butter in a large bowl
until the mixture resembles
fine breadcrumbs.

Spread the mixture
evenly in the tin,
packing it down well
to make a firm base
with a 2.5cm (1in)
side. Bake the biscuit
base for 10 minutes.
Remove from the heat,
leave to cool, then chill
until needed.

2

3
For the filling, pulse the ice
cream in a food processor,
a little at a time, until thick,
creamy, and smooth. Transfer
it to a large bowl.

Fold in the marshmallows and nuts.
Spread the filling in the biscuit case
evenly and freeze for at least 1 hour,
until firm. To serve, thaw the pie in the
fridge for 20–30 minutes, remove from
the tin, and top with marshmallows and
nuts. You can store the pie, covered in
the freezer, for up to 2 months.

4

50 mins
plus cooling and freezing

SERVES 8

ICE-CREAM PIE triple chocolate

The whisked sponge in this ice-cream pie does not harden in the freezer, giving the dessert a yielding texture that you can eat straight from frozen. Other flavours of ice cream, such as cherry, could also work very well with the chocolate cake.

INGREDIENTS
3 eggs

125g (4½oz) caster sugar

60g (2oz) plain flour

30g (1oz) cocoa powder

For the filling

500g (1lb 2oz) chocolate ice cream

500g (1lb 2oz) vanilla ice cream

60g (2oz) Oreos, filling removed, finely crushed

SPECIAL EQUIPMENT
20cm (8in) deep springform cake tin

PLAN AHEAD
You can store the unfilled sponge cake in an airtight container up to 2 days ahead.

1 Preheat the oven to 190°C (375°F/Gas 5). Line the tin with baking parchment. Whisk the eggs and sugar in a bowl for 5 minutes, until the mixture is pale, thick, and has tripled in size. Sift in the flour and cocoa and fold gently, until combined.

2 Pour the batter into the prepared tin evenly. Bake for 20–25 minutes, until the sponge cake is well risen and an inserted toothpick comes out clean. Leave to cool in the tin for 10 minutes, before turning out onto a wire rack to cool completely.

3 For the filling, place the chocolate ice cream in a bowl for 10–15 minutes, to soften. Then whisk it briefly with a hand-held whisk until smooth. Slice the cake in half, lengthways.

4 Place the bottom slice, cut-side up, in the tin and spread over the chocolate ice cream evenly. Top with the second cake half, cut-side down, and freeze for at least 30 minutes.

5 Soften the vanilla ice cream in a separate bowl (see step 3). Remove the cake from the freezer and spread over the vanilla ice cream evenly. Sprinkle over the Oreo crumbs evenly. Cover the pie with cling film, and freeze for at least 4 hours, until frozen solid.

6 Remove the pie from the freezer at least 10 minutes before serving and turn it out onto a large serving platter. Serve immediately. You can store the pie, covered in the freezer, for up to 1 month.

ICE-CREAM PIE
pear and ginger

Three forms of ginger combine to give a complex warmth to the refreshing pear and cream filling of this ice-cream pie.

INGREDIENTS

75g (2½oz) unsalted butter plus extra for greasing

250g (9oz) ginger biscuits, crushed

For the topping

1 litre (1¾ pints) good-quality vanilla ice cream

5 pieces stem ginger, preserved in syrup, drained, plus extra to decorate

2 tbsp stem ginger syrup, plus extra for drizzling

415g can pear halves in natural juice, drained and finely chopped

SPECIAL EQUIPMENT

23cm (9in) springform cake tin

PLAN AHEAD

You can store the blind-baked biscuit base, wrapped in cling film, in the fridge up to 2 days ahead.

1 Grease and line the tin with baking parchment. Place the ice cream in a bowl, and leave to soften. Place the biscuits in a separate heatproof bowl. Melt the butter in a saucepan and mix with the biscuits.

2 Spread the biscuit mixture evenly in the tin, pressing down with the back of a spoon to form a firm base. For the topping, pulse the ice cream, ginger, and ginger syrup in a food processor, until smooth, thick, and creamy. Stir in the chopped pears.

3 Pour the topping over the biscuit base and freeze for at least 2 hours, until completely frozen. Before serving, leave to soften in the fridge for 30 minutes. Transfer the pie to a serving plate. Drizzle over a little ginger syrup, scatter over the ginger pieces, and serve. You can store the pie, covered in the freezer, for up to 2 months.

Index

Entries in **bold** indicate ingredients.